Mediating Divorce

Mediating Divorce

A Step-by-Step Manual

Marilyn S. McKnight, M. A.

Stephen K. Erickson, J. D.

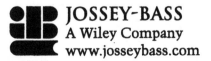
JOSSEY-BASS
A Wiley Company
www.josseybass.com

Published by

JOSSEY-BASS
A Wiley Company
989 Market Street
San Francisco, CA 94103-1741

www.josseybass.com

Copyright © 1999 by John Wiley & Sons, Inc.

FIRST PAPERBACK EDITION PUBLISHED IN 2002.

Jossey-Bass is a registered trademark of John Wiley & Sons, Inc.

Jossey-Bass books and products are available through most bookstores. To contact Jossey-Bass directly, call (888) 378-2537, fax to (800) 605-2665, or visit our website at www.josseybass.com.

Substantial discounts on bulk quantities of Jossey-Bass books are available to corporations, professional associations, and other organizations. For details and discount information, contact the special sales department at Jossey-Bass.

We at Jossey-Bass strive to use the most environmentally sensitive paper stocks available to us. Our publications are printed on acid-free recycled stock whenever possible, and our paper always meets or exceeds minimum GPO and EPA requirements.

Library of Congress Cataloging-in-Publication Data
McKnight, Marilyn S.
   Mediating divorce : a step-by-step manual / Marilyn S. McKnight,
Stephen K. Erickson.
      p.   cm.
   Includes bibliographical references.
   ISBN 0-7879-5849-2 (paper : acid-free paper)
   ISBN 0-7879-4485-8 (client's workbook : acid-free paper)
   1. Divorce mediation -- United States. 2. Divorce settlements--
United States.   I. Erickson, Stephen K.   II. Title.
KF535.Z9M38 1999
346.7301'66—dc21
                                                             98-42715
                                                             CIP

PB Printing   10 9 8 7 6 5 4 3 2 1

Dedication

This work is dedicated to the memory of one of Steve's divorce clients: Lorraine Brown, a mother of four children who was killed in 1976 by her husband two days after their temporary hearing. The tragedy of her death propelled us to work diligently to create something that would prevent such losses in the future. We hope that our model of client-centered mediation will begin to reduce the number of violent outcomes to divorce and that no more children will lose their parents to the acrimony of divorce as Lorraine Brown's children lost both of theirs.

Contents

1   Introduction

This manual is intended for the therapist or family law attorney who wishes to engage in divorce mediation, a process through which clients create their own divorce settlement with a professional mediator. Mediation offers divorcing clients an excellent alternative to the typical adversarial approach. It is much less expensive, it yields fair, satisfactory results, it gives clients power over the process and ownership of the results, it helps them to heal, and it leaves them with a sense of respect for themselves and each other.

The manual is used in conjunction with *Mediating Divorce: A Client's Workbook*, which is given to both clients seeking a divorce. It lets them know what to expect from the process of mediation. Extra copies are available from Jossey-Bass.

The mediator's manual guides you through the mediation process step by step. The following paragraphs present a brief summary of the contents following this Introduction.

Part One: Elements of Divorce Mediation

Part One consists of three chapters:

- Chapter Two explains client-centered mediation and the four basic ways to resolve conflict. It also discusses the differences between the adversarial process, which emphasizes competition, and mediation, which emphasizes cooperation.
- Chapter Three describes the competencies you need as well as the skills necessary to be a divorce mediator, which includes managing the mediation process, promoting cooperative behavior, maintaining impartiality, and demonstrating a positive, non-judgmental attitude.
- Chapter Four explains the emotions experienced by people going through a divorce and how you as a mediator can help them understand those emotions. It is important to know the enormous impact of these emotions. Your task is to be especially understanding, caring, sensitive, and respectful toward clients at this time when they are particularly vulnerable.

Part Two: The Mediation Process

Part Two consists of seven chapters. The first of these, Chapter Five, explains how to conduct the initial consultation with prospective clients. It offers information on screening for abuse, forming a relationship with the couple, providing information about what to expect from mediation, and contracting for mediation services.

The next five chapters describe the five subject areas of divorce mediation. Although each of the five subject areas includes unique features, the general process used in each is as follows:

- Identifying all issues and reviewing and understanding all information that might affect the clients' decisions on the subject (parenting, finances, or property)
- Defining the standards of fairness that the clients will use in making their decisions
- Creating options through discussion and brainstorming
- Considering all options and then selecting ones that will not only resolve the issues but also meet the clients' own personal sense of fairness

The contents of the five chapters are as follows:

- Chapter Six describes Subject Area 1, Establishing a Parenting Plan. This presents a more realistic and more humane approach to what is commonly known in adversarial divorce as determining "custody." The chapter offers information on child development, what happens to children when their parents divorce, the effects of spousal abuse on children, the underlying causes of custody contests, how to create a parenting plan, and the procedure you will follow to assist them in establishing that plan.
- Chapter Seven describes Subject Area 2, Planning Future Living Expenses. Clients usually embark on a divorce fearing that they will not have enough money to live on in the future. In this section you help them resolve their financial issues so neither suffers financial disaster. You address monthly expenses, net income, the shortfall between expenses and income, ways to decrease expenses as well as ways to increase income, and determining the payment of spousal support and child support.
- Chapter Eight describes Subject Area 3, Dividing Property. In this section you assist the clients in identifying all of their property and its value, identifying nonmarital property (non-community property), deciding who gets what, and assisting clients in division of property that seems fair to both clients.
- Chapter Nine describes Subject Area 4, Reviewing Progress and Pulling it All Together. During this step you discuss the tax implications of various decisions that the clients may have made or may be contemplating. The clients also address the legal requirements of their divorce. Subsequently you review all of the previously generated data with the clients in preparation for creating the first draft of the Memorandum of Agreement. At this time the clients revisit their original decisions and make any necessary adjustments.
- Chapter Ten describes Subject Area 5, Finalizing the Memorandum of Agreement. During this final stage you and the clients carefully review the entire draft copy of the Memorandum of Agreement, concentrating particularly on the wording. Any necessary revisions are made so that the final document can be prepared.

Although this manual presents the mediation process as five discrete subject areas, most often you will find that these areas overlap. You may start on one subject area and discover that the clients need additional information from a CPA, for example, before you can proceed with it. Or you may need to address an immediate crisis related to the emotional divorce process. When this occurs, you and the clients may decide either to delay mediation or to proceed to the next subject area while waiting for the necessary information or while waiting for the emotional crisis to wane. Changing focus keeps the process moving forward while satisfying clients' needs.

Chapter Eleven, Mediator Strategies, presents a variety of strategies that you will find useful to apply in the mediation room. They have been put together in this chapter so that you can use the chapter not only to learn about the various strategies that mediators use to promote cooperative agreements, but also to look up information on how to manage particular questions. Three kinds of strategies are offered: basic mediator interventions, protocols for managing special situations, and strategies to avoid impasse.

Part Three: Appendixes

Part Three has two appendixes. Appendix A consists of forms that are used during the mediation process. Some of these forms you may want to reproduce as is, and others you will want to modify for your own unique situation. Appendix B presents recommended readings that you will find useful as you build your career as a mediator.

Part I

Elements of Divorce Mediation

2 What Is Client-Centered Mediation?

There are four ways to resolving the conflict inherent in divorce: litigation, arbitration, negotiation, and mediation. Litigation and arbitration are adversarial processes, and negotiation can be either adversarial or cooperative. Only mediation is by its nature cooperative, and we believe that client-centered mediation offers greater benefits for those involved in divorce than does a directive or law-centered mediation process.

Approaches to Resolving Conflict

Litigation

Despite its many drawbacks, litigation is a common approach to divorce, because it is an adversarial contest in which each person's goal is to win at the expense of the other. The two people relinquish control over the process by hiring attorneys to speak for them and to plan case strategy. The attorneys control settlement discussions, including which settlement options are considered.

A judge determines the winner and the loser or the case is settled based on the prediction of what a judge might do. Formal rules (of "discovery" and "evidence") are followed at all stages of the contest. These rules are used to determine how issues are defined, what evidence can be examined, and what solutions can be considered.

If the case is tried, the judge sits behind a desk, usually elevated, signifying power and authority. Communication is between the judge and the lawyers, between the lawyers, and between the lawyer and the client. Generally the decision-maker has no direct communication with the divorcing clients. Similarly, the divorcing clients do not communicate directly with each other.

Instead, the attorneys stake out rather extreme positions, each working hard to prevail. This process, known as "positional bargaining," adds to the competitive, win-lose nature of litigation. However, at the conclusion of this process usually neither person feels like a winner.

The following are some other important characteristics of litigation:

- In the adversarial litigation system, the divorce has become a high stakes contest over children, money, and property. Standards of fairness, based on state laws, are frequently changing and applied differently, depending on the judge or lawyer who is interpreting the law.

- The focus is on the past and on assigning fault or blame to one of the divorcing spouses, in an effort to determine who is right and who is wrong.
- Discussions emphasize differences between the divorcing clients, and the transaction cost of the adversarial process leaves clients emotionally damaged and financially drained.

Arbitration

Although less formal than litigation, arbitration is still closely related to litigation. When applied to divorce issues, each divorcing person's goal is to win at the expense of the other. The clients are seated around a table. One divorce client and his or her attorney sit on one side of the table, and the other divorce client and attorney sit on the other side. (Occasionally there are no attorneys involved, but the divorce clients still sit on opposite sides.) An arbitrator (or sometimes an arbitration panel) is seated at the head of the table in a position of authority. The divorce clients defer to the arbitrator or panel; arbitrators have complete control over the issues to be examined, the evidence that can be presented, and the outcomes that can be considered.

The communication is between arbitrator and attorneys, between attorneys and witnesses, and between each attorney and his or her client. Even in particularly informal arbitration, the divorcing parties may communicate directly with the arbitrator but usually do not communicate with each other.

Some important characteristics of arbitration are as follows:

- As in litigation, the focus of arbitration is most often on the past, and each divorcing person's goal is to assign fault to the other, or to achieve their own positional outcome.
- State law is applied as the standard of fairness, rather than a tailor-made standard of fairness created by the couple.
- The arbitrator frequently "splits the difference" in an attempt to please both divorce clients, but this approach often results in dissatisfaction on both sides.

Negotiation or Settlement Conferencing

Negotiation is another approach in which the parties are seated around a table. Clients sit on opposite sides, either with or without their lawyers. When attorneys are involved (as in the practice of collaborative law), they speak for their clients; the clients speak to their attorneys but not usually to each other. When attorneys are not involved, clients communicate directly. In either case, the two clients and their attorneys make all decisions without relinquishing authority to a third party.

Following are some of the main characteristics of negotiation:

- Both divorcing clients enter the process voluntarily.
- The clients decide whether to speak for themselves or to hire attorneys to negotiate for them.
- The clients create their own rules of fairness.
- The focus can be on the past, the present, the future, or a combination of all three.
- The process can be either adversarial or cooperative. When the process is adversarial, positional bargaining is used; often each client gives up something (compromises), and neither feels like the winner. When the process is cooperative, both people seek solutions that address their own and each other's needs; the outcome is generally satisfactory to both people.

Divorce Mediation

The process of mediation is managed by a mediator, who functions as an impartial third party. Both people are the mediator's clients, and the goal of this cooperative approach is a settlement that is satisfactory to both people.

Other important characteristics of divorce mediation are as follows:

- Procedural rules concerning confidentiality, disclosure of information, using attorneys, caucusing (meeting with one person in private), and the like are established by the mediator in consultation with the clients.
- Standards of fairness are based on either the state's divorce laws and/or the divorcing couple's own concepts of fairness.
- The clients speak for themselves, unless their attorneys are present and clients want their attorneys to speak for them.
- The mediator assumes control of the process, directing the clients in their examination of issues, assisting them in communicating, clarifying, and developing options and resolving conflict.
- Each client may include in the process various professionals (attorneys, appraisers, and so on) who serve as advisors.
- After thoroughly exploring options, the clients are encouraged to make their own decisions. Creative thinking is encouraged. After the clients have reached a settlement that both deem satisfactory, the mediator drafts their Memorandum of Agreement, which specifies the details of the settlement. The clients then present the memorandum to their respective attorneys, who use it as the basis for constructing the legal documents that terminate the marriage and implements their mediated decisions.

Client-Centered Mediation

Our approach to divorce mediation includes the following beliefs and assumptions as the foundation of a client-centered approach:

- The clients' fears, beliefs, concerns, values and ideas are the focus of the process.
- The adversarial system is harmful to families because it focuses on winning or on the law, or on something other than the clients.
- The vast majority of people seeking divorce desire to work cooperatively to create a divorce settlement, but it is the adversarial process that encourages them to behave combatively.
- Cooperation can be learned by those who are divorcing if they choose to function in an environment that imposes the elements of cooperation rather than the elements of competition.

We term our approach client centered because of the following assumptions about our clients:

- All divorcing clients are worthy of respect, regardless of their past behavior.
- Divorcing clients can achieve a resolution that is acceptable to both when the process emphasizes their similarities and shared needs rather than their differences.

- All divorcing clients are capable of developing their own standards of fairness if they are given a safe, structured environment in which to do so, though some with a history of abuse may need special protocols.
- All divorcing clients with children have the opportunity to continue to be active parents to their children, rather than being labeled visitors or non-custodians.
- All divorcing clients have a need for some measure of economic security in the future.

The differentiating elements of our approach grow from these beliefs and assumptions. Consequently, the process of client-centered mediation differs from other mediation approaches in the following ways:

- Procedural rules are tailored to meet the clients' specific needs. The mediator may offer simple "protocols" for consideration.
- The mediator focuses discussions on the present and how best to plan for the future. Blame and guilt are subject areas that are discouraged. Past history is de-emphasized except in cases of abuse.
- The mediator helps the clients examine their interests and explore various options for a settlement that addresses everyone's needs, including those of their children.
- The clients may occasionally confer with various neutral experts (CPAs, appraisers, and so on) who serve in an advisory capacity to the two of them and assist them in making certain decisions. However, these experts do not serve as the clients' advocates during mediation.
- The clients make their own decisions; the mediator does not advise them or make decisions for them.

Client-centered mediation promotes honesty, self-reliance, respect, and empowerment. Clients are encouraged to ask questions and to address all of their concerns and fears so that they can make well-informed decisions. The emphasis on results satisfactory to both makes clients appreciate the process and the outcome.

Competition Versus Cooperation

It is important for both you and your clients to understand the specific ways in which the competitive emphasis of the adversarial process differs from the cooperative emphasis of the client-centered mediation approach to divorce. The following paragraphs explain the differences involved in filing for divorce, procedures and time required, representation, temporary hearings, discovery, cost, standards of fairness, and compliance.

Filing for Divorce
An adversarial approach generally involves the court system, and the two parties make the legal decision to divorce when they petition the court for divorce. For the court to have jurisdiction of the case, a civil action must be started and a petition for divorce filed and served.

When people choose client-centered mediation, they need not make an immediate decision to divorce, nor do they have to start any kind of legal action. Filing a petition for divorce is usually one of the last steps in a mediated divorce, after all their agreements have been reached.

Procedures and Time Required

An adversarial divorce, depending on the state, may take six months to several year to complete, not counting any waiting period that a state might require! A Final Decree of Divorce is either negotiated through the attorneys, or imposed by the court if the attorneys cannot reach an agreement.

If a settlement has been reached, one spouse's attorney prepares a legal document that terminates the marriage (sometimes called the "stipulation for settlement" or "marital termination agreement"). This document spells out the details of the divorce decision, including the division of property, the parenting plan, the method of sharing support for the children, and sometimes spousal support. The other spouse's attorney scrutinizes the document for accuracy. If he or she finds parts that need to be changed, the two attorneys start a back-and-forth process of amending and reviewing the document.

If the attorneys are not able to resolve those issues, the case goes to the judge for a decision. If the attorneys reach an agreement that they both find acceptable, however, the settlement is submitted to the court for its review and approval.

Then, if no waiting period is required by the state, the divorce becomes final when the court approves and enters the document-generally several weeks or so after the document has been submitted. The court notifies the clients of the official date of divorce. If the court tries the case, the clients must wait for the judge's official ruling.

Client-centered mediation usually takes up to approximately three months, not counting any state-required waiting period. After contracting with you, the divorcing couple spend approximately six to ten hours in mediation (in three to five two-hour sessions). After all the issues have been decided, you prepare a preliminary Memorandum of Agreement of the clients' decisions. This copy is first marked "Draft—For Discussion Only," and each person takes a copy to his or her attorney for review.

If one or both attorneys suggest changes, the clients generally ask their attorneys to resolve these issues; if the attorneys are unable to reach agreement quickly, however, the clients may discuss the proposed changes on their own and determine whether to include, amend, or reject them. If necessary, the clients may attend another mediation session, with or without the attorneys present, to resolve the issues raised by the attorneys. If neither attorney has changes to the preliminary memorandum, however, you simply prepare a clean copy of the document without the "preliminary" and "draft" notations.

Subsequently, the clients have one of their attorneys prepare the legal termination documents, which are based on the memorandum, and submits them to the court.* If no waiting period is required, the divorce is final when it is signed by a judge and entered into the court record.

---

*State laws on divorce are also used as the standard of fairness in settlement and law-centered mediation but not in client-centered mediation unless the clients wish to adopt the state law as an acceptable standard of fairness.

The law does not dictate fairness in client-centered mediation because what might happen if the case went to court is less important than their joint agreements about fairness. The clients are asked to determine their own *standard of fairness based on their unique needs*. After the parties have applied their standard in the form of decisions recorded in the Memorandum of Agreement, and that agreement has been used to create the legal termination documents, the court does not usually change them. However, we have numerous reports from across the country of judges refusing to approve a couple's choice of equal time sharing of children because the judge would prefer one parent to have custody and be in charge.

A mediated divorce not only saves time but also spares the clients the emotional strain of a prolonged divorce process.

Representation

In an adversarial divorce, the attorneys representing the two persons often use an adversarial, competitive process. In fact, each attorney has an ethical duty to be a zealous advocate for his or her client. Unfortunately, this adversarial posturing encourages each person to view the other as "the enemy" making it even more difficult to settle divorce issues and greatly alienating them from each other.

In contrast, you do not represent either client. In client-centered mediation, your ethical duty is to remain impartial and to serve the needs of each person involved, including any children. The mediator helps establish an atmosphere of cooperation.

Temporary Hearing

The rules of divorce in all states permit a temporary hearing or "pedente lité" hearing. This early step in the adversarial divorce process occurs when spouses have been unable to agree upon issues that have immediate impact, such as parenting schedules, support payments, or occupancy of the home, so their attorneys schedule a hearing. The hearing process requires each client to file an affidavit containing sworn testimony which often includes negative statements about the other. Many clients get so wounded by this process that they find it even more difficult to negotiate constructively than before. The hearing also involves extra expense, of course, and always takes place in the adversarial atmosphere of a courtroom where both persons engage in intense efforts to "win." The outcome of the hearing is binding on both people, and often the resulting hostility escalates, alienating spouses throughout the divorce process and beyond.

With client-centered mediation, part of your job as mediators to help clients avoid the need for a temporary hearing. Any disagreements are discussed early on and resolved during the mediation sessions with temporary agreements about parenting, support, and occupancy of the home.

Discovery

An adversarial process includes what is called "discovery," where each party attempts to learn or discover the strength of the other's case. Formal discovery consists of written interrogatories, scheduling of oral depositions with a court reporter and attorneys, and demands for production of documents. Discovery can be not only very costly, but also demeaning to the divorcing clients. Since discovery is carried out in the adversarial atmosphere of a contest, the goal is often seen as "give the other side as little information as possible and make them work for it."

With a mediated divorce there is no need for formal discovery as the information is exchanged voluntarily in the mediation room. As a part of the rules of mediation, spouses agree to exchange financial information. This exchange is closely monitored by you, the mediator, to ensure completeness and fairness. Verification of income and assets is accomplished through the voluntary exchange of documents as well as occasionally asking a neutral accountant to assist when there are concerns about trust and complete disclosure. When one spouse is unsure what happened to certain accounts or has not been informed about the marriage finances during the relationship, they may hire a forensic accountant to trace the money.

With a mediated divorce there is no need for costly formal discovery. The vast majority of couples willingly exchange information and cooperate with each other. Consequently, they save money and retain their dignity.

Cost

The adversarial approach is expensive, primarily because of the high cost of legal services and the cumbersome and contentious nature of the decision-making process itself. In addition to the fees of two attorneys, the divorcing clients must pay court filing fees. There is no average cost information available, but it is not uncommon for each side to pay more than $10,000 for contested divorce proceedings. Consequently, an adversarial divorce can cost the couple thousands of dollars.

As a mediator, you will generally charge about the same amount per mediation hour that a divorce attorney in your area would charge; in our experience the hourly rates charged by divorce attorneys vary from $75 to $300 per hour. In addition, the mediator often charges a one-time administrative fee to cover case setup, word processing, copying, and phone calls. That fee may vary from one to five times the hourly fee, depending on how the mediator charges and the complexity of the case.

The clients may spend in the range of $750 to $3,000 on mediation sessions, depending on your geographical area and assuming that six to ten hours are required to mediate the divorce; $75 to $1,500 on the mediator's administrative fee; and approximately $300 to $3,000 on combined attorneys' fees to prepare and file the legal documents terminating the marriage. In addition, the couple may need to pay some fees to neutral experts such as CPAs, psychologists, and appraisers; those fees vary widely in cost, but they could expect to pay as much as $800 to $10,000, depending on the number of experts and the complexity of the issues. As you can see, the entire sum required for a mediated divorce is significantly less than that required for an adversarial divorce. You may wish to find out the range of these fees in the geographical area where you practice to help you decide what your fees will be.

Standards of Fairness

The standard of fairness applied in an adversarial process is legal—the state laws and case law governing divorce control how your clients end up in divorce. You may need to help your clients understand that divorce laws are not always fair. They are rather a patchwork quilt of rules and customs that vary from state to state and county to county. THEY CANNOT ALWAYS BE APPLIED FAIRLY, particularly when the discussion about how to apply these laws is held in an adversarial contest. Because state divorce laws vary greatly, the couple's outcome will differ depending on where they live. Even when a court trial is not involved, the attorneys will attempt to settle the case from the perspective of what the outcome would be if the case were tried before a judge who followed the law of the jurisdiction or precedence set by case law. Unfortunately, although the intent of these laws is fairness, current divorce law is vague and inconsistently applied in a contested action making it impossible to create fairness for each couple seeking a divorce.

Compliance

Given the power and prestige of the court, one might assume that the adversarial system would enjoy an excellent record of compliance with court orders due to the fact that the court's power of contempt stands behind the document. However, statistics show high levels of noncompliance. Even the "winning" spouse is often dissatisfied because he or she continues to experience difficulty with the former spouse. In addition, in some jurisdictions as many as 70 percent of all divorce trials are appealed to a higher court.

In our experience, most couples are satisfied with the outcome of client-centered mediation because the results are beneficial to both sides. Research has shown a high rate of compliance with mediated settlement agreements, no doubt because people are less likely to violate a settlement that they participated in creating. In fact, most people include in their legal divorce document an agreement to return to mediation if future disputes arise.

3

Your Role As a Mediator

As a mediator, you will begin to understand that you have a great deal of power, but you must use that power wisely. Just as we ask the clients to let go of some of the pain and anger of the past conflict, so too must the mediator let go of the tendencies to give advice and direct the outcome.

Qualifications

This book is written for counselors, therapists, and attorneys who wish to mediate divorces. To be effective as a mediator, you do not need to be an attorney. However, you do need to be familiar with your state's divorce laws so that you can be aware of how the attorneys might react when a couple chooses unconventional solutions, such as 50/50 time sharing with a joint checkbook for children's expenses.*

If you are already licensed by your state in your profession, you understand licensing procedures. Mediation is still a relatively young profession without formal licensing. The Academy of Family Mediators has recommended training requirements for mediators but appropriate credentials and standards are still being developed. If you are a counselor or therapist, you have probably had extensive training in human behavior, and if you are an attorney you have an expertise in practicing law. However, mediation encompasses aspects of both professions. So in addition to learning divorce mediation from this manual, we recommend that you develop skills and knowledge in the "other" profession mentioned above. If you wish to receive referrals from the court, find out about requirements for those credentials by checking with your state court administrator's office.

Responsibilities

Your role as a mediator is to assist your clients in developing mutually beneficial agreements. You will be helping your clients use their knowledge, creativity,

---

*There is nothing wrong with clients making choices outside the norms, but you need to explain in your memorandum of agreement the basis for the departure as the attorneys and judge raise questions about any departures from state laws.

strength, and good intentions in a productive manner. Fulfilling this role consists of the following:

- Managing the mediation process
- Promoting cooperative behavior
- Understanding conflict
- Maintaining impartiality
- Demonstrating listening skills and a non-judgmental attitude

Managing the Mediation Process

Managing the mediation process—keeping it cooperative and focused on the task at hand—is your primary responsibility as a mediator. Meeting this challenge requires that you

Know and use a variety of techniques and strategies.   Several techniques are discussed under the headings "Listening and Responding," "Reframing," and "Asking Questions" in this chapter. In addition, we discuss many mediator strategies in detail in Chapter Eleven. Becoming thoroughly familiar with these techniques and strategies will enable you to use them constructively. Obviously, they cannot cover every situation that might arise during mediation; however, being familiar with them will help you mediate common situations and will encourage you to use your own creativity in dealing with extremely unusual situations.

Narrow the issues.   Some of the issues facing clients during mediation can seem overwhelming. If you help your clients break down such issues into their smaller, more manageable components, they will find them easier to manage.

Ensure the participation of both clients.   You will need to manage the flow of the discussion so that both people are able to express their thoughts on all issues.

Encourage openness.   If you perceive that a client is withholding information or avoiding a particular subject, encourage that person's thoughts and comments. Open and honest discussions are essential in establishing effective agreements.

Listen and Respond

As a mediator you need to listen and respond effectively. The following are some useful guidelines:

- Use body language that invites openness: smile, maintain eye contact, keep your arms unfolded, and lean toward the client who is speaking.
- Use a tone of voice that is respectful, kind, and interested.
- Listen with your heart. Show your clients that you care about them. Heartfelt listening is a gift that clients gratefully receive. It changes attitudes, demeanor, thinking, and their responses.
- Empathize with your clients. When a client is speaking, try putting yourself in his or her place. Consider, for example, how it must feel to participate in a divorce media-

tion when you do not want the divorce to happen. Be careful about bringing up similar feelings and problems from your own experience, however, as they may not be appreciated by your clients.

- If you do not understand something that is said, either attempt to restate the words and feelings you heard or simply say that you do not understand and ask the client to repeat the statement. Never ignore a misunderstanding; if you do not understand a particular comment, the other client may not understand it either. After the comment is repeated, try restating. Make it your habit to clarify, clarify, clarify.
- If you offer suggestions, make sure that you frame them as options, not as advice.
- Remember that you do not have a vested interest in the outcome of the mediation. Accept your clients' decisions without judging them.
- Encourage your clients to listen to each other. To promote understanding, occasionally ask one client what he or she heard the other person say. Also encourage each client to express his or her needs and why those needs are so important, so that each can more fully understand the other.
- If a client expresses frustration, support their frustration as an opportunity for growth. Although this mode of expression is not necessarily productive, the underlying motivation is what needs to be understood and resolved, if possible. Similarly, if a client becomes angry, accept the negative energy of that anger and help the client turn it into a positive opportunity for understanding and growth. If you challenge a client's anger, the discussion will only become more negative and aggressive. When you learn underlying causes of frustration and anger, you can help your clients make better choices.

Reframe

An impending divorce often cripples people's ability to communicate with each other. Their emotions interfere and cause them to say things that are not helpful. When this happens, the mediator needs to intervene.

When a client says something that is obviously colored by emotion, you can use a technique called reframing, which consists of rephrasing the comment in order to better understand the message. The exact approach you will take and the degree to which you reframe will depend on your ability to hear the message and respond accurately.

Suppose, for example, that you are mediating the divorce of your clients Bob and Jane. Bob says, "I want the kids with me because Jane is an unfit mother."

You can reframe this in any of several ways:

- If you want to clarify the outcome that Bob seems to want, you might say, "Bob, I think I hear you saying that you believe you have to prove Jane unfit so you can have a significant parenting relationship in the future."
- If you want to address Bob's concern but remove the aspect of blaming Jane, you might say, "So . . . , Bob, you want the kids to be with you more of the time than with Jane because you have concerns about her parenting."
- If you want Bob to specify his concern about Jane's parenting but alleviate any fear that Jane might be feeling, you might say, "Bob, you say that you want the kids. But you're not trying to terminate Jane's parental rights, are you?" (Wait for Bob's

response, assuming it will be no. In our experience no one has ever said yes.) "Then what is it that troubles you about her parenting?"

- If you suspect that Bob has an underlying fear that has nothing to do with Jane's ability to parent, you might say, "Bob, although I hear you comparing your parenting abilities to Jane's, I sometimes hear a client make comments like that because he doesn't want to lose his relationship with the children."
- If you believe that Bob is trying to pick a fight about custody with Jane, you might say, "Bob, I hear you getting caught up in a contest. Would it help to talk about a parenting plan instead of Jane's fitness as a parent?"
- If you believe that Bob and Jane are both getting caught up in a custody contest, and you want to encourage creativity and productive action instead, you might say, "Let's look at custody from another angle. How about figuring out a parenting agreement that will allow both of you to be the best, most active parents you can be?"

Asking Questions

There are significant differences between the way the basic questions in an adversarial divorce are framed and the way in which they are framed in client-centered mediation. For example, consider the adversarial question, Who will be awarded custody of the minor children? This question assumes that it is necessary to determine ownership of the children, with one greater and one lesser level of ownership; therefore, it results in labeling one parent as less important in some sense.

Also, beginning the discussion on parenting by interjecting the word custody creates the wrong focus and motivation for dealing with children. The focus is on the past and on determining which parent has been "better." Courts generally award custody to the parent who can produce evidence of the more appropriate parental behavior in the past. Mental health professionals know that developing a future parenting plan based on the concept of custody is unhealthy and generally results in an acrimonious foundation for the future parenting relationship. It is no wonder, then, that so many couples who experience custody trials or adversarial custody negotiations have difficult problems with their future parenting relationship.

Instead, in client-centered mediation avoid the term custody until your clients have established a parenting plan for the future. (For that matter, also avoid the term visitation.) Your question then becomes, What future parenting arrangements can you agree to so that each of you can be the type of parent you want to be? When framed in this way, the question creates a different focus and leads to a very different outcome. Cooperative attitudes and mutual planning are necessary to answer this question.

In all phases of mediation, be sure to ask questions that

- Are future oriented
- Encourage mutual understanding and cooperation
- Lead to options and solutions
- Are open-ended and cannot be answered with a simple yes or no
- Build from the general to the specific, working toward greater clarity

In mediation, couples are required to look toward the future because it is the future that can be planned and built in such a way that past problems do not recur. Asking future-oriented questions enables clients to work through the difficult task of planning how to be separate, single adults and parents.

Another aspect of asking questions is the importance of being prepared to explain why you are asking a particular question. Also ask hypothetical questions beginning with "What if" as a way of expanding clients' thinking and encouraging creativity.

One of the most important skills of a mediator is asking questions, and the way in which you ask them is one of the most critical factors for success. This is a skill that takes practice, but it can be learned. Throughout this book, in the chapters that deal with the different subject areas and in Chapter Eleven, you will see examples of constructive questions.

Promoting Cooperative Behavior

People respond to conflict in a number of different ways. As a mediator you need to examine your own comfort with conflict in order to understand the range of responses that clients exhibit so that you can intervene effectively.

Morton Deutsch, a professor at Yale University, points out, "Conflict is determined by what is valued by the conflicting parties and by what beliefs and perceptions those parties hold. But values, beliefs, and perceptions are not always unalterable" (1973, p. 17). A major part of your role as mediator consists of (1) identifying when the clients' values, beliefs, or perceptions are interfering with progress and (2) intervening in such a way that you encourage the clients to look at issues differently.

You will find that many of your clients have had only negative experience with conflict. They do not know how to manage it or channel it into productive behavior. Consequently, they view it with distaste or even dread, and they believe the common myths about conflict. Figure 1 presents these myths along with the corresponding realities. You may want to share this information with your clients as you urge them to view conflict differently. (Note that this information on conflict also appears in Chapter Three in the client's workbook.) Encourage the clients to think of conflict as an opportunity to increase their options and to grow.

The two most frequent responses to conflict are avoidance and aggression. Frequently you will find that one client tries to avoid conflict while the other takes a combative stance. Your task is to intervene with any of a number of strategies (see Chapter Eleven) to influence the clients' communication, attitudes, bargaining process, and goals in such a way that cooperative problem solving can occur.

Figure 2 presents the three basic responses to conflict—avoidance, problem solving, and aggression—along with some of the behaviors that characterize each response. When you can move your clients away from avoidance and aggression and toward problem solving, they will begin to think of creative ways to resolve the issues that confront them.

Mediators, like all people who work with those in conflict, have an important responsibility. Deutsch (1973) offers valuable advice: "The point is not how to

Figure 1. Myths and Realities About Conflict

MYTH	REALITY
CONFLICT IS NEGATIVE	"CONFLICT IS NATURAL, NEITHER GOOD NOR BAD, IT JUST IS" (Crum, 1987)
CONFLICT IS A CONTEST	CONFLICT IS NOT A CONTEST CONFLICT IS OPPORTUNITY FOR GROWTH CONFLICT IS OPPORTUNITY FOR CHANGE CONFLICT IS OPPORTUNITY TO LEARN
CONFLICT MEANS YOU HAVE FAILED	VIBRANT, LIVELY, SUCCESSFUL, HEALTHY RELATIONSHIPS HAVE CONFLICT. IF NO CONFLICT, RELATIONSHIP IS STATIC OR MAY BE DEAD.
CONFLICT IS PAINFUL	USING ADVERSARIAL TECHNIQUES TO RESOLVE CONFLICT IS QUITE PAINFUL. USING COOPERATIVE TECHNIQUES TO RESOLVE CONFLICT IS CHALLENGING, EXCITING AND PRODUCTIVELY CREATIVE.
CONFLICT SHUTS DOWN PRODUCTIVITY, CREATIVITY AND DESTROYS RELATIONSHIPS	ONLY IF CONFLICT IS LEFT TO FESTER UNRESOLVED

eliminate or prevent conflict but rather how to make it productive" (p. 18). In addition, Robert Baruch Bush and Joseph Folger (1994), authors of *The Promise of Mediation*, note that conflict affords opportunities for moral development and that mediation captures those opportunities "by helping people respond with compassionate strength as they address difficult and often painful disputes" (p. xv).

Maintaining Neutrality
In mediation you will be leading your clients toward settlement without making decisions for them. To be effective as a leader, you must be perceived as absolutely impartial.

Figure 2. The Three Basic Responses to Conflict

AVOIDANCE	PROBLEM SOLVING	AGGRESSION
Is silent, uninvolved	States feelings and needs	Attacks the other
Withdraws	Asks mutual questions	Interrupts
Allows interruption	Speaks for self	Subordinates the other
Allows stereotyping of self	Neither stereotypes nor allows stereotyping of self	Stereotypes the other
Does not make eye contact	Maintains eye contact	Glares
Exhibits poor posture	Exhibits open posture	Exhibits invasive posture
Withholds information, opinions, and feelings	Discloses information, opinions, and feelings	Conceals information, opinions, and feelings
Listens ineffectively	Listens effectively	Listens selectively
Is indecisive	Is able to look at options	Is dominating
Is apologetic	Investigates interests and needs	Is loud, abusive, blaming, and sarcastic
Has no confidence	Is confident	Is overconfident, acts like a "big shot"
Is passive	Is assertive	Is aggressive
Sees conflict as negative	Sees conflict as an opportunity	Sees conflict as a contest
Hides	Cooperates	Competes

Strategies for establishing and maintaining the necessary impartiality include the following:

- Periodically check with your clients to make sure they feel that both the process and the outcomes are meeting their standards of fairness. For example, keep in mind that fairness in a property settlement does not necessarily mean equal bottom lines for the clients; it means that the clients perceive the settlement as a whole to be "fair" according to their own sense of fairness. Generally you will find, too, that your clients' definition of fairness includes some reconciliation of emotional feelings as well as facts and figures.
- Sit equidistant from each client. Sitting closer to one person than the other may be perceived as taking a side.
- Make sure that you treat your clients courteously and as equals.
- Address both clients; ask each to respond to your questions.
- Ask questions that invite rather than interrogate.
- Ask questions that assist the less-knowledgeable client in learning more.
- Ask future-oriented questions that require a mutual effort to answer.
- Move the discussion back and forth between the clients. Use body language and eye contact as well as conversation to give equal time to the clients.
- Make sure that no one dominates the conversation. If one person tries to dominate, carefully turn your attention from that person and invite comments from the other.

- Resist stating your opinions; allow your clients to create their own outcomes. If they press you for your view, respond with a comment such as, "It really makes no difference what I think. What is important is what each of you thinks and what the two of you can eventually agree on."
- Never accept a favor from a client.
- If you practice another profession, never form a different professional relationship with either client after mediation.
- Refuse to make judgments about what or who was "right" or "wrong." You may find it useful, for example, to suggest that they might never agree on what or who was right or wrong in the past, but they can agree on what will happen in the future.
- Retain possession of the marker. Although the idea may seem strange, the felt-tipped marker with which you list clients' ideas on a flip chart seems to hold special powers. Clients almost always view the mediator's relinquishing the marker as favoritism, or giving up of control to the more dominant spouse.
- Maintain an intense focus on resolving issues. If the discussion starts to go off-track (for example, by focusing on one client's past behavior), explain that the clients need to redirect their efforts toward resolving their differences so that they can get on with their lives. Such a reminder can help to create a sense of security and stability for your clients at a time when they may feel that their lives are in chaos.

Demonstrating a Positive Non-Judgmental Attitude

The phrase "unconditional positive regard" was coined by psychotherapist Carl Rogers to describe the central concept of his person-centered therapy model. It is also one of the most powerful tools that a mediator can use. Treating clients with a positive non-judgmental attitude means showing that you believe they are worthy, you respect them, and you accept them, regardless of their character, demeanor, statements, presentation, or any other personal traits or behaviors. When you treat your clients with a positive, non-judgmental attitude, you not only empower them but also model the behavior that contributes to the positive resolution of conflict. You will also benefit from this approach: when you give respect, you receive respect.

Suppose, for example, that one of your clients has a personality trait that you find especially disagreeable. Maybe you see him as stingy or irascible or mean spirited, and maybe his wife shares your view of him. But you treat him with the same respect, caring, and concern that you would any client. You are patient with him, you always allow him to complete his thoughts, and you find something in his character to appreciate and acknowledge.

In a very short time you find that he responds as best he can with respect toward you and perhaps even his wife; he becomes involved in the mediation sessions as best he can. When his wife sees the change in his behavior, her disdain for him lessens, her demeanor changes, and she begins to communicate with less resentment, hurt, and anger. Both husband and wife participate more positively, and the mediation is not contaminated by the personality trait that you originally thought might cause a problem. Both parties save face and are empowered to go forward with a hopeful attitude.

Exercising patience, in particular, not only enhances unconditional positive regard but also offers other benefits during mediation:

- It has a calming effect on clients. Using a soft voice when clients are raising theirs, for example, encourages them to lower their voices so they can hear you.
- It indicates that you are not willing to buy into one client's demands or attempts to gain power over the other client.
- It creates a safe environment for your clients. They will feel secure in the knowledge that even in stressful situations they can count on you to stay in control.

References

Baruch Bush, R. A., & Folger, J. P. (1994). *The Promise of Mediation: Responding to conflict through empowerment and recognition.* San Francisco: Jossey-Bass.

Crum, T. F. (1987). *The Magic of Conflict: Turning a life of work into a work of art.* New York: Simon & Schuster.

Deutsch, M. (1973). *The Resolution of Conflict: Constructive and destructive processes.* New Haven, CT: Yale University Press.

4 Emotions Involved in Divorce

The impact of the emotions related to divorce is enormous. You must learn to be understanding, caring, sensitive, and respectful toward clients when they are emotionally "at their worst."

The emotions of divorcing people are like a temporary mental illness caused by their separation and their fears. These emotions usually diminish as the divorce is mediated. It is not at all uncommon to meet former clients years after mediation and have them apologize for their "craziness" at that time. But if you buy into the craziness by taking sides or if you show even a hint of a judgmental attitude during mediation, you may lose your impartiality, delay the clients' healing process, or even lose your clients just when they so desperately need a mediator.

To succeed at mediation and to help your clients deal with the emotional onset of divorce, you need to understand the psychology of the marriage breakdown and the different perspectives that each client brings to mediation. This short chapter is designed to help you acquire this understanding.

The Emotional Divorce Process

A marriage does not break down overnight. It takes time for the relationship to deteriorate. Many believe that the breakdown happens when people do not put their marriage first and nurture it as something very intimate and very important. Often the early signs of discontent go unnoticed, and negative intimacies cloud their interactions.

There is no research that indicates how long it takes for a marriage to break down; the amount of time differs with every couple. But after a period of discontent, incompatibility, arguments, and predominantly destructive behaviors, one party begins to consider the possibility of divorce. For purposes of this discussion, we refer to this person as Spouse A and to the other spouse as Spouse B (see Figure 3).

At some point during the breakdown of the marriage relationship, Spouse A begins to consider divorce as the solution to the problems. This is a personal time to contemplate the idea of divorce. The length of time varies for every spouse A. After some time passes, Spouse A makes a decision to divorce. This is a private decision, not yet shared with Spouse B or anyone else. Spouse A may mirror this

Figure 3.   The Emotional Divorce Process

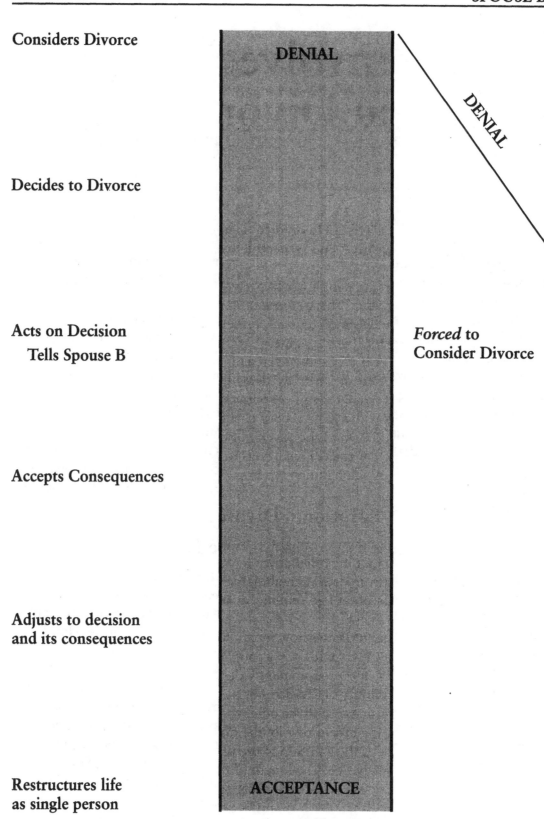

SPOUSE A   SPOUSE B

Considers Divorce

Decides to Divorce

Acts on Decision
   Tells Spouse B

Forced to
Consider Divorce

Accepts Consequences

Adjusts to decision
and its consequences

Restructures life
as single person

DENIAL

DENIAL

ACCEPTANCE

decision, however, by exhibiting distancing behaviors, moving emotionally and psychologically away from Spouse B. Spouse A may no longer be engaging in arguments or fights with Spouse B and may even show signs of relief or happiness at having made the decision. These behaviors of Spouse A may be misinterpreted by Spouse B—who has been in denial all along—as evidence that their relationship is improving.

More time passes, and Spouse A decides to act on the decision to divorce by telling Spouse B. Spouse B reacts with shock, anger, or fear, or by staying in denial. Spouse B's are often described as being like "a deer caught in the headlights," and their emotional responses are often filled with anger and fear.

This is a significant point in the emotional process of divorce, because this is often when Spouse A initiates the legal divorce process by scheduling an initial consultation with a mediator or filing a divorce petition. This has a tremendous impact on mediation. Often you, the mediator, will be faced in an initial consultation with Spouse A, who wants the divorce to happen as soon as possible, and Spouse B, who absolutely does not want to be sitting in your office. Clients are most emotionally ready to begin mediation when they have spent time with a counselor, are physically separated and have had time for each to adjust to the idea of divorce. Then they have both adjusted to the emotional divorce process and are more able to begin the process of making divorce decisions. Even in a situation in which both spouses say that they want to divorce quickly, one spouse is usually moving much faster than the other.

The Relationship Circle

It can be useful to display the relationship circle on the flip chart in order to help clients see that they can move away from intense negative intimacies by discussing and creating rules about their future conduct. When clients understand this process, often they change their behavior and begin to cooperate with each other because they see that they have the same goal: to establish a more businesslike relationship with written agreements about their conduct in the future. Their new understanding facilitates mediation by helping them to move away from the negative intimacies they have been experiencing and toward the new and different relationship they will be forming.

We have found that sharing the Relationship Circle (Figure 4) with our clients and explaining it to them is an excellent way to build their understanding of the changes in their relationship and the potential to make it better in the future. (Note that this figure also appears in Chapter Two of the client's workbook. See the section "The Relationship Circle" in Chapter Five of this manual for information on when to present this figure).

Friendship
The first quarter of the circle, Friendship, represents the beginning phase of the clients' relationship. That early phase was characterized by courtesy, fun, compatibility, and respect; it was casual, positive, enjoyable, and increasingly more exclusive and meaningful. Eventually, the two people marry and committed themselves to an exclusive, long-term relationship.

Figure 4. The Relationship Circle

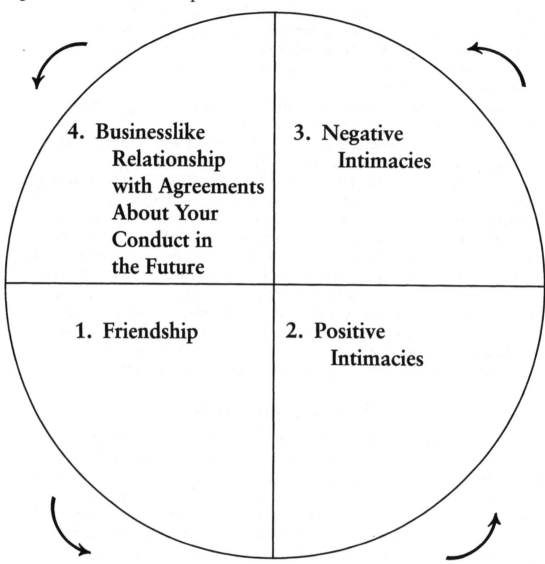

Positive Intimacies

The second quarter of the circle, Positive Intimacies, represents the second phase of the clients' relationship, the early part of their marriage. New chores, roles, and expectations were added to the partnership. This phase was probably dominated by a continuation of the characteristics of the friendship quarter, perhaps with greater depth and intensity. Positive intimacies were the things the partners shared that were unique to their relationship: each person got to know the other's habits and what the other was thinking or feeling; one said the same thing or had the same idea at the same time as the other; the two shared private jokes and language.

They may have had conflicts during this phase, but they resolved these conflicts and forgave each other. They were able to confide in each other with secrets and with life issues and had a deep, abiding trust in each other.

With some relationships this phase lasts a lifetime. With others, as in the case of a couple seeking a divorce, it ends when the negatives dominate the relationship.

Negative Intimacies

The third quarter of the circle, Negative Intimacies, represents the third phase in the continuum of the clients' relationship, the phase when they generally seek the services of a mediator. Negative intimacies are behaviors such as criticism, putdowns, name calling, power struggles, cheapshots, and displays of abusive anger. This phase can begin under any of several different circumstances, including the following:

- When there has been a major breach of trust such as an affair or physical abuse
- When deep emotional pain has resulted from arguments that escalated into fights that were not resolved or forgiven
- When the relationship has been overburdened with stress, disorder, addiction, financial problems, or other potentially destructive problems
- When the services of a therapist have not resulted in a reconciliation.

Of course, a healthy marriage also experiences negative intimacies. But in a healthy marriage the partners play out these experiences differently; consequently, the negative intimacies do not dominate the relationship. For example, when the partners engage in negative intimacies but quickly recognize them as potentially destructive to the relationship, they work together—with or without professional help—to eliminate the negative behaviors, resolve the underlying problems, and forgive each other. They make a conscious effort to ensure that positive intimacies dominate their relationship, and the relationship endures.

But negative intimacies can cause irreparable damage when they are not quickly recognized and addressed. Once they dominate the relationship, that relationship becomes irreparably damaged, and the result is usually divorce.

Businesslike Relationship

The fourth quarter of the circle, Businesslike Relationship, introduces the clients to your role as a mediator. It represents a positive ending to a marriage relationship that results in divorce. When two people leave a marriage overwhelmed by negative intimacies and have family and friends in common, they need to develop a functional relationship so that both of them can be present at events attended by their family or friends without detracting from everyone's enjoyment.

By building a businesslike relationship with agreements about their conduct in the future, the clients will be able to feel emotionally safe in each other's presence. A businesslike relationship is especially important when children are involved, as parents have to relate to each other as parents for the rest of their lives.

Using the relationship circle allows the couple to see clearly the goals of the mediation process. By focusing on building agreements about their conduct in the future, the mediator can use the relationship circle on the flip chart to show that there is really no need to investigate or re-hash the past. Although some history is certainly important during mediation, the couple begins to see that it is useless to conduct a custody investigation, for example. After all, a custody investigtion concentrates on the blame and fault of the past to judge who is the better parent. It also heightens both parents' fear of loss. The mediation process on the contrary focuses on their building a plan for the future that avoids the mistakes of the past. With this subtle but powerful shift in focus, the mediator may say to Mary, "I appreciate your concerns about his past parenting, but could you now describe what you want him to do differently in the future that will address your concerns and assist him in becoming a better parent in your eyes so you won't have the same complaints in the future?"

Most couples experience the emotional divorce process much as the grief process so aptly described in the book, *On Death and Dying*, by Elisabeth Kubler-Ross, M.D. As in death, divorcing people experience major losses in their lives such as their family, home, neighborhood, in laws, friends, role as spouse and/or parent, routines, and even religious congregation, to name a few. For many, including Spouse As, the deepest loss is the loss of a dream—their hopes and images of a shared life. So the mediator needs to understand and recognize that these losses are real, and they underlie the emotions and behaviors exhibited by clients in mediation.

Reference

Kubler-Ross, Elisabeth (1969). *On Death and Dying*. New York, NY: Macmillan Publishing Co.

Part II
The Mediation Process

5  Initial Consultation

A potential mediation typically begins when one person inquires about your services. Your first response to the person needs to be compassionate, factual, impartial, and professional.

You can handle an initial inquiry in different ways. For example, sometimes a person will phone, and you will find it convenient and easy to answer his or her questions at that time. At other times you may want to send the person an informational letter and a brochure about your services along with an offer of an initial one-hour consultation at no charge.

Occasionally you may be approached by a person who has been referred by the court. The person may or may not be well informed about the court's recommendation of mediation. In any case you may phone the court or the attorneys to ascertain or clarify the following:

- The reason for the referral
- The expectations of the judge
- Any time limits that the court has imposed
- What reports the court expects on conclusion of the mediation.*

In your contact with the court you may need to explain the rules of confidentiality in mediation. Do not include confidential information about the clients without their agreement in a memo to be submitted to the court or others. (See the Rules of Mediation in Appendix A). You are welcome to use these rules as they stand or to adapt them in any way that you feel is appropriate. When you contract with clients, both you and they agree to abide by these rules, which are incorporated into the contract.)

After you are contacted, if the couple decides to follow through with an initial consultation, you then phone or write each of them to set up the initial consultation. The couple does not need to make a firm decision until the end of the initial consultation or possibly later, if they need additional time to decide whether to use the mediation process.

---

*In this situation be absolutely clear about what information the court expects and the confidentiality of mediation if the couple reaches impasse.

The initial consultation is a face-to-face meeting with the couple. This meeting takes forty-five minutes to an hour and includes these elements:

- Administering the Intake Form
- Screening for abuse
- Forming a relationship
- Providing information about the mediation process
- Closing the consultation

Administering the Intake Form

An Intake Form, which appears in Appendix A, is completed by each person.

Screening for Abuse

Important Note: If you are just beginning to mediate divorces and you have no previous training in mediating couples with a history of domestic violence, we strongly recommend that you not accept such a case until you have acquired special training in recognizing abuse and mediating these cases. For recommendations about domestic violence training programs, contact the providers of services to victims and perpetrators of abuse.

Also understand that you must never mediate the abuse occurence itself.

After they have completed their Intake Forms, privately review them prior to beginning the consulation and before meeting with them separately. If one has disclosed or implied the existence of abuse, you should meet with each client separately for a few minutes to clarify and assess the abuse in the relationship.

If you do not perform this assessment before you mediate, you run the risk of causing more harm: the abused spouse is already misunderstood, and the mediation process can become another setting in which he or she is not listened to or believed or understood. Also, without an assessment, you might find yourself in a situation that makes mediation difficult, if not impossible, for both you and the clients.

When you verify abuse, you may proceed with mediation only under specific conditions described later in this chapter. If you decide not to mediate, you may want to refer the prospective clients to another mediator, or a therapist or program that specializes in working with people in abusive relationships. Keep a list of those professionals to whom you can refer clients. Talk with other mediators and ask their recommendations of therapists or programs that work with abusers and abused people. Begin to make your own list of referral resources.

Sometimes clients will not disclose or imply the existence of abuse, but you will recognize signs that indicate you should meet with the parties separately. The following paragraphs provide you with some essential information on abusive behaviors and indicators of abuse that you need to be able to recognize.

Common Behaviors of Abusers

Domestic violence is the emotional, sexual, psychological, economic, or physical abuse (or a combination of these) carried out systematically or routinely by one spouse toward the other. It is motivated by the abuser's need to control and to have power over the other spouse. It is intentional and, therefore, can be controlled by the abuser. Although there is never an excuse for abuse, the abuser frequently attempts to rationalize the behavior by blaming the other spouse.

The following is a list of behaviors that an abuser commonly exhibits outside the mediation environment:

Isolating the other.   Isolating behavior consists of controlling what the other person does, whom the other sees and talks to, and where the other goes. Frequently, the other is homebound without phone or transportation, and totally dependent on the abuser.

Emotionally or psychologically abusing the other.   These behaviors include putting down or insulting the other, engaging in "cheap shots," making the other feel bad about himself or herself, name calling, yelling at the other, ridiculing the other, and playing mind games.

Using money to control.   Behaviors in this category include trying to prevent the other from obtaining or keeping a job, making the other ask for money, giving the other an allowance, and taking the other's money.

Using the children as a weapon.   These behaviors include making the other feel guilty about the children, using the children to give messages to the other, and using visitation as a way to harass the other.

Threatening.   Threatening behaviors consist of making or carrying out threats to hurt the other emotionally, threatening to take the children, threatening suicide, or reporting the other to a government welfare agency.

Using "gender privilege."   This kind of abuse includes treating the other like a servant, making all of the "big" decisions, and acting like the supreme authority.

Intimidation.   Intimidating behaviors consist of putting the other in fear by using looks, a loud voice, gestures, and actions (smashing things, destroying the other's property).

Physical abuse.   Physical abuse includes pushing, shoving, bodily throwing, beating, hitting, slapping, choking, pulling hair, twisting arms, tripping, biting, punching, kicking, grabbing, and using a weapon against the other.

Sexual abuse.   Sexual abuse includes such behaviors as unwanted touching or viewing, withholding sex or affection in order to punish, using sexual labeling ("bitch," "whore," "slut"), humiliating the other, forcing the other to strip, having affairs, behaving promiscuously, forcing the other to watch sex, raping, forcing the other to have sex after battering, and engaging in incest.

Indicators of Abuse

During the initial consultation and throughout the mediation process, you need to be aware of the following general indicators of abuse:

- One party exhibits dominating or intimidating behaviors.
- One party speaks softly, carefully, and timidly, making little eye contact.
- One party speaks for the other party, discounting anything said by the other.
- One party reluctantly agrees to things that may not be in his or her own best interest (for example, agreeing to accept no financial support despite having no income).
- One party manipulates or threatens the other.

In addition to these general behaviors, you need to watch for any of the following situations, especially when abuse has not been disclosed. (In the following examples the husband is presented as the abuser and the wife as the abused. Of course, men are also the recipients of abuse but only in a very small percentage of relationships.)

- The husband is angry and speaks mostly about his wife. He has little to say about himself and gives the impression that his wife is the entire problem.
- The wife is the initiator of the divorce, and the husband clearly communicates that he is adamant about not wanting the divorce to occur.
- The wife speaks in low and measured tones, taking great pains not to disagree openly with the husband.
- The husband and wife fight over who should move out of the house. The husband says that if the wife wants to leave, she should be the one to move out. Any attempt to discuss the husband's moving out is met with great resistance and anger.
- The wife has difficulty expressing her needs. She often makes veiled comments, such as "Things have been difficult," "We can't continue to go on like this," and "It's hard on the children," but never openly mentions abuse.
- The husband exhibits controlling behavior: he is the one who scheduled the mediation session. He is the one who has managed the finances. The wife may comment that she has not hired an attorney because she does not have any money.
- The body language of the wife indicates fear and tension, and she is unable to make direct eye contact with the husband.
- The husband denigrates the wife, putting her down as a mother and threatening to obtain sole custody or to take the children away from her.

You may see one or two of these indicators in a nonabusive relationship. But when several or all of these indicators are present, inquire further about possible abuse. Remember that spousal abuse, like incest, alcoholism, and drug abuse, is a family secret that most couples have extreme difficulty acknowledging openly.

Separate Meetings with Clients

When you determine that abuse definitely or probably exists in the relationship and you decide to meet with the clients separately, your goal is to acquire the information to help you decide whether and how to mediate the divorce.

In both meetings, ask the following questions:

- What abuse has taken place in your marriage?
- Who has done what?
- How long has this been going on?
- How often does it happen?
- What happens to you and your family afterward?
- Are you seeking this divorce?
- Are you ready for your marriage to end?
- During the mediation sessions, you and your spouse will be together in the same room. What are your concerns about mediating your divorce settlement at the same table with your spouse?
- Is anyone pressuring you to mediate? Who? Why do you think this person is pressuring you?
- How do you assess your ability to participate in mediation?
- In what ways are you afraid of your spouse?
- What threats have been made by your spouse?
- What physical danger do you fear from your spouse?
- Is there now a court order for protection presently in effect? Has there ever been any in the past?
- What threats has your spouse made regarding the children?
- What are your concerns about the children's physical safety when they are with the other parent?
- Has a child protection agency been active with your family? If so, what was the complaint? Was the complaint adjudicated?

Following are some additional questions to ask the abused spouse:

- What do you know in general about spousal abuse?
- Are you able to negotiate with your spouse in your own best interest?
- How do you identify the times when you are most at risk?
- Do you have a safety plan for yourself and your children? If so, what is it? Do you need to develop one?
- Are you able to resist your spouse's controlling behaviors? If so, how do you resist?
- What signal will you give me to tell me you feel threatened or unsafe so I can stop the session and meet with each of you separately?

There are also additional questions for the abusive spouse:

- Do you recognize that your behavior toward your spouse has been or is abusive and controlling?
- Are you able to negotiate with your spouse without name calling, threatening, coercing, bullying, or intimidating?
- How do you get along with others—neighbors, relatives, and co-workers, for example?
- Divorce evokes many emotions. How will you control your emotions in mediation sessions?

- What will you do to let me know that you are having difficulty controlling your negative feelings?
- As a condition of mediation, would you agree to having your spouse leave each session fifteen minutes before you so that the two of you do not have an opportunity to get into an argument or fight as you leave?

Ask any other questions of either party that may be helpful in determining whether or not you are comfortable undertaking their mediation. Some of their answers may lead you to believe that it is not appropriate for you to mediate. For example, the abused party may be so fearful that he or she will not sit in the same room with the abuser; the abuser may be very threatening in demeanor; either party may refuse to mediate; or you may not feel qualified to handle the situation.

If you do not wish to proceed with mediation, tell them about your decision. You may tell them separately or together. Regardless of which approach you choose, take responsibility for the decision even if it is based on the abused person's decision not to mediate. It is important not to disclose any of the actual answers that appear on the Intake Forms.

Although such a meeting can be difficult, it is important that you appear comfortable in asking the screening questions. As you acquire more information during each meeting, you will be able to ask more specific questions about the nature, extent, frequency, and impact of the abuse.

If you are aware of the existence of abuse before the initial consultation (for example, as a result of information disclosed by a prospective client while inquiring about your services, as a result of your contact with the court, or indicators on the intake form), you may choose to meet separately with each prospective client just before the initial consultation in order to gain more specific information.

Note that holding separate meetings with the two parties is a technique that should be used only when there are indications of abuse or as a strategy to avoid impasse later in the mediation process.

Forming a Relationship

After screening for abuse, you again meet with both prospective clients in the same room. If you have not already done so, introduce yourself and briefly describe your qualifications as a divorce mediator. A good opening question is to ask the clients if they are, in fact, getting a divorce. This question is used to clarify the purpose of the mediation consultation. At some point, you can ask each client to identify his or her greatest area of concern about the divorce, as this information will be important if you decide to mediate the case.

At this time you should also give each person a copy of the client's workbook. As you provide information, you can start forming a relationship with the prospective clients by:

- Demonstrating your neutrality
- Modeling honesty
- Validating and addressing the prospective clients' concerns about fairness

- Establishing control
- Demonstrating professional competency

Demonstrating Neutrality

The prospective clients will be looking for clues that you do not favor one over the other. It is important to assure both of them that you are impartial and unbiased. This is accomplished by maintaining equal eye contact, positioning yourself approximately equidistant from the prospective clients, and responding to all of their questions by focusing on both of them when you answer. For more detailed information on demonstrating impartiality, see "Maintaining Neutrality" in Chapter Three.

When spousal abuse exists in the relationship, the abuser is often very angry about being forced to consider divorce and either may be suspicious of your impartiality or may not understand it. During the initial consultation, you may have to take more time to explain mediation.

Modeling Honesty

Prospective clients are looking for answers to the difficulty they are facing. Do not "hard sell" yourself or mediation, but let them know that you believe mediation can work for them because they are well-intentioned people who are capable of making their own decisions.

Although there is nothing mysterious about the legal process of divorce, prospective clients need to be reassured that you can and will help them through the decision-making maze. Above all, make sure that you respond directly and honestly to each and every question they raise. Your honesty and respect will put both of them at ease.

Validating Concerns About Fairness

Prospective clients considering mediation often have an overriding concern that they may not be able to achieve a fair result through mediation or that they will reach impasse. Acknowledge that you have not experienced their marital history, but assure them that you will assist them in arriving at a fair settlement. Help them develop options and use techniques to decrease the possibility of impasse.

When spousal abuse exists in the relationship, it is important to empower the abused to participate in defining what is fair. The abuser may try to dominate by stating that they have already reached agreement about almost everything without permitting the other to comment.

Establishing Control

Every couple you meet is looking for professional guidance and assistance, so it is important to establish control of the session. Be willing to ask questions about the positions taken by one or both prospective clients. Many couples want to tell you about the ugly details of the past by blaming the other. Always control the initial consultation by ensuring that the discussion focuses mostly on the goals you wish to accomplish during the consultation.

When spousal abuse exists in the relationship, exert more control if necessary and be very aware of the prospective clients' behaviors and body language.

Taking Time to Interact

During the initial consultation, the prospective clients will be looking for signs of your competence so that they can determine whether to hire you. Provide them with your professional mediation credentials, and recognize that they need some time to interact with you before engaging your services. Make sure that you give them the time and interaction they need to appraise your competence and their comfort with you.

When spousal abuse exists in the relationship, the abuser may challenge your abilities. Do not be intimidated; stay confident and kind.

Providing Information

You need to provide prospective clients with information on the following subject areas:

- The emotions involved in divorce
- A comparison of an adversarial divorce with a mediated divorce process
- The benefits of client-centered mediation
- An overview of the subjects covered in the mediation process
- Your role as mediator
- The Rules of Mediation and the Contract to Mediate
- Your fees

Emotions of Divorce

Give each prospective client a copy of the client's workbook.* Using the information in Chapter Four of this manual (which is also found in Chapter Two of the client's workbook), briefly explain the emotions involved in divorce. Emphasize that the emotions the clients are now feeling are normal and temporary; they will diminish as they make progress towards a settlement. To assist in making this point, show and explain Figure 4, "The Relationship Circle" (Figure 2 in the client's workbook).

Also explain that the mediation process itself helps to alleviate some of the pain that the clients are experiencing. As they discover that they can work together cooperatively to make decisions about the future, they will begin to heal.

Two Common Approaches to Divorce: Comparison of an Adversarial Divorce with a Mediated Divorce Process

Use the information in Chapter Two of this manual (which is also found in Chapter Three of the client's workbook) to explain the two common approaches to divorce

---

*You can use the client's workbook in any way you wish. We recommend giving each prospective client a copy during the initial consultation. We have found that people appreciate receiving this information and tend to come back to contract with us. If you prefer, however, you may sell the workbooks to prospective clients and then subtract the price from your fees if the couple subsequently contracts with you.

that are available to clients: adversarial litigation, and mediation. Discuss how these approaches differ from one another.

Point out that the adversarial approach to divorce emphasizes each party's competing for what he or she needs even at the expense of the other party, whereas mediation emphasizes both parties' cooperating to meet the needs of both. When spousal abuse exists in the relationship, stress that the cooperation required of both parties during mediation is for the purposes of (1) dissolving the marriage without further abuse and (2) reaching an agreement on how the parties will function separately, with specific rules governing their communication and interactions in the future.

Benefits of Client-Centered Mediation

Again use the information in Chapter Two of this manual (also in Chapter Three of the client's workbook) to explain what is meant by client-centered mediation. Point out that the primary goal is to create a detailed Memorandum of Agreement of *their* decisions that will serve as the basis for creating *their* legal documents that terminate *their* marriage.

Then demonstrate the value of client-centered mediation for them. Assure the prospective clients that neither of them will be victimized during mediation. They will not be required to sign any papers that force them to give up any of their rights, and they will be asked to consult with their respective attorneys before the Memorandum of Agreement is finalized and implemented.

Emphasize that divorce creates a problem, not a contest, and although contests require winners and losers, problems require solutions. Emphasize that they will work together on the parenting, support, and property division problems, and that they can only achieve fairness by attacking the problems rather than each other. When spousal abuse exists in the relationship, the abuser may see this as an opportunity to attempt to encourage the other to drop the divorce because the two "can cooperate." In this case empower the abused spouse by stating that you understand the difficulty that working together might cause but that both of them need to maintain an ongoing relationship after divorce in order to raise their children from their two separate households. Emphasize that courts rarely terminate the parental rights of abusers.

If the prospective clients have difficulty in understanding what is different about client-centered mediation and how they will benefit from the process, consider asking each to identify some of their areas of disagreement and then explain how you would guide them toward mutual decision making in these areas. You can then contrast mediation with the way the adversarial system might approach these areas. However, if there is spousal abuse, be careful to not allow the abusive person an opportunity to re-victimize the abused person. Instead, emphasize that the mediation will concentrate on mutual decision making, and validate them for interest in learning about mediation.

Also, to reinforce the importance of cooperation, listen throughout the initial consultation for statements that indicate cooperation and always be quick to recognize any cooperative efforts you observe. If you cannot find an opening, acknowledge their willingness to meet together to consider mediation.

Overview of the Mediation Process

The following paragraphs offer some general information about the mediation process and a step-by-step overview that you can share with prospective clients. (Note that this overview also appears in Chapter Four in the client's workbook.)

Mediation is scheduled in two-hour sessions, each of which covers a specific subject area. Occasionally a session can be completed in less time; occasionally more time or an additional session will be required for a given subject area. The amount of time required and the order in which the subject areas are addressed are affected by such factors as the level of conflict between clients, the length of the marriage, the level of trust between clients, and the complexity of the issues involved. Sometimes you will skip a session (for example, with a childless couple or a couple whose children are adults, you will skip the session on parenting).

The prospective clients also should be informed that each session will involve homework on their part and that the homework assignments can be found in the client's workbook. Emphasize that the clients are to complete their homework assignments independently, not together. When spousal abuse exists, resist the abuser's offer to complete the other's questionnaire in addition to his or her own, explaining that there is not a right or wrong way to do the work and that each need only independently provide the information that he or she is aware of and has access to. Indicate clearly that the need to complete homework does not give the abuser the right to enter the abused party's home to obtain information.

The sessions, their content, and their usual order are described in the following:

Subject Area 1: Establishing a Parenting Plan

If there are minor children, it is often a good idea to begin with a discussion about parenting. During this session, the prospective clients will be discussing all aspects of their parenting plan, such as: a schedule of exchanges, future parenting concerns, a holiday schedule, a summer vacation schedule, and so on. As they work through these issues, tell them you will write their ideas, options, and decisions on a flip chart, and tape each flip chart sheet to the wall as it is completed.

After the session, you will gather all of the flip-chart sheets and use them to write a memo of their decisions and send the memo to each of them to review.

Subject Area 2: Budgeting for the Future

Explain that during the budgeting session, clients will plan their separate living expenses. You will be listing their budgeted expenses on the flip chart and then helping them ascertain their available net income. They then consider options for child support and spousal support. As they work, you will be writing their budgets, incomes, ideas, and decisions on the flip chart sheets displayed in front of them.

Tell them this step sometimes requires the help of a neutral expert, or accountant who can help them determine net income when someone is self-employed or owns a business. However, most of the time, you will be able to help them establish their net income from pay stubs or tax returns.

Explain that after the session, you will gather all of the flip chart sheets and use them to write a memo of their progress, options or decisions. Then you will be sending them a memo listing their budget and income numbers for their review.

Subject Area 3: Dividing Property

Mediation offers the opportunity to greatly reduce the time and cost of what the adversarial system referes to as the 'discovery process." During the property session, the clients focus on listing their marital and nonmarital property. They discuss every asset and liability they have, check documentation to verify values, and decide how to divide the marital property. Record all the data on the flip charts and after the session, collect all of the flip-chart sheets and send a memo showing the property listing and division options.

Subject Area 4: Addressing Tax and Legal Issues and Reviewing Agreements

Next, focus the clients on tax and legal issues involved in their divorce; note any issues that will affect their settlement. This is a good time to run the Divorce Tax Planner to address some of their "legal concerns." Then review all of their information, options and decisions from the previous sessions, discuss the contents and make their changes.

After the session, review all of the flip-chart sheets, and prepare a preliminary Memorandum of Agreement. Send a copy of this preliminary memorandum to each client for review.

Subject Area 5: Finalizing the Memorandum of Agreement

Since the end result of mediation is a memorandum similar to the legal stipulation for settlement, review the entire draft copy of the Memorandum of Agreement with the clients, concentrating especially on the wording but also making any necessary revisions and fine-tuning as requested by the two of them.

After the session, update the Memorandum of Agreement as agreed during the session, and send it to each client, asking each to review the memorandum with his or her attorney. If either attorney desires changes, and both clients agree, incorporate them into the memorandum. If neither attorney wants changes, the memorandum can be used by one of the attorneys to prepare the legal documents terminating the marriage.

The Mediator's Role

Use the information presented in Chapter Three to describe your role as mediator. Explain that you are not there to make decisions for them but to show how they can reach their own solutions. You can remind them that you do not have the power to help them change the past but that you do have the ability to help them shape the future in a way that is fair to both of them.

If their marriage relationship is characterized by a lot of fear, hurt, or anger that prevents one or both from mediating effectively, suggest that they consider marriage-closure counseling as a way to address such feelings. Give them the names of several competent therapists in the area who do this kind of therapy.

In summary, explain that by keeping them on task, you will manage their communications, create a safe environment in which they can interact and help them to create options and solutions that will benefit both. When there is spousal abuse, emphasize the safety of mediation. Also talk about any special conditions necessary for the abused party's safety and how those conditions will benefit the abusive party as well (see "Handling an Abusive Relationship" in Chapter Eleven).

Rules of Mediation and the Contract to Mediate

This section assumes that you will be using the Rules of Mediation that appear in Appendix A; these rules are incorporated into the Agreement to Mediate, which also appears in Appendix A. Give each client a copy of the Rules of Mediation and provide a brief explanation, drawing attention to any section of the Rules you think may address concerns expressed by one or both of them about full disclosure, misuse of mediation discussions, or other concerns they may have. When there is spousal abuse alleged, implement the following protocols:

- Mediation is a choice. A spouse must not be coerced by a message from the court or from the other spouse stating that mediation is the most appropriate alternative for a given reason (for example, because it will best serve the interests of the children).
- The choice not to mediate cannot be used against a spouse in any court proceeding to show lack of cooperation.
- Each spouse must be represented by an attorney, even though the attorneys might choose not to formally commence the divorce proceedings until mediation has been completed.
- Each may take advantage of the services that are available for victims and perpetrators of abuse. Explain how to obtain these services.
- Each may avail himself or herself of protection orders. Agreements reached in mediation can be incorporated into a stipulated court order. Explain that attorneys or legal advocates can provide information on how to obtain and use such orders.
- Each may ask neutral experts (child psychologists, CPAs, business appraisers, real estate appraisers, and the like) to attend the mediation sessions to offer information and recommendations. The abuser may attempt to challenge the use of neutral experts. If this occurs, explain with confidence the usefulness of neutral experts; do not become defensive.

Carefully explain the mediation rules regarding confidentiality, full disclosure, verification and valuation of assets, and the fact that no assets or debt may be significantly changed except by mutual agreement. When spousal abuse exists in the relationship, explain that you may terminate mediation if there is a recurrence of any abusive behavior. Explain that if the clients choose to mediate, each will need to sign a copy of the Agreement to Mediate, which incorporates the Rules of Mediation. By signing, the clients agree to adhere to the rules.

Review the Agreement to Mediate with the prospective clients. The sample contract in Appendix A contains a statement that should one or both of them wish to drop out of mediation, they agree to schedule a session to discuss this action. We highly recommend that you include this statement in your own contract. Emphasize that making a strong commitment to the process is an important factor in success.

Mediation Fees

Use the information presented under the heading "Cost" in Chapter Two to explain your fees. Explain to the clients that mediators generally charge a fee that is similar to that of divorce attorneys in the area. Mediation fees are due at the end of each session.

Explain that the administrative fee, discussed in Chapter Two, is paid when the Agreement to Mediate is signed, which may be at the end of the initial consultation if the clients feel comfortable in doing so. Often, however, prospective clients like to take their copies of the Agreement to Mediate home after the initial consultation so that they can thoroughly read it before they sign. Then, at the first mediation session they sign the agreement and pay the administrative fee. Fees for neutral experts are paid directly by the couple to those experts.

Sharing the fees in some manner is part of the commitment that the clients make to mediation. Take time to discuss with them how they will share fees (for example, by paying from a joint account or by splitting the cost). When spousal abuse exists in the relationship, the abuser may refuse to participate in paying fees or may insist that the abused spouse does not have any money. These response need to be discussed before you proceed with the fee payment arrangement. Regardless of the level of conflict, it is always best to have them share the fees in some manner, even if they pay them out of a joint savings account.

Closing the Initial Consultation

Not all couples will require detailed explanations about all the issues addressed in this chapter. However, we suggest you do try to cover most of these issues in some way. You will soon learn to use your own judgment in assessing how much information to give, just as you will develop your own style of mediating. The most critical skill to practice during the initial consultation is listening. Only by listening closely to what your prospective clients say can you respond to their concerns and adjust your presentation to emphasize some points more than others.

At this point, ask whether the prospective clients have decided to enter into mediation. If one or both of them is reluctant to commit, ask them to agree to a time by which they will make their decision.

As mentioned previously, when abuse or high conflict exists in the relationship, you may need to be more directive. Let the prospective clients know that you are in charge; answer their questions with nonthreatening, nonjudgmental, and nondefensive responses. Tell them to inform you or your office of their decision, not each other. Explain that you will then contact the other person.

If both parties have decided to proceed, they may sign a copy of the Agreement to Mediate, or they may sign it at the first scheduled working session.

At the conclusion of the initial consultation, regardless of whether the parties have contracted with you, you will have taken the first step toward empowering them to let go of the negative past so they can create a positive, respectful, safe manner of interacting.

Assigning Homework for Next Session

Before the clients leave, review their homework for the next session (see "Homework" in Chapter Five in the client's workbook). Give each a copy of the

Mediation Questionnaire. (Explain that the copy of the Mediation Questionnaire in the workbook is a sample only and should remain in the workbook. Also explain that you will need to make and keep a copy of their questionnaires for your use throughout the mediation process.)

Encourage the clients to make notes about questions or particular issues they would like to discuss at the next session. Remind them to bring materials with them as indicated in the same "Homework" section of the workbook.

6   Subject Area 1: Establishing a Parenting Plan

One of the basic assumptions of client-centered mediation is that most parents have a need to be recognized as full-time parents and not simply part-time visitors. In fact, for your clients with minor children, the subject area of post-divorce parenting probably weighs most heavily on their minds. For this reason we recommend that you consider taking some time at the first mediation session helping them to establish a parenting plan, while at the same time addressing other immediate needs.

To succeed in mediating this, you need a basic understanding of child development and what happens to children when their parents decide to divorce. The purpose of this chapter is to provide you with that understanding and to explain: the effects of spousal abuse on children; the underlying causes of custody contests; how to approach the creation of a parenting plan; and the mediation process used to help your clients establish that plan.

Child Development and the Effects of Divorce

Divorce in and of itself does not harm children; the intensity and duration of the conflict between parents is what negatively impacts children's adjustment. Even when parents do not divorce, intense conflict between them can harm their children.

Divorce does, however, affect children's behaviors. Children's reactions to divorce vary widely, depending on many factors, especially their age. These reactions can include denial, hoping that the parents will get back together, fears of abandonment, anger, hostility, depression, regressing in behavior or abandoning childhood too early, blaming themselves for the divorce, or acting out and treating their parents disrespectfully.

Be aware that divorcing parents usually do not know what is best for their children at this time. In fact, when their children exhibit what they consider to be negative behaviors, they frequently attribute those behaviors to the other parent's bad parenting practices. This means that in the process of working out a parenting plan, you need to educate your clients about the ways in which their children's behaviors are likely to change as a normal response to divorce. The following information is provided for your own understanding and as background for educating your clients. (Note that the material included in this section on child development and the effects of divorce on children also appears in Chapter Five in the client's workbook.)

Newborn to Six Months

In infancy, one of a child's primary developmental tasks is to learn how to trust. Babies need a lot of nurturing, attention, care, and admiration from their parents. As these needs are met, babies respond with eye contact, facial expressions, gestures, and certain movements. They need their parents to provide consistency in the environment, to adhere to routines, and to develop an emotional connection with them.

From birth to six months, infants need consistency in caregivers, the people they meet, and their routines. If parents must change their environment or the people around them, they should try to do so gradually. Babies this age need lots of physical attention, and eye contact, and talk that is kind and loving.

Parents should try to avoid angry outbursts and fighting in front of the baby. Optimally, each parent should spend time with the baby at least every other day; if they must have overnight exchanges, they should experiment first to see if the baby can tolerate such changes in environment and routines. Young babies may exhibit changes in their sleeping and eating habits as a reaction to the changes.

Seven to Eighteen Months

These are the months when babies develop attachments and begin to notice differences between caregivers and strangers. They need consistency in caregivers so that they can develop emotional connections with those caregivers. They still need a great deal of physical affection from their parents, and nurturing as they begin to develop their social skills.

Like younger infants, babies from seven to eighteen months need a high level of consistency not only from the people with whom they spend time but also in their routines. Parents need to take a gradual approach to introducing changes in caregivers and routines.

Infants at this age also begin to notice the differences between themselves and others. They get to know their surroundings and can communicate some of their physical needs through gestures and sounds. During this time they begin to develop language. Beginning at about nine months of age, babies begin to remember certain things within a context and their long-term memory begins to develop.

What Divorcing Parents Need to Know About Infants

The important things for divorcing parents to remember are as follows:

- The parents need to control their fights and angry or emotional outbursts in the presence of the baby.
- Parental cooperation is very important in coordinating the baby's care. The parents need to create a parenting schedule that specifies when each will attend to the baby—in its familiar surroundings if at all possible. As the baby gets older, a schedule of overnights with the other parent may gradually begin.

- If one parent is sometimes absent, parents should make sure that the baby always has some toys and belongings that will remind him or her of the absent parent. Even hearing the absent parent's voice on the phone or a tape is helpful to a baby.
- The baby may react to the divorce by changing eating and sleeping habits. The baby also may have difficulty in separating from a parent and may cling to the parent.

Eighteen Months to Three Years

Children in this age group continue to need consistency in parenting, environment, caregivers, and routines. They gradually become more independent and begin to test their limits. They need to learn self-control without losing self-esteem, and they need to learn to deal with doubt and shame.

As they learn these developmental tasks, they need continual reassurance of their parents' love. Their parents need to nurture them and set reasonable limits on them in a respectful manner. All children of this age develop fears of being abandoned, and these fears are exacerbated by separation from parents. In a parent's absence, a child may even fear that the parent has disappeared.

At this age, children are also concerned about security and who will care for them. When there are changes in routines and consistency, parents need to assure the child, in words that the toddler can understand, that he or she will be cared for.

What Parents Need to Know About Children Eighteen Months to Three Years

The important things for divorcing parents to know are as follows:

- Parents need to communicate frequently about the child's needs and any changes in the child's behavior.
- Parents need to allow the child to express feelings and fears in words and behavior. Parents, however, must not fight or use angry expressions in front of the child, who at this age is very aware of the parents' body language and how they treat each other. Parental conflict can cause the child to become distraught.
- Children at this age are particularly sensitive to being shamed. Consequently, parents must avoid doing anything that may cause the child to feel shamed.
- Children in this age group may cling to their parents and be attached to special objects such as toys or blankets. This is part of their normal development, not an indication that a child does not want to leave one parent and go with the other. Parents should begin to understand and respect this need, take time for nurturing during the exchange process, and not lose patience.
- If the toddler is being exchanged from home to home, the parents need to ensure that the child always has photos and special mementoes as reminders of the absent parent.
- The passing of time for a child of this age is very slow, so the child needs a schedule with more frequent exchanges between homes. Parents need to keep consistent schedules of exchanges and must help the child to understand when he or she will see the other parent.
- At this age, children may react to divorce by regressing in toilet training and sleeping habits. They may become more fearful or more aggressive. They may test the limits of their feelings and their security, especially in their parents' presence. It is important for parents to understand that these reactions are normal, and not indications of poor parenting.

Three to Five Years

The developmental tasks for children in this age group call for learning self-motivation and how to overcome guilt and to develop their own identities. They accomplish these tasks through play and exploration. Their parents need to set safe limits for them in a kind, understanding way.

At this age, children fear being abandoned and rejected. They also develop imagination and fantasies. In the midst of divorce, their fears and fantasies translate into insecurity about their own lovability. They may believe that a parent left the home because they (the child) did something wrong or bad or because they (the child) were not "good enough."

These children may create fantasies and tell stories about their parents' reconciliation. This is from their desire to have their parents back together. A parent who does not understand this may blame the other parent for "putting things in the child's head" because the other wants to reconcile. These children may also have gruesome fantasies about some horrible demise of a parent as a way of explaining why they believe that parent has disappeared.

Children at this stage may react to the divorce by regressing in their sleeping, eating, and toilet habits and even their talking. They may be very clingy and have difficulty going from one parent to the other. They may also become more aggressive in their activity and play, or more withdrawn.

What Parents Need to Know About Children Three to Five Years

The important things for divorcing parents to know are as follows:

- They need to be punctual when exchanging the child.
- They need to avoid jumping to conclusions about the stories the child is telling.
- They need to recognize the child's need to be with the primary caregiving parent at least every three or four days.
- They need to understand that their child is creative and will tell stories to alleviate anxieties about abandonment.
- They need to develop a consistent parenting schedule in order for the child to feel secure and to adjust.
- The child will naturally be on his or her best behavior when staying with the parent who moved out. This is because the child fears doing something that may make that parent disappear altogether. Then, when the child returns to the parent in the family home, he or she may feel more secure and may act out because the home is a safe place in which to do so. Sometimes parents misinterpret this behavior and suggest that the child just gets along better with one parent than the other. Parents need to understand that this is not always the case.

Six to Eight Years

The developmental task for children in this age group is to achieve a sense of competence by bonding with peers, by learning to compete with peers, and by trusting that their parents will be there for them when needed. At this stage, they are working on friendships, learning interpersonal and academic skills, and developing morals.

When their parents divorce, they have a strong yearning for the absent parent and a strong interest in parental reconciliation. They have loyalty conflicts, because they know they are part of both parents; when their parents fight they feel torn inside. When one parent disrespects the other, they feel that half of who they are is negated or discounted. They sometimes become very concerned about their parents' well-being and take care of a parent who is distraught or unhappy, even to the extent of denying their own needs.

These children do not want to be in the middle of their parent's conflicts and do not want to carry messages from one parent to the other. Consequently, the parents need to develop their communication protocols for separately parenting the child, without having the child carry any messages between parents.

The reaction to divorce for children at this stage is deep sadness, which may be revealed in crying and withdrawal. Children fear that they may lose their relationship with one of the parents, and they fear a loss of order in their lives. They are also afraid of being deprived of important things in their lives, such as food and favorite possessions; in their minds, if they can lose a parent, they can certainly lose other important things as well. They may show more anger than they did previously, become more aggressive, and have difficulty playing and experiencing pleasure.

What Parents Need to Know About Children Six to Eight Years

The important things for divorcing parents to know are as follows:

- The parenting schedule needs to be consistent, and the parents need to cooperate in adhering to the schedule.
- Posting the parenting schedule on the refrigerator at the child's eye level gives the child the security of knowing that he or she is not losing either parent.
- The parents need to help the child be organized so that parent exchanges can go as smoothly as possible. They need to have the child's clothing packed and school or other information enclosed with *The Children's Book*.
- Parents often do not understand the child's behavior at this stage and misinterpret it to mean that the other parent is lobbying for the child's support. Instead, the parents need to reassure the child that both of them are capable of caring for themselves and for the child.
- Both parents need to spend time with the child regularly so that the child does not feel he or she is losing one of the parents in the divorce. The child needs permission from each parent to have and love the other parent. It is important for the child to have pictures of both parents in the child's room at each parent's home.
- Sending messages through the child because the parents feel the child is old enough to remember is not appropriate. Children are not messengers for parents; parents must communicate with each other.
- Each parent must encourage the child in his or her relationship with the other parent so that the child does not experience loyalty conflicts.

Nine to Twelve Years

Children at this age are just beginning to confront changes in their own identities when their world is upset by divorce. Their sense of identity is tied to what seemed secure—home, family, neighborhood, school, and friends. They are confused by divorce because it interferes with everything they depended on. At a time when they would normally be developing academic and athletic abilities, becoming aware of gender, and beginning to experience attraction to others, this development is threatened by the divorce.

At this age, children may be ashamed or embarrassed by the divorce and may feel powerless to do anything about it. They may experience somatic symptoms based on their conflict about the divorce. They may complain of headaches, stomachaches, fatigue, and generally feeling out of sorts. They may experience intense feelings of anger and direct this anger at the parent perceived to be at fault for the divorce. They may side with one parent and shut out the other. Their school performance may deteriorate, and they may have difficulties with peers.

What Parents Need to Know About Children Nine to Twelve Years
The important things for divorcing parents to know are as follows:

- Loyalty conflicts are not unusual for a child at this stage. If the child chooses to side with one parent, that "chosen" parent must not use this behavior as an opportunity to reinforce a contention in a custody dispute that this choice shows the child's preference. Children can be fickle and most divorce therapists warn against allowing children to choose between their parents.
- Parents can assist a child at this stage by listening to the child's needs, fears, concerns, and complaints without making judgments. Unfortunately, parents caught in a custody contest often use this intimate sharing by a child as an indication of parental fitness or unfitness. However, using the child's words in this way fails to meet another extremely important need of the child, which is to know that the parents respect each other.
- Speaking poorly of the other parent is one of the worst mistakes a divorcing parent can make. This negativity not only makes the child very uncomfortable, but also serves as a personal attack on the child's self-image. (Remind the parents that their child knows that he or she is a product of both of them.)
- Each parent should encourage the child's relationship with the other parent.
- Parents must not send messages to each other through the child nor pump the child for information about the other parent or about the child's relationship with the other parent.
- The child may try to look "cool," to be very active, to make good impressions on friends, and to seem oblivious to the divorce. However, the parents need to know that this facade often masks the child's intense hurt and pain. The child needs the parents to understand this pain and not simply see the child as "going through a stage."
- For the sake of security, the child needs consistency in the application of the rules and expectations that the parents have agreed to. However, at this age the child also may need more flexibility in the parenting arrangement if he or she is not coping well.
- Parents are not only welcome in the child's world but also necessary to the child's survival.

Teenagers: Thirteen to Eighteen

Just when adolescents are developing into adulthood and planning their eventual exit from the family, they are upstaged by their parents' divorce. They need support from their parents when their parents are least emotionally available. Parent-adolescent relationships are normally tenuous, and a divorce makes them more so.

At this age, children may accelerate their independence from the family or delay it because of the divorce. While they are working on developing their further individuality, the divorce interferes. Some children in this age group take on the responsibilities of the absent parent and side with the parent who is present. If the parent who is present takes the child's side in this situation, the absent parent is alienated, and the child is damaged by the alienation.

In reaction to divorce, adolescents begin to feel insecure about their own relationships. They often fear that they may never be able to have a happy marriage.

What Parents Need to Know About Teenagers

The important things for divorcing parents to remember are as follows:

- The parents must put away their resentments and disrespect for each other for the sake of the adolescent. If the parents have difficulty in doing this, a therapist specializing in marriage closure therapy may be very helpful.
- Parents often assume that their adolescents can handle divorce, yet this is a very vulnerable time for children. They may retreat to their own rooms to hide their depression. They may turn up their music to drown out their crying. They need their parents' care but will not ask for it; instead, they confide in their friends about what is happening. Some adolescents withdraw and become so depressed that they need professional help. A few attempt suicide; some are successful.
- When the adolescent sides with one parent against the other, the parents need to join forces to assist the adolescent in adjusting to the divorce and in confronting the loss of the way things (family, home, parents, and his or her own importance) used to be.
- The adolescent's room is not absolutely off-limits to either parent. Each parent should ask to visit the child in their room when the child is at home, overlook the disarray, and sit down with the child and talk heart to heart. It is even more important that each parent listen without interrupting, judging, or advising.
- The parents need to open the communication between the adolescent and themselves and not expect the adolescent to initiate communication.

Effects of Spousal Abuse on Children

As a mediator you must understand how the behavior of the abusive spouse affects the couple's children and, therefore, the outcome of the parenting plan. Most of the abuse cases you encounter will involve the husband as the abuser. Consequently, the information presented here deals with what is known about husbands as abusers.

Research has shown that men who batter have more than likely witnessed the battering of their own mothers and learned from the role modeling of their fathers.

The following are some of the effects of abuse on children as reported by Hart (1990):*

- At least half of all battering husbands also batter their children.
- Battering of mothers usually predates the infliction of abuse on children.
- Older children are frequently assaulted when they intervene to defend or protect their mothers.
- Daughters are more likely than sons to become victims of the battering father.
- A father may turn to abuse and subjugation of the children as a way to dominate or control their mother.
- When the mother is assaulted by the father, daughters are exposed to a risk of sexual abuse 6.51 times greater than girls in families not characterized by spousal abuse.
- Children who witness violence inflicted on their mothers exhibit behavioral, somatic, or emotional problems similar to those experienced by physically abused children.
- Custodial interference (kidnapping) is one of the few abusing behaviors available to an abuser after separation.
- Wife and child abuse are commonplace in families in which children are killed.
- Eighty percent of fatal cases of child abuse are attributable to men.
- The investment of the abuser in pursuing custody is usually an attempt to preserve continued access to and control over the mother and the children.

Although this information is important for divorce mediators to know, it does not negate the fact that mediation can work in settling many divorces involving abuse. These are factors to be considered throughout the entire mediation.

The "Custody" Contest Is Always About Something Else

Fights over "custody," are rarely about children, but almost always about something else. Usually that something else is one of the prizes or assumed benefits parents believe flow from winning the "custody" label. It is your role as mediator to identify the real issue. The following is a list of the more common prizes that people seek to win when they say they want custody of the minor children:

The family home.   In the initial stages of divorce, parents realize that they must separate and that one of them must leave the family home. Their attorneys may advise them not to move out because doing so might jeopardize their rights to custody. At a temporary hearing, the person who gets temporary custody of the minor children is usually also awarded the home. Therefore, the fight over custody of the children sometimes is really about who gets possession of the home. The solution to this dilemma is to work in mediation on providing adequate residences for both parents.

---

*Adapted from "Gentle Jeopardy: The Further Endangerment of Battered Women and Children in Custody Mediation," by B. Hart, 1990, *Mediation Quarterly, 7*, pp. 317-330. *Used with permission of the publisher.*

Child support. In all states as well as in Canada, the parent who wins temporary custody of the children is entitled to child support from the other parent. Therefore, the fight over custody of the children sometimes is really about who will get child support.

The solution is to separate the issue of money from the issue of parenting. As you are assisting your clients in completing their budgets (see Chapter Seven), you can help them to see that there is a great deal more involved in setting child support than simply trying to determine some percentage of the non-custodial parent's net income and then awarding that amount to the parent who stays in the family home.

The right to move out of state in the future. In many states the parent who wins physical custody in the original divorce action is in a better position to move out of state later and take the children with them. Therefore, the fight over custody of the children sometimes is really about preserving the right to move with the children or trying to prevent the other parent from moving in the future.

The solution to this dilemma is to encourage both clients to consider an agreement about remaining in the same area. If they establish success early in the mediation process, the chances are that neither parent will want to geographically escape the actions of the other. Instead, both parents will recognize that it is important to be nearby to help each other with parenting.

The parenting schedule. In jurisdictions that allow for "reasonable visitation" instead of requiring a parenting schedule, the parent who wins custody is permitted to determine the other parent's visitation times. Therefore, the contest over custody of the children sometimes is really about who will be in charge and who must ask to see the children. The solution to this dilemma is to ensure that the clients create a weekly and a holiday schedule. The schedule has the power.

Punishing or hurting the other. In every divorce, there is anger. The anger is sometimes so great that the custody contest is really about punishing the other parent. Even after the ruling is made, the parents continue to wage a type of guerrilla war using the children as weapons. Therefore, the contest over custody of the children sometimes is really about one parent's attempts to hurt the other or both parents' attempts to hurt each other as much as possible.

The solution is to focus on the effects of the battle on the emotional health of the children. Ask the clients to consider having a neutral child psychologist or therapist attend a mediation session. Professional assistance will help the parents see the harm that their negative efforts are causing the children. Ask the parents to consider marriage-closure therapy to resolve the emotions of their relationship so that they can get on with the task of parenting.

Protecting the children from poor-quality parenting. One parent may have concerns about poor quality parenting of the other. Concerns may range from alcohol and drug abuse, gambling, religious practices, or moral conduct. Attorneys frequently advise that parent to try to win custody so that the other parent is prevented from negatively influencing the children. This approach is faulty because the so-called defective parent can have just as much influence on the children during two weekends per month as he or she can with fifty-fifty sharing of parenting. Therefore, the contest over custody of the children sometimes is really about protecting the children from bad influence.

The solution is to focus on the real problem, whether it is alcohol or drug abuse, inattentive parenting, inconsistent discipline, or whatever concern is expressed. Make sure that the parenting plan specifically addresses the real problem through agreements about future parental conduct. (See the sample language in Figure 5.)

Figure 5.   Sample Agreement About Parental Problem Behavior

> The two of us agree that neither will ever transport the children while impaired.
>
> If either of us suspects that the other parent has transported the children while impaired or is about to transport the children while impaired, the other can request an immediate intoxicyzer test. Should the parent not be found to be legally intoxicated, the cost for the test will be paid by the person requesting the test. Should the parent be found to be legally intoxicated, that parent will pay for the test; furthermore, he or she will immediately enter a thirty-day treatment program and thereafter resume daily attendance at A. A. meetings.

Who has the greater fear of losing?   Often the contest over custody is fueled by societal or cultural norms. A mother has greater difficulty agreeing to joint custody because mothers are expected to have custody of their children. A father who seeks joint custody often face strenuous objections from the mother because her attorney will advise her that joint custody is the first step toward losing custody. Therefore, the contest over custody of the children sometimes is really about the mother's fear that it will appear as if "something is wrong with her" if she does not have sole physical custody.

The solution is to focus on building a parenting plan and building some trust between the two parents so that neither will have to fear the worst from the other, thereby decreasing the significance of the custody labels.

How to Create a Parenting Plan

In an adversarial divorce, the technique currently used to resolve custody and parenting disputes consists of determining which party will be the sole custodial parent and which will be the visitor. This determination is based on the relative faulty conduct of each parent. Unfortunately, this technique turns the parenting question into a contest about who is better or worse and, therefore, who is entitled to a higher or lower level of ownership of the children.

Mediating Divorce

Client-centered mediation offers a radically different technique: the mediator helps the clients develop future parenting arrangements that meet the needs of the children and of both parents to the greatest extent possible.

The following are some guidelines for using this technique:

Learn the stages of child development and how divorce affects children. Study the information provided in this chapter so that you will be better equipped to assist the couple in building a parenting plan.

Avoid legal terminology. Avoid the word custody and similar terms that the adversarial system uses in divorce. These terms are unhelpful and potentially inflammatory. Discourage your clients from using this language, too. Use "parenting" or "parenting plan" instead of "custody," "parenting" or "living with" instead of "visitation," "obligations" or "responsibilities" instead of "rights," and "each home" instead of "primary and secondary residences."

Focus on the future and avoid the entire issue of "custody." Refuse to act as a custody investigator seeking fault. Instead of asking who should have custody, ask a future-focused question requiring a mutual effort to answer: "What future parenting arrangements can the two of you agree to so that you can both be the type of parents you want to be?"

Avoid assigning blame or fault. Most custody investigators need to know about the past because that is the focus of a custody investigation. As a mediator you need not concern yourself with who was the more unfit parent in the past. Instead, concern yourself with what you can do to help your clients create a parenting plan for the future. If the clients try to pull you into the acrimony of their past, change that focus. The more you allow them to dig into their past, the more you become a part of it and the more you become an investigator instead of a mediator. Instead, ask your clients, "What parenting plan can the two of you develop together that will overcome any concerns that each of you may have about the other's parenting behavior?"

Determine roles and expectations, not "who will be in charge." Ask your clients, "What ground rules can you decide on so that you and the children have a clear understanding of what roles each of you will assume and what expectations each of you has of the other?"

Use neutral professionals to advise about future parenting. "Custody" studies, to determine who measures up to the best-interest test in adversarial divorces, harden parents and prevent the future cooperation that is so necessary to overcome the pain and trauma of divorce. Instead of trying to ascertain who should "win" the parenting "contest," suggest that the clients ask a professional child psychologist or therapist to help them understand what their children need from them, rather than hiring an expert to show the other as a bad parent at trial. As a mediator it is your responsibility to build a network of trusted professionals as referral sources for your clients.

The following is a list of standard responses a mediator might use to address certain custody issues during a mediation. Please note that these responses or interventions are often best incorporated into the process through dialogue as opposed to lectures or long statements.

Goal: Creating a Positive Atmosphere

To create a positive atmosphere for discussion of parenting issues, recognize clients who are cooperative. Encourage those who are more contentious to take a positive rather than negative approach. Also, consider the following options:

Option 1 (particularly appropriate at the beginning of the session on parenting). "Do you both want to be active, significant parents in the future?"

Option 2 (particularly appropriate at the conclusion of the session on parenting). "You see, it is possible for you two to be in the same room, reach agreement, and make decisions. Both of you have accomplished a great task today. This is a difficult time for you, but you are both to be commended for your efforts."

Option 3. "Would each of you be willing to acknowledge (1) that you appreciate the assurances you have been given by the other, (2) that you understand the other's fears, and (3) that you will take steps to make sure your worst fears and those of the other will not come true?"

Option 4. "For the last half hour, all I've heard from both of you is what hasn't worked in the past. What I think will be helpful now is for you to suggest some things that you believe will work."

Goal: Moving from Competition to Co-Parenting

When you want to move the clients' conversation from a focus on competition to a focus on co-parenting, consider these options:

Option 1. "Would you agree not to use the word custody in our mediation sessions? It serves no useful purpose at this time. You know, the only other time we use the word custody is in connection with prisoners."

Option 2. "You say that the single biggest disagreement between the two of you is who will have the children? No problem, couples in mediation frequently agree that each parent will "have" the children when they are with them according to the parenting schedule. The work in this office is about agreeing on the "when" each of you will spend time with the children. Could the two of you talk about when those times will be?"

Option 3. "The problem with our adversarial system is that it asks all the wrong questions. If we say that your task upon getting divorced is to determine who will have custody of the children, you will be required to find two levels of ownership. How does it feel to have your children treated like pieces of property? The custody question also requires you to determine who will be labeled the non-custodial visiting parent. No parent really wants to spend the rest of their life labeled as a non-custodial visiting parent. The real problem is that the only way to determine custody is to prove who was a better or worse parent in the past. The question you rather need to answer is: "What future parenting agreements can be made so that each of you can be the good, loving type of parents you want to be?"

Option 4. "Would you agree not to use the word "visitation?" Children think of visiting when they visit relatives. Most parents do not want to visit their children. They want to parent their children. Try to define when you will each be with the children in place of visit."

Goal: Moving from Positional Bargaining to Meeting Needs and Interests
When you want to move the conversation from positional bargaining to meeting the clients' individual needs and interests, consider these options:

Option 1 (addressed to both). "If you could write the script all by yourself, what kind of schedule would you want for the future?"

Option 2. "What do you think your spouse needs to do differently so you could be a better parent?"

Option 3. "I really believe that if you can first take care of the children's needs, your needs will also be met."

Option 4. "When you say that you want to have custody of the children, are you saying that you want to be able to care for your children in a way that makes sense to you as a parent? If you can figure out a way for both of you to achieve that goal, aren't both of you *and* the children the winners?"

Option 5. "Sharon, when you say that you don't want John to see the children because he is a `bad' parent, you're saying that keeping him from the children will solve the problem. There are a thousand other ways to solve the problem. After all, a parent can still negatively impact the children two days a month as well as four days a month. Why not figure out what the problem really is and then see if there is any way to solve it other than by restricting John's access?"

Goal: Abandoning Conflict and Concentrating on Better Parenting
When your clients seem stuck in conflict about the children, and you want to move the conversation toward better parenting, consider the following options:

Option 1. "From your previous comments and exchanges, I can tell that there's a great deal of hostility and anger between the two of you. Can you discuss what that source of anger is for each of you?"

Option 2. "You both have to remember that you will be parents forever. You have two small children, and you will be having weekly contact with each other for the next fifteen years. When your children graduate, get married, and have your grandchildren, wouldn't it be great if you both could participate in family events without your presence detracting from everyone else's enjoyment? You say that you want to end the contest. What do you think is preventing that from occurring?"

Option 3. "Many couples report that after divorce, the father, who may have been a less active parent in the marriage, assumes an entirely new role and in fact becomes a very effective parent."

Option 4. "It is absolutely essential that the two of you separate your anger toward each other from your roles as separate parents."

Option 5. "Both of you said earlier that you would like to be cooperative parents. That can't happen overnight because the two of you haven't yet had an opportunity to practice living in two different homes. It's hard enough to be parents living in the same house. Think of the recent difficulties you have had because of two facts: first, you are going through a divorce, which places a great deal of stress on both of you; and second, you are rookies at the difficult task of being separate parents. Would you like me to help you create a plan for being the best parents you can be, when you're living separately?

Option 6. "Research shows that children whose parents divorce fall into three categories. Those children whose parents have an amicable divorce settlement generally experience few adverse effects as a result of the divorce. Those children whose parents experience a lot of turmoil, such as that caused by acrimonious litigation, will most likely experience a negative psychological adjustment. Those children who experience the most severe problems are the ones who are abandoned by one parent.

"Now, for the sake of the children, would you agree that you must find some solutions that will work for both of you?"

Goal: Rebuilding Trust Through Small Steps
When you begin the process of rebuilding the clients' trust in each other as parents, consider these options:

Option 1. "As your mediator, I can't just wave a magic wand and suddenly create trust between the two of you. What I can do is offer to help you make small agreements that have a high likelihood of success and then hope that the two of you will see that this can work. Now what are some small steps that each of you wants the other to take in the next two weeks to build trust between the two of you?"

Option 2. "Small acts of violence often lead to larger acts of violence. It's also true that small cooperative acts lead to greater trust and more cooperation."

Option 3. "You two are in this situation together, and you don't seem to realize that everything one parent does affects the other. You can continue to disrespect each other, which will prolong your struggle, or you can agree to cooperate and start rebuilding some measure of trust."

Option 4. "Now that you have agreed to a temporary schedule for the exchange of the children, will you both try your hardest to make this work? Your trust in each other can't grow if you fail in the early stages of using this new schedule. Would you agree not to change the schedule unless it is a dire emergency? Later, as you become better at the task of separate parenting, you will find it less difficult to call the other and work out changes. At this point, though, you may be more successful if you follow the schedule without deviating from it."

Option 5. "The reason a schedule seems to be so important for couples is that it eliminates complaints such as `He never sees the children' or `She never encourages the children to see me.' With a schedule you both have certainty, and there are expectations set for the children. Remember that if the children don't know when they will be seeing you, they are walking a tightrope. Schedules seem to have a way of creating trust by eliminating the uncertainty and the use of children as `weapons' against each other that so often happens in the early stages of divorce."

Option 6. "What is the greatest fear you have as you think about the future relationship you'll have with each other as parents?" (If each client has expressed a fear, turn to the other client and ask what assurances he or she can give so that the fear will never come true.)

Option 7. "It is very difficult to rebuild trust if there isn't some measure of openness and sharing. One thing some couples have done to improve their communication about the children is to agree that on every Sunday evening at a set time, the two of them will have a phone conversation about the children. They set rules for the phone call, such as `We will not talk about finances, our lawyers, or anything except the children.' Do you think this is something that would be helpful for you?"

The Process of Establishing a Parenting Plan

If this is the clients' first session, make copies of their completed Mediation Questionnaires for yourself; return the originals to them. Let the clients know that they will need to bring their completed questionnaires to each mediation session.

The process of establishing a parenting plan consists of the following elements:

- Reducing the clients' fears
- Discussing special needs
- Gathering information
- Defining standards of fairness
- Creating a parenting schedule

- Addressing child-related issues to be covered in the plan (education, health care, dating and remarriage, and communication between parents)
- Planning for contingencies
- Eliciting the children's feedback
- Choosing custody labels

Reducing the Clients' Fears

Your clients need to know that it is not damaging for children to move back and forth between two homes. There is no credible research to support the notion that children cannot be with both parents at different times during the week or, for that matter, during different parts of the year if the parents live in different states.

However, there is a lot of research concluding that children are harmed when they go back and forth between the homes of parents who are in great conflict. It is the level of the parents' conflict—not the moving back and forth—that causes the harm. In addition, you should let your clients know that the most severe problems experienced by children have nothing to do with the arrangements that their parents make to exchange them; instead, the most severe problems occur when children are abandoned by one parent, or when children are caught between two highly conflicted parents.

If the parents are in extreme conflict, they may want to consider having the parent who is experiencing less anger or pain be in charge and restricting the children's time with the parent who is feeling more anger or pain, so that the children will not be hurt by that parent's bad feelings. However, this should be a last resort taken only after the parents have tried everything possible to reduce their conflict.

You also need to inform your clients that children want to know what is happening during a divorce. In order to prepare for changes, the children may need to know about the divorce process and what to expect. The parents need to be honest, but they must also be careful to communicate this with each child at his or her age level.

To allay your clients' fear about what will happen to their children, suggest that after the session they reread the material on child development in Chapter Five in their workbooks. Emphasize that they have the power to keep their children from being harmed by the divorce. You might also want to suggest some readings on parenting from the list in Appendix B. In addition, offer the following comments:

> It is true that most children are hurt by their parents' divorce. However, parents are responsible for the extent to which their children are hurt. The most harmful thing to children is a highly charged, negative conflict that exists between their parents.
>
> You hold the key to your children's adjustment to the divorce. If you choose to set aside what you hold against each other, your children will be positively affected. If you choose to cooperate as parents even when you are dissolving all other aspects of your marriage, your children will greatly benefit.
>
> If each of you gives your children permission to have a meaningful relationship with the other parent, your children will feel respected. If you respect each other as parents, your children's self-images will be more positive despite the divorce.

When you are struggling with the issues of separation and divorce and are so emotionally overburdened, your children need you more than ever before. They need your love, your respect, your ears, and your hearts. It's not easy, but it is critical that both of you recognize your children's needs and meet those needs to the greatest extent possible.

Discussing Needs

Ask each client to discuss his or her needs regarding a future parenting relationship with the children. Then ask both clients to discuss the special needs of the children and any concerns they have about the children.

Gathering Information

Next obtain information from the parents as a basis for discussing parenting schedules. Find out where each parent lives, the schools that the children attend, the parents' work schedules, and the parents' work obligations. Also ask the parents to discuss the new roles that each will assume as a "separate"—not "single"—parent. Finally, ask the clients what they consider the optimum parenting arrangements to be so that you can learn about their parenting values and philosophies.

Defining Standards of Fairness

The clients will find their problems easier to solve if you assist them in developing and applying one or more standards of fairness by which to evaluate the consequences of their options. First ask them to state what they believe is fair with regard to the issue at hand (in this case, parenting). Encourage them to take advantage of the safety of the mediation setting by fully discussing all of their concerns about fairness.

Help them discuss their ideas about fairness until they are comfortable and can reach an understanding. During this process, acknowledge that fairness is often a trust issue. Also acknowledge their differences and encourage them to separate these differences from the task of understanding each other's fairness.

Offering examples of standards of fairness that other couples have created is often useful. Here are two examples of standards of fairness with regard to parenting:

- "Regardless of what has happened between us, we wish to keep our children from being unduly harmed by the divorce process."
- "Each of us will have significant contact with the children, and the children will have a significant relationship with each of us: Therefore, we will follow a schedule of approximately equal time with the children."

When spousal abuse exists in the relationship, however, these examples may not be appropriate. Instead, you may have to move the discussion in a direction of more general standards such as, "The children will have a *relationship* with each parent, though limited with the abuser." Also, be prepared to tell the clients what research has shown: when there is great conflict between the parents, and they are unable to cooperate in parenting, it may be harmful for children to have equal time with the parents. In fact, it may be best for children to have miminal contact with the abusive parent until that parent has successfully completed some type of treatment.

Determining a Parenting Schedule

Although most couples fight over the labels of "custodial parent" and "noncustodial parent," they are likely to agree on most aspects of the parenting plan. Your job as the mediator is to suggest that they use their energy to help each other carry out the parenting plan rather than to fight over who is assigned which labels.

There are several strategies that you can use to encourage the couple to avoid the conflict that labels cause:

Delay using the labels. Encourage the clients not to decide who is to be the "custodial parent" and who is to be the "noncustodial parent" until they have agreed on all aspects of the parenting arrangements. After the parenting plan has been created, the clients will have less difficulty choosing labels for themselves.

Avoid court action in the future. It is more likely that parents will avoid problems with custody labels if they do not fear returning to court in the future. Suggest that they can stay out of court by including a binding arbitration clause in their Decree of Divorce, requiring the use of therapists as arbitrators.

Avoid the "Disneyland parent" syndrome. Sometimes the parent who does not live in the family home is "visited" by the children and ends up always showing the children a good time instead of engaging in routine parenting. Suggest that both parents think of themselves as routine parents not visitors or entertainers. When they use this mind-set and create a parenting schedule, each parent is "on duty" with the children according to the schedule; there is then more of an expectation that each parent will participate in the chores of parenting and will not treat the children as visitors.

Avoid the issue of deciding who is "in charge." The adversarial process suggests that one of the parents must be in charge and that parent is the sole physical custodian of the children. When the parents have a detailed schedule and follow the on duty/off duty agreement, the schedule has the power, and each parent will be in charge of the children when on duty.

If clients avoid some of the traps that custody labels create, they will be in a much better position to cooperate in creating a parenting schedule.

Alternatives for Parenting Schedules

Usually there are two components to the schedule: (1) the weekly recurring schedule and (2) the holiday schedule, which includes vacations, school breaks, and special arrangements for visiting with grandparents if desired.

Figures 6 through 9 illustrate alternatives that your clients might want to consider as they work on establishing a weekly schedule. Another option for the parenting schedule is the school-vacation split. This schedule has the children primarily with one parent during the school year; they are with the other parent for designated weekends, three-day weekends, school breaks, and summer vacation from school. Note: It is important to use the flip chart to display any schedules that parents are considering in mediation. Use the format of Figures 6–9. Figure 10 is a sample holiday schedule.

Figure 6. Traditional Parenting Schedule

M–Mom; D–Dad

	MON	TUES	WED	THUR	FRI	SAT	SUN
WK 1	M	M	M	M	M/D	D	D/M
WK 2	M	M	M/D/M	M	M	M	M
WK 3	M	M	M	M	M/D	D	D/M
WK 4	M	M	M/D/M	M	M	M	M

Figure 7. Variation of Traditional Parenting Schedule

M–Mom; D–Dad

	MON	TUES	WED	THUR	FRI	SAT	SUN
WK 1	M	M	M/D	D/M	M/D	D	D
WK 2	D/M	M	M/D	D/M	M	M	M
WK 3	M	M	M/D	D/M	M/D	D	D
WK 4	D/M	M	M/D	D/M	M	M	M

Figure 8. Fifty-Fifty Shared Parenting Schedule Number 1

M–Mom; D–Dad

	MON	TUES	WED	THUR	FRI	SAT	SUN
WK 1	M	M	D	D	D	D	D
WK 2	M	M	D	D	M	M	M
WK 3	M	M	D	D	D	D	D
WK 4	M	M	D	D	M	M	M

Figure 9. Fifty-Fifty Shared Parenting Schedule Number 2

M–Mom; D–Dad

	MON	TUES	WED	THUR	FRI	SAT	SUN
WK 1	M	M	M	M	M	M	M
WK 2	D	D	D	D	D	D	D
WK 3	M	M	M	M	M	M	M
WK 4	D	D	D	D	D	D	D

Figure 10. Sample Holiday Schedule

HOLIDAYS	Even-Numbered Years	Odd-Numbered Years
Easter	Mom	Dad
Memorial Day	Dad	Dad
Fourth of July	Mom	Mom
Labor Day	Dad	Mom
Thanksgiving	Mom	Dad
Christmas Eve	Mom	Mom
Christmas Day	Dad	Dad
Childrens' Birthdays	(According to schedule and the other parent	
Parents' Birthdays	will have some contact, as requested)	
Mother's Day	Mom	Mom
Father's Day	Dad	Dad

Note: Do not assume Christian holidays. Ask for a different set of holidays when families celebrate non-Christian holidays.

Addressing Child-Related Issues

A number of other issues related to the children may need to be considered. (Sometimes parents elect not to address some of these issues, but you will at least call them to their attention.) The parents may discuss these issues and come to agreement, and their decisions would then be included in the parenting plan. These issues include education and related concerns, health care, dating and remarriage, and communication between the parents.

Education

Ask if they have any concerns about the children's education. This category may also include religious education. They may need to discuss and include the following in their parenting plan:

- How they will inform the school about the particulars of the divorce (separate residences and parenting schedule, for example.)
- How each of them will learn about school events
- How each will receive information about progress
- How each will convey educational concerns to the school
- How they will address the children's extracurricular activities
- How they will share costs and transportation responsibilities for those activities
- How they will share the costs of higher education, if any

Health Care

Ask the parents who will provide medical insurance for the children in the future and whether or not there is dental insurance. If no insurance currently exists, the clients need to discuss how they will pay for any of the children's medical and dental expenses in the future. Even with insurance coverage, they need to address how they will share the uncovered medical and dental expenses.

Dating and Remarriage

Discuss how each parent will introduce a new relationship to the children. Also encourage them to agree on a way to inform each other and their children, should one of them remarry.

Communication Between Parents

Ask the clients how they will communicate with each other in the future about issues concerning the children. Offer them copies of *The Children's Book* and encourage them to read and use this book as a resource.

Planning for Contingencies

As the future cannot be predicted or even fully anticipated, it is important to ask the clients to reach agreement on a process for addressing future changes or new problems of parenting.

Eliciting the Children's Feedback

After the clients have reached agreement on a parenting schedule, education, health care, dating and remarriage, communication between themselves as parents, and contingency planning, they may wish to have the children attend a mediation session to discuss these arrangements. Getting feedback from the children can be helpful in finalizing the parenting plan.

Choosing Custody Labels

After the clients have made decisions on all of the aspects of parenting covered in this chapter, discuss their options about the custody labels. By this time they have made logical, workable decisions that fit their situation. The labels are then only for the purpose of satisfying the court. Generally parents who communicate well and cooperate in parenting choose "joint legal and physical custody." When parents choose to have one parent primarily in charge and the other to have the children every other weekend and Wednesday evenings, they often choose "joint legal custody and sole physical custody" (with the physical custody assigned to the parent who has the children the majority of the time). If parents live in a state that has recently adopted "parenting plan" legislation to replace custody laws, your work as a mediator has just become easier.

When there is spousal abuse, there is usually great conflict between the parents well beyond the divorce, even when they have resolved some of their differences in the process of mediation. One parent usually has "sole physical custody" or primary care of the children after the divorce because of the toxic relationship between the parents.

The discussion about custody labels is the last task of mediating the parenting plan. This task is usually easier after all of the details of the parenting plan have been determined.

Assigning Homework for Next Session

Before the clients leave, review their homework for the next session (see "Homework" in Chapter Six in the client's workbook).

Explain that during the next session, the clients will be working on planning their future living expenses as single people (and as separate parents, if they have minor children). Encourage them to jot down notes and questions concerning budgets. Remind them to bring with them all materials described in the "Homework" section of Chapter Six in the workbook.

After the Session

After the session, use all flip-chart sheets to write a memo about the options and decisions the clients generated. (Later you may use this memo as well as those from the other mediation sessions to help construct a preliminary or draft copy of the Memorandum of Agreement.) Send a copy of the memo to each client along with instructions to review the content and jot down notes about any questions or proposed changes.

Write the Memorandum of Agreement as clearly and succinctly as possible while still capturing the meaning that the clients attach to each subject area (in this case, the meaning they attach to their parenting roles). See Figure 11 for a sample agreement.

Figure 11.   Sample Parenting Agreement

PARENTING AGREEMENT
Smith, Doug and Sylvia

Doug Smith and Sylvia Smith have made a decision to live separately and seek a dissolution of their marriage relationship. As a result of that decision, both have agreed to enter into mediation conducted by Erickson Mediation Institute for the purpose of settling all issues which might otherwise be the subject of contested litigation. Prior to entering mediation, they signed an agreement with each other and with Erickson Mediation Institute to be fair and equitable throughout the mediation process.

They understand that neither Erickson Mediation Institute nor the mediator legally represents either or both of them. Both agree to retain attorneys of their own choice to legally represent them and to provide each of them with an independent judgment about the decisions reached in mediation.

Mediation was conducted by Marilyn S. McKnight for Erickson Mediation Institute. The following represents their intended decisions reached in mediation after careful review of all facts and options. Both have made a full disclosure to each other of the full nature and extent of their assets, and they wish their attorneys to incorporate the following into a legally binding settlement agreement. Both intend to incorporate this mediation agreement to the fullest extent possible in their legal documents of divorce. However, both understand that there may be some word changes based upon review by their attorneys.

Doug and Sylvia were married on June 7, 19XX in Robbinsdale, Minnesota. They were separated in October, 19XX.

Social Security Numbers: Doug: 999-99-9999 Sylvia: 999-99-9999.

Birthdates: Doug: 2-10-XX, age 43; Sylvia: 7-17-XX, age 39.

PARENTING ARRANGEMENTS: Doug and Sylvia have three minor children of the marriage relationship: Heather L. Smith, born 6-15-XX, age 17, Joshua M. Smith, born 10-12-XX, age 12 and Susan F. Smith, born 11-14-XX, age 5.

Doug and Sylvia have agreed to share Joint Legal Custody of the minor children. They agree to Joint Legal Custody as a way of sharing joint decision making in the future regarding the children. They understand that Joint Legal Custody means that they will continue to cooperate in making decisions regarding education, medical treatment, religious training and other important parenting decisions. They also agree that Joint Legal Custody means that each of them will continue to have equal access to all medical, educational and other important records of the children. Should they have any disagreements concerning parenting of the children, they agree to first try to resolve such differences between themselves, and to return to mediation if they are unsuccessful.

As to the requirement that their Decree contain a clause designating physical custody, they agree that they will have Joint Physical Custody of the children.

Doug and Sylvia agree that joint legal and joint physical means the following:

They will confer with each other before making a decision on a matter involving a major aspect in the lives of their children, such as religious training, education or health care. The parties shall make sincere efforts to cooperate and shall put the best intersts of the children first.

Neither of them will do anything that would alienate the children from the other parent or perform any act that would hamper the natural development of love and affection of the children for each parent.

In the event that the parent with whom the children are residing or scheduled to reside has other obligations at the time, it is the responsibility of that parent to make arrangements for the care of the children. If the other parent is not available to assist in providing such care, then the parent with whom the children are residing or scheduled to reside at that time will have ultimate responsibility for making alternative arrangements for the care of the children. If the parties cannot agree upon a schedule change, then the schedule will be followed.

Doug and Sylvia have agreed to a time sharing arrangement in which the children are home-based with Sylvia, with Doug having the children with him every other weekend and one or two evenings each week depending on their activities. Doug and Sylvia will talk with each other each Sunday evening at 9:00 p.m. to discuss the next week's schedule.

Sylvia and Doug agree that future exchanges of the children will be flexible based upon each of their travel and work schedules, but they will always alternate the weekends and provide for Doug to have the children at least one evening per week. The weekends will begin after school on Fridays and continue overnight Sunday until Monday morning. They agree that the weekend times with Doug will also include taking the children directly to school on Monday morning.

They have agreed to a time sharing arrangement that calls for an initial weekly schedule as follows:

M–Mom; D–Dad

	MON	TUES	WED	THUR	FRI	SAT	SUN
WK 1	D/M	M	M/D/M	M	M	M	M
WK 2	M	M	M/D/M	M	M/D	D	D
WK 3	D/M	M	M/D/M	M	M	M	M
WK 4	M	M	M/D/M	M	M/D	D	D

Both are willing to follow the above schedule and if it is not agreeable, to experiment with different schedules in order to try to find an exchange schedule that does not unduly disrupt the children's daily schedules but still allows for significant parenting contact by both parents.

They will assist children in remembering Mother's and Father's days. They both agree that a deviation from the regular schedule can occur on these days.

HOLIDAYS	Even-Numbered Years	Odd-Numbered Years
Easter	Mom	Dad
Memorial Day	Dad	Dad
Fourth of July	Mom	Mom
Labor Day	Dad	Mom
Thanksgiving	Mom	Dad
Christmas Eve	Mom	Mom
Christmas Day	Dad	Dad
Childrens' Birthdays	(According to schedule and the other parent	
Parents' Birthdays	will have some contact, as requested)	
Mother's Day	Mom	Mom
Father's Day	Dad	Dad

When Mondays are a legal holiday, unless otherwise indicated in the above Holiday Schedule, the children will be with the parent they are normally scheduled to be with on the Sunday before until Tuesday morning.

For purposes of this agreement, since we each plan to travel over the Thanksgiving weekend in the future, it will begin at 5:00 p.m. on the Wednesday preceding, and end on the following Monday morning.

They agree that each Christmas they will each build special traditions when they are with the children. They agree that they will always be within a reasonable driving distance of each other to accomplish the Christmas schedule.

Easter will begin on the Saturday before at 5:00 p.m. and end on Monday morning.

They agree that the schedule will alternate each year. In the event it is necessary to deviate from the above holiday schedule, they will try to give the preference to the parent listed in the holiday schedule, but in any event, it is their desire to share the holiday periods on an approximately equal basis. Both agree that there should be at least one month's planning around the holiday schedule. For summer vacation, they agree that they will each have up to two weeks for vacation with the children, and to have a preliminary discussion about summer plans for the children by February of each year with final plans being decided upon by May of each year.

Sylvia and Doug understand that the regular schedule as well as the holiday schedule may need to be revised due to special circumstances in the future. They agree to be flexible in responding to the needs of the other parent about parenting and scheduling, but they also agree not to use flexibility as a way of defeating the intent and purpose of the schedules.

CHILDREN'S HEALTH INSURANCE: Doug has health insurance through his employment. He agrees to continue to name the children as dependents of that policy and will be primarily responsible for providing health insurance coverage and dental insurance coverage for the benefit of the children until he no longer has an obligation to share in the cost of raising the children.

Uncovered medical and dental expenses will be shared equally by Doug and Sylvia. Both agree to discuss non-emergency or elective medical or dental needs of the children before assuming the other parent will share in those costs. Doug agrees to ensure that Sylvia is supplied with current health insurance identification cards for the children.

RELATIONSHIPS WITH RELATIVES: Doug and Sylvia recognize that the children will benefit from maintaining ties with their grandparents, relatives and people important to them and they will help the children maintain their relationships with these people from time to time.

ON DUTY, OFF DUTY PARENTING: They agree to the concept that each of them will provide parenting during the times they are scheduled to care for the children. This means that if the children are ill or either of them have other obligations during the scheduled time with the children, it will be the responsibility of the on-duty parent to make arrangements for the care of the children. They each welcome the on-duty parent to request assistance during their scheduled times with the children, but they each understand that if the off-duty parent is not able to assist the on-duty parent during the scheduled time, it will be the responsibility of the on-duty parent to make alternative arrangements for the children.

EDUCATION: Each of us will communicate with children's schools to remain informed about children's needs and progress and special events including parent-teacher conferences. They also agree to share information about children's school progress, behavior and events with each other. They realize college or technical training is important and they will encourage and support children's efforts for further education. Major decisions about children's education will be made by both of us together.

HEALTH CARE: In emergencies each of us may consent to emergency medical treatment for our children as needed. Our intent is to take care of the medical emergency first and communicate with the other parent as soon as possible. They each have the right to the children's medical information and records, and they will communicate with each other on major health care for children, and major decisions about health care will be made by both of us together.

RELIGION: They will communicate with each other on major religious ceremonies involving our children, and major decisions about religious upbringing will be made by both together.

If either is away from our children, they will maintain frequent contact with them by phone, letter, post cards, video or audio tapes. They will also encourage and assist the children to communicate frequently with the other parent by phone, letter, etc. They agree to give the other parent the address and phone number where the children can be reached anytime they are away from home for more than 48 hours.

They each agree not to compromise the safety of children. They will not leave Susan unattended for more than an hour until she is twelve years old. They agree not to operate a vehicle when under the influence of alcohol or non-prescription drugs when children are in the vehicle, or use these substances carelessly when any of the children are in our care.

They each agree the parent who is receiving children will transport them. They will make sure the children have their belongings when they deliver the children. Remembering is sometimes difficult for Susan, so they will cooperate and help Susan remember to take her belongings with her so she will have with her the personal belongings and school supplies she needs.

If a move from a current residence makes it impossible to continue our parenting schedule, they each agree to renegotiate this Parenting Agreement prior to a move. They will always consider how they can still be involved as parents in a way that would best meet the needs of our children.

They agree that this will be in effect until they make another agreement to replace this and our agreement is amended by the court. They agree any changes to this Agreement will be made in writing, dated and signed by each of us, and they will each retain a copy. Until such a written change is approved by the Court, they understand that our agreements made herein will govern any dispute.

They agree that neither of them will move the residence of the children from the State of Minnesota without the prior permission of the other parent or a change in this agreement and the parenting schedule. They further agree that they will be reasonable when the other parent requests to take children out of Minnesota for trips or vacations.

CHILDREN SUPPORT: Doug will pay child support to Sylvia for the support of the minor children in the sum of $1,250 per month payable in two equal installments on the first and fifteenth days of each month, commencing in the month of the entry of the judgment and decree herein. A child shall remain entitled to support until the child reaches eighteen (18) years of age, marries, is emancipated, self-supporting, deceased, or in the armed forces of the United States of America, whichever shall occur first, or until further order of the Court. In the event a minor child is attending high school at the time of his eighteenth (18) birthday, the child support obligation shall continue so long as the child is attending high school, but in no event after the child becomes twenty (20) years of age. The parties will not subject their child support obligations to biennial cost-of-living adjustments as they intend to review and adjust their direct in kind contributions from time to time.

FUTURE CONFLICT RESOLUTION: Doug and Sylvia agree that should they have disagreements in the future about scheduling exchanges or any other parenting disputes, they will first try to resolve such disagreements on their own, returning to mediation should they have difficulties in resolving these new issues on their own. The future costs of returning to mediation if needed will be shared equally.

BINDING ARBITRATION: Should they have any major parenting disputes in the future that cannot be resolved after making a good faith effort in mediation, they agree to submit the parenting dispute to binding arbitration. The arbitrators will be chosen from a panel maintained by Erickson Mediation Institute. The arbitrators will consist of two mental health professionals and a family law professional who will have the right to interview the minor children as well as the parents.

The arbitration hearing will be subject to the terms and conditions of the Minnesota Arbitration Act and the Rules of Arbitration for Parenting Disputes published by Erickson Mediation Institute and in effect at the time the arbitration is commenced.

Reference

Hart, B. (1990). Gentle jeopardy: The further endangerment of battered women and children in custody mediation. *Mediation Quarterly, 7,* 317-330.

7
Subject Area 2: Budgeting for the Future

> ***Important Note:*** The tasks involved in this session occasionally require the assistance of a neutral accountant who can help determine important net income numbers, especially when that income is earned from a business or from self employment.

Your clients will probably begin the divorce journey fearing that the worst financial scenario will become a reality—that they will be unfairly treated by the courts or each other and not have enough money to exist. If you can help them to view their situation not as the beginning of a contest but as a problem that can be addressed in manageable pieces, both will begin to see how they can create a mutually acceptable resolution.

This chapter offers information on the budgeting session, the stage where you help your clients plan their separate future living expenses.

Why the Budgeting Process Is Necessary

The objective of the budgeting process is to determine each spouse's separate future expenses for the next 12 months. This process is an essential step of every client-centered mediation for the following reasons:

- Couples who have been pooling their money together for many years need to now unhook and determine what amount of money each of them will need to meet their separate monthly expenses. This step helps them begin to build boundaries around their relationship with each other. They may have already been living in separate parts of the house and asking them to build separate budgets helps them establish another new boundary around finances, paying bills and managing their own accounts.
- One or both will be in new living arrangements, and it is essential to determine whether they will each have enough money to pay their bills.
- The budgeting process is a diagnostic tool that helps determine the subsequent roadblocks to settlement for both clients.

- The budgeting process enables you and the clients to see what levels of child support and spousal support are needed. It makes more sense to have the couple examine and then try to meet projected monthly expenses than to put the decision in the hands of a judge who is reading a budget written by each attorney, often prepared in an exaggerated fashion due to their advocacy perspective.
- The budgeting process affords each client an opportunity to respond to the question "What is it that you really need?" and to be taken seriously.
- If the budgeting process is skipped, and no rules about money are established, the spouse with fewer financial resources will probably consult an attorney to make sure that he or she gets the help needed. Because the client's needs have not been met in mediation, the intervention of an attorney at this stage usually results in a motion for temporary relief.
- Completing the budgeting process can help the clients determine whether the family home should be sold as well as what type of housing each can afford in order to accomplish the separation.
- The budgeting process allows the numbers—not you—to tell them what they need to do about child support and spousal support.

The Process of Budgeting for the Future

Managing this session requires the mediator to focus on the following:

- Defining standards of fairness
- Budgeting expenses
- Determining net income
- Assessing the shortfall (the difference between the clients' expenses and their available income)
- Considering ways to decrease expenses
- Considering ways to increase income
- Establishing child support
- Addressing the issue of spousal support (when one spouse is currently dependent on the marriage relationship for support)

Defining Standards of Fairness
The clients need to define standards of fairness for child support and spousal support. (See "Defining Standards of Fairness" in Chapter Six.)

Budgeting Expenses
This part of the process involves helping them create separate monthly budgets and displaying the budgets on the flip chart. By building the budgets side by side, line item by line item and then talking about each expense item, it will be easier for them to understand and accept the reality of their individual living expenses. In order to determine how they will share the costs of raising the children, they must first know and agree to the amounts that each of them needs each month to pay bills.

Budgeting (arriving at bottom-line monthly expenses) is accomplished through the following steps:

Record budgets on a flip chart.   Ask them to refer to their completed Mediation Questionnaires and read off their monthly expenses while you write. Write their budgets side by side on the flip chart. This process takes from one to two hours to complete. Recording the numbers in this way transforms the budgets into a jointly owned statement of the their new situation. (Sitting around a table with clients looking at their separate budgets side by side does not have the same effect; creating the flip-chart document is essential to the success of client-centered mediation.)

Each may ask questions about the other's budget items for the purpose of clarification only. Discourage each from criticizing the other's budget levels by pointing out that it may not be possible to find the money to meet each and every budget need, but list the need anyway. The budget process will also not work if one completes a budget for the other.

Mark items to be reconsidered.

Discuss the marked items.   As you lead the discussion, ask each to speak for himself or herself and to restrain from making value judgments about the other's information.

Help them, not you, determine whether the budgets are reasonable.   You can ask "Do the two of you agree that these expenses are fair and reasonable?" If one objects to the numbers being suggested by the other for a particular expense, allow them an opportunity to discuss the concern briefly. (Each may certainly question whether a particular amount on the other's budget is accurate or appropriate. However, you want to discourage arguments over the amounts each says it costs for a particular item by suggesting that the numbers should first be put up on the chart; then we will try to find the money if possible.) If a client's budget items is questioned and he/she has no data to support that amount, encourage that client to double check the figure. Be very respectful and avoid negative judgments about their efforts.

Try to find opportunities to recognize their efforts as this is a very difficult task to complete jointly. When finished, you might ask them what the numbers mean to them.

On occasion the clients' immediate concerns may cause you to deviate from the budgeting task. While it is your goal to keep them focused on the budget task as much as possible, it is also important that you attend to any emotional difficulties that arise. For example, if it becomes obvious that one of them is upset about some new issue concerning the children, put the budget task aside and address their concern. As soon as the clients are ready, return to the budget task.

> *Important Note:* The budget expenses can change while the couple is in mediation, so allow them the opportunity to present any new or changed budget information at later sessions, before you complete the final Memorandum of Agreement.

Determining Net Income

The next step is to determine what net income is available to meet the budget expenses.

In client-centered mediation, the disclosure and exchange of accurate income information is necessary to determine how much money is currently available to the couple for meeting their own needs as well as sharing the costs of raising the children. As mediator, you take responsibility for managing the exchange of information.

The income data, when written on the flip chart next to the couple's previously agreed-on expenses, will help both of them see whether there is enough money available to support two households. Pay stubs and income tax returns are the basic documents used to establish incomes.

Assessing the Shortfall

In those cases where there is a shortfall between agreed-to expenses and available income, it is helpful to use the flip chart to display how large the combined shortfall is. The clients have not yet decided the support exchange amount and, therefore, do not know what each will be able to spend each month.

Considering Ways to Decrease Expenses

The next step is to ask, "Can the budget expenses be decreased?" Help them think about ways in which they can jointly attack the problem of not having enough money to pay for the costs of two households. Brainstorming may be appropriate at this point. Although it is dangerous to encourage them to decrease what already may be bare-bones budgets, they should be encouraged to review and eliminate any nonessential expenditures they may have listed.

If you manage this part of the process properly, the clients can work together effectively to determine whether expenses can be reduced. If both the husband and wife, in each other's presence, can indicate several areas in which they can reduce expenses, they will begin to build the trust that is essential to a positive, businesslike relationship in the future.

Considering Ways to Increase Income

Clients are also asked: "Can the combined income now being shared by both of you be increased?" It would not be fair to ask them to consider cutting their budgets without asking this question as well. The ensuing discussions frequently concentrate on future plans for the dependent spouse, who has an opportunity to present his or her thoughts about employment, training, and education. This is also a good time to begin a preliminary discussion about possible tax planning to create additional income. (The major tax implications of divorce are discussed in Chapter Nine.)

In most cases available income cannot be immediately increased, but this question opens the door for a discussion about how the dependent spouse can eventually become more financially self-sufficient.

Even in a situation where the clients agree that it is presently impossible for the primary parent to work, they will still face the reality that at some point in the future, divorce requires both parents to work full time, except for the very wealthy.

Determining Child Support

You should obtain child-support guidelines* from your state's support and collection offices to familiarize yourself with their procedures. When clients decide in mediation to deviate from the state child support guidelines, you will need to provide reasons for the deviation in the Memorandum of Agreement. (Most courts require a clear explanation for deviating from the child support guidelines.)*

To help the clients decide more easily about what to do concerning child support, ask, "What special costs in your monthly budgets are attributable to the children only?" These costs are such things as private school tuition, day-care expenses, orthodontia costs, fees for extracurricular activities, and special medical costs. Some couples find it useful to create a separate budget for all costs related to the children. Others prefer adding the expenses for the children to the flip-chart budgets by simply adding and filling in columns headed "Dad" and "Mom." Figure 12 offers an example of a budget with these columns added. (This figure includes marginal notes explaining some important aspects of the subject clients' expenses.) In any case, having the clients consider the children's expenses separately helps to make this issue more manageable.

"How will you two share in the cost of raising your children?"   Answering this question would be easy if all couples agreed to a fifty-fifty, shared parenting arrangement and the husband and wife earned exactly the same salaries. Usually one parent earns less than the other, which means that a dollar spent by the parent with the smaller income represents a larger percentage of that income than a dollar spent by the parent who earns more.

Even though most clients with whom you mediate will usually settle their child-support issues by using a monthly transfer payment of child support, having them complete the budgets allows them to see more clearly why a transfer payment is needed and how that amount will be spent by the recipient of child supoprt. Usually clients readily understand that the spouse with a higher income will likely pay something to the other spouse—especially if the spouse with the lower income has greater responsibility for children's costs, as is often the case with women, who tend to earn less in our society and who often have more responsibility for care of the children.

One couple with whom we worked created an innovative mechanism for solving the child-support issue. While working on options for division of their duplex, the clients noticed that their duplex checkbook was lying on the table we used for mediation sessions. One of them said, "Why don't we go to the bank and open a `child's account'?"

As all of us thought about the idea, it began to make sense. The clients had already agreed that a separate budget for the one child, age fourteen months, amounted to $740 per month, which included formula, baby-care items, some furniture for the baby's room, clothing, day care, and all other costs they could think of at the time.

---

*We prefer to use a software program to help us determine child support amounts. This program, called "FinPlan," is available from FinPlan Co., 100 E. Cuttriss Street, Park Ridge, IL 60068; phone 800-777-2108, fax 708-554-1769.

Figure 12. Sample Budgets

Start by noting that each client can raise questions about the other's budget, but if that becomes too contentious, you will ask clients to save all of their remarks until the end.

Although it is not necessary to allocate housing costs to the children, all budgets should contain a children's column in order to help clients see the actual costs of the children.

Housing and utilities are usually straightforward and do not create a great deal of controversy.

Part of determining whether one client should stay in the house is ascertaining what the house costs each month. This is the essence of future planning.

Cleaning assistance could be needed if one of the spouses is disabled. Be careful; this is a hot issue. If there is any dispute, just put up their numbers.

Because Alice will have the children more than Frank, she spends more on groceries.

Alice has always purchased the children's lunch tickets.

The clothing budget anticipates that Alice will buy most of the clothing for the children. It also allows for Frank to buy $10 of children's clothing per month, because part of parenting is sometimes taking a child out and buying some item.

Budget Item	Frank	Alice	Dad	Mom
Rent	650			
Second mortgage		150		
Mortgage Payment		628		
Real estate taxes		incl		
Homeowner's ins.		incl		
Maintenance/Repair		65		
Utilities Electricity	35	81		
Heat	incl	76		
Telephone	26	37		
Water		18		
Refuse Disposal		25		
Cleaning Assistance				
Lawn Care		20		
Snow Removal				
Housing Subtotal	**711**	**1100**		
Other Prop. Mortgage	185			
Utilities	nom			
Taxes	120			
Maint/Rep				
Food/Groceries	170	225	50	150
Lunches at Work/School	40			37
Eating Out	30	30	30	25
Clothing	50	50	10	120
Dry Cleaning, Laundry	30	10		

Frank, living in an apartment, is likely to have higher costs for laundry done at a laundromat.

Alice could pay as much as $150 to $200 per month for COBRA continuation, depending on her age and the provisions of the policy.

Frank will cover the two minor children on his policy.

Frank is currently taking Prozac for depression and not all of the expense is covered by his insurance policy. Alice expects some dental work for herself.

Alice has a car payment. She and Frank are thinking of paying it off, as there is only $2300 left on the debt. This will improve the ability of each to cash flow the budget.

Recreation, vacation, and travel are often volatile categories. Couples should be encouraged to put some amount into the budget, as the budget is a goal for a new life.

Frank and Alice have a five-year-old and they will be paying day-care expenses of $200.

In this case Frank would rather give the child support and have Alice pay the sports fees and buy the equipment for the children.

Budget Item	Frank	Alice	Dad	Mom
Medical Insurance	Thru work	$_?	60	
Uncovered Doctor	10	10		10
Uncovered Dental	20	20	15	20
Prescriptions	15	5		3
Eyeglasses/Exams	30			
Orthodontia			75	
Car Payment	325	350		
Gas and Oil	60	75		
Insurance	50	55		60
Maintenance/Repairs	20	35		
License	15	12		
Parking	10			
Life Insurance	28	35		
Recreation/Ent.	30	20	40	40
Vacation/Travel	75	30	75	50
Personal Care	10	15		20
Dues and Clubs	35			
Reading Materials	15	10		5
Hair Cuts/Hair Care	10	20		25
Children Day Care				200
Activity Fees				30
Allowances				86
Dance Lessons				20
Sports				25
Religious Contribut.	30	30		

Each will be contributing about one-half of what they formerly pledged to their church as a couple.

It is useful to keep the clients' personal living expenses side by side to avoid creating the illusion that Alice's total expenses are much greater than Frank's. She has higher housing and higher children's expenses than Frank will have.

Budget Item	Frank	Alice	Dad	Mom
Gifts	40	50		
Totals Below				
Housing Now	711	1100		
Cabin (if kept)	305			
Personal Living	1106	1022		
Children Total			355	926
Monthly Need	2022	2232		
Plus Children	355	926		
Total Monthly Need	2377	3158		

Although the clients had agreed to joint custody, the child would be with the mother about 75 percent of the time. In addition, the husband's full-time earnings were approximately twice the amount of the wife's full-time earnings. They agreed that the husband would contribute $500 per month to the account, and the wife would contribute $240 per month. From the "child's account" the wife would purchase all items necessary for the care of the child. In addition, they agreed that the wife would be the accountant for the child's expenses and would use the checkbook to keep a record of all expenses. This record would make it easier for them to make adjustments to the amounts in the future when child-related needs increased or decreased, such as changes in day care costs.

Although this arrangement may not work for all couples, it is a viable option for many. The record of canceled checks, periodically reviewed by both parents, provides detailed information needed to support any future modifications. Additionally, as their incomes change, they can alter their proportional contributions to the children's checkbook.

The process of establishing child-related costs and devising a plan for sharing those costs might result in exchanges of support that are higher or lower than the guidelines; or it may result in an agreement to pay expenses directly or into a child's checkbook. Whatever their choice, they will probably realize that the state guideline formula used is never an exact science.

Addressing the Issue of Spousal Support

Many couples approach a divorce with one person partially or totally dependent on the marriage relationship for financial support. In the adversarial system, the question: "What amount of alimony or spousal support should the payor pay to the payee and for how long? is played out with posturing and aggressive offers and counter-offers.

In client-centered mediation, different questions set the stage for understanding and cooperation: Following are a series of small questions that help you narrow the issues when discussing spousal support.

Do you two agree that one of you is now dependent on the marriage relationship for financial support? It is necessary for the clients to agree that one of them is dependent on the marriage relationship. Although the dependence may seem so apparent that the question need not be asked, the clients usually need to discuss how it came to be that one of them earned all the money and the other stayed home and took primary responsibility for the children.

This discussion is important. The clients must see and understand that they both made the choices that led to the fact that now one of them is unemployed or has very little earning capacity. If they can agree that they both participated in creating this situation, the higher income spouse is less likely to blame the other for needing support.

Do you agree that a goal of mediation is for the two of you to create a plan to allow the more dependent spouse a greater measure of financial self-sufficiency? When you ask this question, you are likely to hear the dependent spouse respond with a comment such as, "I would certainly like to be able to stop getting support as soon as is humanly possible, but I can't predict the future." In most cases, the spouse with little or no income considers alimony to be a sign of continued dependence on a person with whom he or she would like to cut financial ties. Generally we have found that the client who is currently paying support feels a great deal of relief on hearing that the other wants to become financially independent. However, in those cases where fault is used as a factor by one, the spousal maintenance issue is frequently converted to a question of entitlement to the future earnings of the higher income spouse.

If clients can agree that financial self-sufficiency is a goal for both of them (and not all will agree on this), they begin to see the possibility for a new beginning as separate people who share a businesslike but cordial relationship.

How will the two of you share responsibility for helping the dependent spouse to become more self-sufficient? What plan can you create to bring about self-sufficiency? The adversarial system would ask different questions, as it commonly sees the payor as having primary responsibility for solving the other spouse's problem. But when you frame the alimony issue in this way, you help the clients to see that the responsibility for solving the problem rests with both of them. Although the higher income spouse cannot tell the other spouse what to do, he or she will participate in the process of searching for a mutual solution, and as a result of jointly building the plan, each is more committed to following the plan.

At this point the clients engage in brainstorming or creative thinking to generate ways of creating a greater measure of financial independence for the spouse with less income. Encourage them also to consider educational and retraining possibilities. If the clients consider retraining to be a viable option, you may want to refer the dependent client to employment counseling or to career-development counseling. (The adversarial system defines this concept as rehabilitative alimony, a term that conveys the proper goal but is not used in the mediation room because it seems to have the effect of further degrading the status of the spouse with fewer financial or educational resources.)

How long will it take the dependent spouse to become more financially self-sufficient? The adversarial system may answer this question in a number of ways: In some states, the courts rule that alimony ends immediately on the dependent spouse's graduation from a course of education or retraining. In other jurisdictions, the courts rule that alimony is awarded for a length of time equal to half the duration of the marriage. The legal guidelines followed in any jurisdiction depend on the political process (as state divorce codes are the product of the legislature) or on the rulings of the state courts.

In mediation the situation is different, but the duration of spousal support can still evoke strong emotions and fears for both clients. The dependent spouse is sometimes willing to have alimony terminate or be reduced when he or she finds adequate employment but is unable to say exactly when that will be. The payor is generally willing to pay what is necessary but wants some certainty for his or her financial future and, therefore, requests a definite end point to the length of the alimony obligation.

However, if your clients have successfully created a plan for self-sufficiency and if you have successfully encouraged them to be sensitive to each other's needs, and in addition, have involved both in developing the plan, the answer will be easier to determine, even though this is the most difficult of all divorce issues.

Assigning Homework for Next Session

Before the clients leave, if you plan to work on property next, give them copies of the Household Furnishings and Personal Property Form and review the homework assignment in Chapter Seven in the client's workbook. Note that the clients have to complete a considerable amount of homework and collect a lot of data, so they will need a reasonable amount of time to do everything required.

Explain that during the next session, the clients will be working on dividing their property, including both assets and liabilities. Encourage them to jot down notes and any questions they have. Tell them to note the items they need to bring with them to the next session. (These items are listed in the "Homework" section of Chapter Seven in the workbook.)

After the Session

After the session, review all flip-chart sheets and write a memo about the decisions the clients made regarding budgets, income, child support, and spousal support (see Figure 13 for a sample report). Send a copy of the memo to each client along with instructions to review the content and make notes about any questions or proposed changes.

Figure 13. Sample Financial Decisions

Expenses

During the mediation process, Doug and Sylvia have examined their individual expenses as well as the expenses for the children. Their basic monthly expenses are as follows:

Monthly Budgets   **CHILDREN—Paid by:**

ITEM	Doug	Sylvia	DAD	MOM
Rent	650.			
Mortgage Payment (PITI)		628.		
Second mortgage		150.		
Utilities				
Electricity	35.	81.		
Heat		76.		
Water		18.		
Refuse disposal		25.		
Telephone	26.	37.		
Home Maintenance and Repair		65.		
Lawn care and snow removal		20.		
Other Property–Cabin				
Mortgage	185.			
Insurance and taxes	120.			
Food/Groceries/Household Supplies	170.	225.	50.	150.
Lunches at work/school	40.			37.
Eating out	30.	30.	30.	25.
Clothing	50.	50.	10.	120.
Dry cleaning/laundry	30.	10.		
Medical Insurance	Thru Wk.	?	60.	
Uncovered medical expenses	10.	10.		10.
Prescriptions	15.	5.		3.
Eye care	30.			

ITEM	Doug	Sylvia	DAD	MOM
Dental Insurance	Thru Wk.	?		
Uncovered dental expenses	20.	25.	15.	20.
Orthodontia			75.	
Automobile Expenses/Payment	325.	350.		
Gas/oil	60.	75.		
Maintenance and repairs	20.	35.		
Auto insurance	50.	55.		60.
License	15.	12.		
Parking	10.			
Life/disability/insurance	28.	35.		
Recreation/entertainment	30.	20.	40.	40.
Vacations/travel	75.	30.	75.	50.
Newspapers/magazines	15.	10.		5.
Dues/clubs	10.	35.		
Personal Items/Incidentals	10.	15.		20.
Hair care	10.	20.		25.
Child Care				200.
Children's School Expenses				
Allowances				30.
Dance lessons				20.
Sports fees				25.
Clubs				20.
Contributions/Charities	30.	30.		
Gifts	40.	50.		
Monthly Expenses:	2,139.	2,227.	355.	860.
Children's Expenses	355.	860.		
TOTALS:	2,494.	3,087.		
TOTAL MONTHLY NET INCOME:				
SURPLUS/SHORTFALL:				

Education and Employment Status

Doug has an M.Ed. degree and is employed by the Robbinsdale Public Schools. His gross annual income from his employment is $52,000. In addition, Doug expects to earn $10,000 gross each year from his consulting. Sylvia has a B.A. degree and is self-employed as a music teacher. Beginning next fall she has a teaching position at the Robbinsdale Junior High School in the Music Department and will earn $22,000. She plans to continue teaching piano part-time, after school and Saturday mornings. Their joint tax returns for the previous tax year will be attached for review by their attorneys.

Child Support

Doug agrees to pay child support to Sylvia in the amount of $1,250.00 per month, which is in line with the percentage required by the state guidelines. This amount is 35 percent of Doug's net monthly income. Child support will continue until each minor child reaches the age of eighteen years; enters the Armed Forces of the United States; is emancipated, self-supporting, or deceased; or reaches the age of twenty years if still attending secondary school; or until further Order of the Court.

Cost of Living Adjustment (COLA)

In the future, Doug and Sylvia agree to include the standard cost of living adjustment (COLA) clause to be calculated every two years using $1,250.00 as the base amount for the calculations.

Each will be responsible for payment of all routine expenses of the children when the children are with him or her; these expenses include clothing costs, food costs, and all other normal costs. If extraordinary expenses related to the children come up, Doug and Sylvia will first meet and agree about whether to spend the money on behalf of the children; then they will decide on a method of sharing such extraordinary expenses.

Doug and Sylvia do not wish to pay their support through the Hennepin County support and collections services.

Post-Secondary Education Expenses

Doug and Sylvia agree to share in some way in the payment of a maximum of four years of post-secondary education (college) provided that the children are full-time students, in good academic standing, and unmarried.

Reservation of Spousal Support

Doug and Sylvia have consulted with their accountant for the purpose of reviewing several levels of spousal support. Their accountant has provided them with information; they have decided, on the basis of this information, that it is not necessary for Doug to pay Sylvia spousal support at this time. They further agree that Sylvia will reserve the right to request spousal support in the future only if it is necessary because of a major loss of income. This stipulation is particularly important in view of the fact that Sylvia will soon be starting her first teaching position and will not have tenure as a teacher for several years.

Doug and Sylvia further agree that this reservation of spousal support is necessary due to the fact that Sylvia is currently partially dependent on the marriage relationship for support. She is now teaching piano but does not make enough income to meet her expenses even with the child support. Nor does Doug's income, after paying child support, meet his needs and those of the children when they are with him. Both Doug and Sylvia are cutting back on their budgets so that they can make ends meet with the income each has.

Doug and Sylvia have been married almost twenty years, and they agree that Sylvia needs some time to build up her teaching income so that it will fully meet her needs in the future. Doug has a high-paying job with annual cost of living adjustments as well as merit increases. The spousal support reservation will terminate on Sylvia's death or remarriage or on the expiration of six years from the date of entry of the Decree of Dissolution.

8 Subject Area 3: Dividing Property

Helping clients divide their property in a way that they perceive as fair is extremely important to the success of the mediation. Some clients will come to the session on dividing property having already worked out most of their property division, whereas others will not have a clue about what they want to do. It is best to complete all steps with every couple, regardless of how much work the clients have done outside the mediation setting. Completing or reviewing all of the property issues is important for the following reasons: (1) the clients may not entirely understand the ramifications of any preconceived arrangements for dividing their property, and (2) you must understand and reflect all aspects of their property division in their Memorandum of Agreement.

The steps involved in dividing property are as follows:

- Listing property and its value
- Identifying nonmarital property
- Defining their standards of fairness
- Deciding who gets what and checking whether the division is fair to each client

Listing Property and Its Value

Ask the clients to refer to their completed Mediation Questionnaires and to discuss the property items listed. As they do so, list the property on the flip chart. (When it comes time to list household furnishings and personal property, ask them about all items listed on their Household Furnishings and Personal Property Forms and for any other personal property not already mentioned.)

List the property on the flip chart in the following categories:

- Bank accounts
- Accounts Receivable
- Stocks, Bonds, and Investments
- Real estate
- Life insurance policies
- Business interests
- Vehicles

- Retirement accounts
- Tax refunds or amounts owed
- Household furnishings and other personal property
- Debts and liabilities

It is important to realize that although clients generally do not experience difficulty in understanding and identifying most of their assets, some items will present questions. For example, many clients do not realize that a retirement plan has value as a marital asset and that it can be divided without incurring a penalty or taxes. It is your responsibility to help them identify and value these assets and to understand that these assets are marital property.

This does not mean that you have to be an expert in valuing business or retirement assets. It simply means that you need to call these assets to the clients' attention and then when necessary refer them to a neutral expert who can help. The client-centered mediation process makes use of experts. These are usually:

- Realtors or real estate appraisers
- Financial planners
- Accountants or CPAs
- Insurance agents
- Specialists in the valuation of businesses
- Actuaries and experts on pension plans

As each property item is mentioned and recorded on the flip chart, ask the clients for the documents that will identify the item and verify its value. These documents are important for the following reasons:

- They are the "physical verification" that creates trust and assists the clients to understand the assets and liabilities of the marital estate.
- Later they will be attached to the Memorandum of Agreement so they can be examined by the attorney who will create the legal document ending the marriage. This avoids the legal discovery process which is costly.
- They may show the original purchase price of the property. This is important for a determination of any capital gains tax that may be owed on a sale. Often, the written verification is also needed to help sort out disputed non-marital claims.

The documents usually show what the items are worth, and the clients agree to the amounts shown on the documents, or they agree to obtain updated verification numbers tracing the history of the account if there have been disputed withdrawals. You simply list the values on the flip chart. However, if there are no documents available for a particular item, and the clients cannot agree on that item's value, make a note by that item indicating that the clients will determine the value later. If they continue to disagree about value, ask the clients to collaborate on choosing an appraiser and clarify which person will be responsible for contacting the appraiser.

The categories of property listed in this section will be found in most divorces. They are discussed in detail in the following paragraphs.

Bank Accounts

With bank accounts, the basic task is to determine what accounts exist and how much is in them. List each account and its present balance on the flip chart. Also ask whether the accounts are joint or separate and record this information.

Most couples in the United States live from paycheck to paycheck. There is usually little asset value to most checking accounts unless those accounts require minimum balances. If the clients list savings accounts or money-markets accounts that have more than nominal balances, you might want to inquire how the accounts will be used during the mediation discussions. If a great deal of mistrust exists and one worries about the other's misuse of the money, they could convert joint savings accounts and joint money-market accounts into dual-signature accounts so that the money is not subject to "grabbing" by either party. (This option is certainly less offensive than the common adversarial practice of withdrawing all of the money from joint savings accounts on the advice of the attorney to keep it from the other spouse.)

By signing the Contract to Mediate with the Rules of Mediation attached, the clients will have agreed with each other not to dissipate their joint assets, including liquid cash accounts, without first discussing the withdrawal and seeking agreement from the other. If they have not yet obtained separate checking accounts, the mediator may ask when they intend to do so. Once they create separate accounts and start paying their own bills, they will have established some financial boundaries and each need not be so worried about what the other might be spending.

From the liquid cash (if any), the clients may choose to fund new-home startup costs (damage deposit for a new apartment, moving charges, phone installation, and so on) for two separate households. Some couples who have already lived apart for some time or are in high conflict may find it necessary, for purposes of building trust, to exchange their canceled checks and bank records from their personal accounts. Doing this allows each client to see where the money is going and alleviates the fear that the other may be mishandling money. A good way to raise this subject is to ask at the time bank accounts are listed on the flip charts, whether either client has any need to review past bank records, canceled checks, or other verification documents.

High-Conflict Issues Connected with Bank Accounts

Following are some high-conflict issues that you might face. Each situation is introduced by a client comment that raises the problem.

1. "I can't trust him, so how do I know he's telling the truth about his income?"
Your response: "You may not really know. However, unless the two of you own a bar or a restaurant with large volumes of cash moving across the table each night, almost every financial transaction creates a paper trail. Would you like to hire a neutral CPA to help complete a detailed review of all records for the past several years? Tax returns are a good place to start. Not many people will lie on their tax returns just to gain an advantage in a divorce."

---

2. "When I moved out, we had more money in that account."
Your response: "Would it be useful for you to exchange canceled checks and bank statements for the past year so that each of you can see how the other has been spending money from that account?"

3. "My attorney told me I need to have a temporary hearing so that he can't control all of the money."
Your response: "One option for the two of you might be a call to your personal banker on the speaker phone right now to start the process of changing joint accounts into dual-signature accounts. Then any money taken from the accounts will require consent from both of you. In this way you won't have to fear that he will control all of the money. This can be done immediately, whereas a temporary hearing would not be held for several weeks. Would any other approaches help you with this concern? In addition, as a result of today's session, you now have a temporary agreement about the exchange of child support. This means, Ann, that you will not have to ask Jason for money each month. And, Jason, you will not have to wonder if you've given enough. In fact, Jason, you can establish a direct deposit mechanism through your bank so that the support is transferred electronically."

Accounts Receivable

This category of property is often overlooked by clients who decide they want to settle their own divorce around the kitchen table. When money has been loaned to friends or relatives or perhaps to the family business, the clients have essentially reduced the value of their marital estate. Therefore, when the loan is repaid, it is considered joint money.

Sometimes you will find that a couple has previously sold property by contract for deed (or, "land contract" as it is called in some states.). Any property that has been sold to a buyer who is making payments to the marriage partnership is considered a marital asset and, therefore, subject to the valuation process.

Ask them to provide documents relating to any such loan, because a copy of the document outlining the loan repayment terms needs to be attached to the Memorandum of Agreement. If the loan is verbal, ask if the clients agree about whether the debt is likely to be paid and whether it will be converted to actual cash. If the loan is truly speculative or if the person who borrowed the loan is unlikely to repay it, language can be inserted into the final decree that calls for division of the money "if, as, and when" received.

High-Conflict Issues Connected with Loans to Others

Following are some high-conflict issues that you might face:

1. "She lent the money to her malingering brother; she can get it back."
Your response: "We're only listing the property. Let's wait until later to determine how you will actually divide all of your assets. Besides, if it is unlikely that the loan will ever be repaid, then the loan isn't worth anything as a marital asset."

2. "He's receiving severance pay from his last job. Shouldn't that be listed as an asset?"

Your response: "That's a good question. On the one hand, the severance pay may be considered property. On the other hand, if he hasn't found another job, you may need to consider it marital income. Perhaps you should decide together how it should be treated."

3. "Shouldn't we be counting the crops in the field as marital property that will be worth something this fall?"
Your response: "Bill, how do you think the crops should be treated? Are they part of your income available for support, or do you consider them marital property to be divided?"

Stocks, Bonds, and Other Investments

This category of property—which includes stocks, bonds, mutual funds, and other investment assets—can be difficult to understand for the spouse who did not manage them. These investments are usually considered a better way of holding cash than putting it in a checking account. Some are liquid, or easily cashed, whereas others may require some delay in converting to cash. Some are reasonably stable and provide slow growth; others are very risky.

One concern in mediation is that some appreciated investment assets create a taxable event when they are sold to a third party. With most investments, the asset appreciates; therefore, a capital gains tax may need to be paid on the profit or increased value of the investment. (*Capital gain is in simple terms the difference between the purchase price or "basis" and the sale price.*) Always have them review any tax issues with an accountant. When one spouse says, "She can have the stocks in exchange for my keeping the house equity," you need to understand that the proposed trade may not be equal because of the different tax implications. The stock may be more "pregnant with taxes" than the house equity.

With stock and brokerage accounts, ask for the monthly summary sheets from the brokerage house. With couples who have large stock holdings, using a CPA, or financial planner as a neutral expert to suggest division options and explain the investment can eliminate any discomfort that might be felt by a spouse who does not understand such assets.

Occasionally, it will be necessary during the divorce to sell an investment that is losing value. At a minimum, the clients might agree that no decisions will be made unless they are joint decisions. As is the case with all property assets, if the couple cannot reach agreement on a voluntary freeze and honor it, the court could order a total freeze on all assets during the divorce process upon the motion of one client. Therefore, a spouse who invades joint money without the consent of the other spouse risks pushing that spouse into court action.

There are many types of investment assets: stocks, mutual funds, municipal bonds, zero coupon bonds, government savings bonds, treasury bills, and so on. The task for the mediator is to list the assets and, at the same time, assemble the documents that verify the existence and current value of each asset. Considerable effort may be required to value some of them—for example, U.S. savings bonds acquired at different times over the past fifteen years will each have a different value. However, it is often not necessary to obtain absolutely exact values for those assets that are going to be divided equally between the two clients; an equal division can be obtained by physically dividing them in half without knowing the exact value.

High-Conflict Issues Connected with Investments

The following are some high-conflict problems that you might encounter:

1. "That 3M stock was a gift from my grandfather, and you have no right to list it because it's mine."
Your response: "Sylvia, I'm only interested in listing everything you have. Certainly, a gift to one of you and not the other is a good reason to declare that property nonmarital and not subject to being included as marital property. Until we can talk about this more, could I just list it on the flip chart with an asterisk? Then later the two of you can decide whether it is marital property or separate, nonmarital property."

2. "I don't know a thing about investments. I think my attorney was right when he said that mediation is not for women."
Your response: "Rebecca, I appreciate your willingness to share your fears. Perhaps it would be a good idea for you and Charles to hire a neutral financial planner to assist both of you in figuring out how to understand and value what may be awarded to you in the property division."

3. "The stocks were always mine, I earned them, and I don't want to divide them with her."
Your response: "Frank, many couples do invest their earnings separately during a marriage. Since they were purchased during the marriage from your income, they are probably marital property. Perhaps you can trade the stock for some other asset that Gloria purchased from her income. You may look at an option awarding you the stock. Once you see how the property is divided in that option, you may feel more comfortable."

Real Estate

Real estate is a bit harder to divide than other liquid investments. With real estate the clients have only three options: (1) they can sell the real estate now and divide the cash proceeds of the sale; (2) one spouse can buy out the other's interest; or (3) they can continue to own it jointly for some period of time, agree on a date to sell or buy the other out, and divide the cash obtained from the sale or buyout at that time.

For most divorcing couples, the family homestead is the single largest marital asset. Some clients react with fear when divorce occurs, thinking they must immediately sell their home. This choice could be premature, and you need to help your clients examine other options before they place the house on the market. Although selling the family home may eventually be necessary, discourage the clients from rushing out and signing a listing agreement out of panic.

The first step in examining the couple's choices concerning the house is to inquire about their goals:

- "Is it important that the children have the stability of the family residence in the midst of the divorce turmoil?"
- "Do you dread the thought of keeping up the house?"
- "Is the house the only stability left in your own life so that without it you would feel that your whole world was collapsing?"
- "Is there enough equity in the home so that if you sold it there would be enough cash for both of you to buy replacement housing?"

By asking these types of questions, you can help your clients decide what to do with the house. Once the clients understand the particulars of their cash flow and what their home is worth, they will be able to make their decision more easily. Therefore, it may be necessary to complete the budget and property discussion before reaching a final decision about the house.

If a buyout of one's interest in the house is a preferred option, the clients will need to have a market analysis done by a realtor or appraisor. (Experienced realtors usually agree to conduct a market analysis without charge because they want to be remembered in case the house is sold in the future.)

Many couples in mediation obtain two or even three market analyses from realtors. A certified appraisal costing several hundred dollars is usually only necessary if the clients plan to present testimony in court or if one of them fears that a realtor might be biased because he or she is looking for a listing.

If they continue to have a controversy over the value of real estate, suggest other options such as averaging three appraisals or splitting the difference between the clients' estimates.

From a process point of view, the price dispute will be easier to solve once the couple has made progress on other property issues. Remember that the agreed-on value of the house is always in relation to other factors, such as how a buyout can occur and whether it will be for cash or for payments over a period of time. With real estate and other kinds of property, try to see everything in relation to the entire agreement that the clients are striving to create. Also encourage the clients to adopt this point of view. Skilled mediators will not let themselves or their clients get hung up on one particular issue; they know that if they leave that issue and come back to it later, it will usually be easier to resolve.

If the couple owns apartment buildings, commercial real estate, or other types of land such as a timeshare or a partnership in a lake cabin with others, values for this kind of property may be more difficult to obtain. In these cases, the clients need to hire an appraiser to provide a written appraisal. The client's workbook outlines this task and advises the clients that some appraisers reduce their fees when they are told that they will serve only as neutral experts with a written agreement that the expert(s) will not be subpoenaed to testify in court.

High-Conflict Issues Connected with Real Estate
The following high-conflict problems might arise:

1. "Michelle just doesn't understand that the house will have to be sold."
Your response: "It may very well be that the two of you will decide to sell the

house. However, I believe that the numbers will tell you what to do with the house—not me, not your attorneys, and not anyone or anything else. Could the two of you wait to make that decision until we complete our discussion of property and when all of the numbers are before us?"

2. "Fred's putting pressure on me to sell the house. But he doesn't understand that with my low income, this is the only house I will ever be able to afford. And with his higher income he can always get a mortgage."
Your response: "Before the two of you make a final decision on the house, perhaps you might consider cooperating in getting Michelle into another house. One of the things that makes mediation so different from litigation is that couples in mediation often cooperate to obtain a house for the spouse with the lower income by securing a mortgage based on both spouses' incomes. If you decide to do this, then the final settlement will have Fred deed over his interest in the home in exchange for other assets. This could mean that the two of you either sell or re-finance the house you are now in, cooperate in getting another house for Michelle that is more suitable for both of your separate cash flows, and then have the Memorandum of Agreement award the new home to Michelle."

Life Insurance
The clients need to ascertain whether they have term life insurance or life insurance that has cash value and dividend value in addition to the death benefit. Whole-life and universal-life insurance accumulates cash value that is subject to property division. Term life insurance provides only a death benefit, but it does have a place in the overall settlement—usually to fund child support or spousal support.

The easiest way to determine the cash value of a policy is to ask the clients to check with their insurance agent or to call the insurance company directly. They need to obtain a letter from the agent or the company, as written verification of the cash value to be included with the Memorandum of Agreement. Most divorcing couples treat the cash value of life insurance just like cash in the bank, and there is no reason for you to do differently even if the insurance company would call a withdrawal of the money a loan. Record all life insurance policies and values on the flip chart.

High-Conflict Issues Connected with Life Insurance

1. "I want him to name me on his life insurance, and he says `over my dead body.' I guess it would be over his dead body, wouldn't it?"
Your response: "Sharon, I don't know if Brad appreciates your humor, but the question of beneficiary designation is a very important issue. At this point in our session, I'm interested primarily in listing the life insurance policy and its cash value if it has any. We will include in the Memorandum of Agreement whatever decision you and Brad make about funding child support with existing or new life insurance. Brad, are you opposed to using some of the life insurance to fund future child support?"

2. "It doesn't really matter anyway. We can't possibly afford to continue paying $189 a month for the policy that her brother sold us. I'm just going to let it lapse."

Your response: "Chuck, before you let anything lapse, could you see if it is possible to keep the status quo? It may very well be that you are overinsured. And, given the stress on family finances during divorce, many couples do scale back their insurance coverage to fit their new, tight budgets. However, I have seen some couples regret letting a policy lapse. Check with the company to see if it is possible to stop paying the monthly premium temporarily and have the policy paid from dividends or cash that resides within the insurance policy. That will buy the two of you a few months' time to figure out what should be done with the policy."

Business Interests

By law in most states, the husband and wife share an interest in any business owned by one of them, even if the other never worked in that business and may not even be listed as one of the legal owners of that business. If your clients own a business, the one who started and operated that business will probably find this law unfair, so be prepared for some possible conflict.

Ask if there are any business interests. If so, list the business on the flip chart. Then ask them what they think the value of the business is. In order to arrive at a value that both clients are willing to accept, they almost always need to have it valued by a neutral appraiser, a CPA, who is retained with the understanding that he or she works for both spouses. (Note that in an adversarial divorce each spouse hires his or her own CPA at great cost.) The neutral CPA is instructed to provide an opinion letter setting forth the value of the business and a brief statement of the information on which the opinion was based

Generally one of them will want to keep the business, so the issue becomes one of determining how the client being bought out will be paid. This issue is addressed when the clients determine who gets what propoerty. (Clients do not usually divide this asset in half by giving each person a one-half ownership interest in the business, because divorced spouses are usually unable to work together after the divorce. In fact, many business agreements will not permit the divorced spouse to become a partial owner of the business.)

High-Conflict Issues Connected with Business Interests

1. "Rita and I have decided it's not necessary to spend the money on a business appraisal, because we've agreed that she will get the house and I will get the business."
Your response: "Ralph, I have an ironclad rule that you can give away anything you want as long as you know the value of what you're giving away. Because both of you told me you wanted an equal division of all marital assets, it sounds as if you believe that the house and the business are equal in value. In your Memorandum of Agreement, it is necessary to show the values of both assets and how you arrived at the valuation numbers. In addition, as manager of the mediation process, I urge you to protect yourselves by getting written appraisals. Then, Rita, if you sell the house next year for three times what the business is worth, I won't get an angry call from Ralph asking me what he can do."

2. "I know the business has to be worth more than the appraiser says, because Jim was always able to lease his cars through the business. And every trip we've ever taken was paid for by the business."

Your response: "Marian, that's why I like to have the business appraiser present a report during a mediation session. Do you remember when the appraiser said that the reason the business has so much debt is because the owners have incurred high overhead costs? When we did the budgets, one of the reasons Jim's monthly living expenses were much lower than yours was because the business pays a lot of his monthly expenses. Because of this, Jim said he would be able to pay you higher support than his attorney advised him to. Maybe you can see Jim's willingness to pay more than he's required to as a way for you to retain the benefit of some of those business perks, at least for a while. Does that make sense, or is something still bothering you about the appraisal?"

Vehicles

Automobiles, boats, motorcycles, motor homes, and other vehicles are listed in a separate heading in the property inventory. Automobiles can be valued by obtaining a copy of the National Automobile Dealers Association (NADA) Official Used Car Guide (available from NADA Appraisal Guides, P.O. Box 7800, Costa Mesa, CA 92628-9924, phone 800-544-6232) and looking up the assigned numbers. You probably know this book as the "blue book" (although it is no longer blue).

Another way for the clients to obtain values on automobiles is to stop at a few used-car dealerships and inquire about what they would pay for the car in question. The answer should be somewhat close to the trade-in value listed in the blue book. Bankers are familiar with these book values; a bank will sometimes look up values for its customers, particularly if they have the car loan with that bank. Similar books are published for older automobiles, boats, motorcycles, motor homes, airplanes and even bicycles.

Suggest that the clients think in terms of what amount of value one of them would be taking from the marriage partnership "pie" if he or she was awarded the car. Help your clients to avoid arguing about who is getting the better car. For example, if a new car is involved, you might point out that the new car may be worth a blue-book amount that is actually less than the amount outstanding on the car loan. Even though both clients may want the new car, they need to realize that it comes with high payments and essentially has no value.

High-Conflict Issues Connected with Vehicles

1. "We used $19,000 from our money-market account to buy her that fancy new car last October, and now it's listed in the blue book as being worth only $14,000. I think it should be valued at $19,000."

Your response: "The car was probably worth $19,000 when you purchased it. I think the problem you raise is a "date-of-valuation" issue. You two need to decide what date you will use as the date of valuation as you list and divide all of your assets—not just the car. Some people use the date of separation, some use today's date. You are free to use whatever date you wish, as long as you use the same date in valuing all assets. Richard, do you want to use October values for everything?"

2. "Our second mortgage was really taken out to purchase the car. Now it looks as if I will get stuck with paying off his car because I get the house."

Your response: "Not necessarily. You could try to get a car loan and pay off the home equity loan. If possible, it is a good idea to try to have the loans repaid by the person who is awarded the asset. What do you think, Valerie?"

Retirement Accounts

The following paragraphs describe the two types of retirement accounts that clients may have.

Defined-Contribution Account

People tend to think that retirement plans are complex and difficult. These plans are easier to understand if you think of a squirrel storing acorns for the winter. When storing acorns in an IRA account, a 401-K account, or any other "defined-contribution" account, the squirrel is essentially storing dollars in a savings account for the long winter of retirement. The reason that these accounts are so valuable (and the reason most financial advisors suggest that everyone should try to emerge from a divorce with some retirement accounts) is that, unlike most other investments, the government does not tax the interest or earnings each year as the account grows. Because the untaxed, compound interest and growth goes back into the accounts, these accounts can grow rapidly.

By depositing money into a defined-contribution account, a person can divert some taxable earnings and not be taxed on them until assets are withdrawn later at retirement. The theory is that when people are in their retirement years, their earnings are significantly less, so the money is taxed at a lower rate than it would have been when it was originally saved. All of the money withdrawn from this account will be fully taxed. The account values are based on how much the plan assets earn income or appreciate and how much is withdrawn.

Defined-Benefit Account

Another type of employee-benefit plan is called a defined-benefit account. Postal employees, state and federal employees, teachers and some employees of large companies have this kind of plan. A defined-benefit plan pays a fixed or formula-based monthly income beginning at a certain age and continuing until the person's death. Some annuities also work this way. For example, a statement brought to the mediation session might say someone is entitled to receive $750 per month beginning at age 65 based upon ten years with the company, or that at age 65 the person will receive, for example, 40% of the average of their highest last three years of pay.

To understand defined-benefit accounts, again think of the squirrel storing acorns for the winter. Assume that one day an agent visits the squirrel and says, "I've been visiting other squirrels in the area, and I have a proposal for you. I'm willing to store your extra acorns in my warehouse, together with everybody else's extra acorns. If you let me do this, I will guarantee that you will receive a defined (fixed or formula) amount of acorns each month for the rest of your life, beginning at your retirement at age sixty-five." You may retire before age 65, but you will get fewer acorns. Then the agent adds, "If you die before you reach retirement age,

I get to keep the acorns you gave me. And, of course, I also get to use your acorns while I have them stored in my warehouse."

The difference between this type of retirement plan and an IRA or a defined-contribution plan is that if the person lives to be quite old, the plan sponsor or the insurance company loses on the deal. Conversely, if the person dies before reaching retirement age, the plan sponsor or the insurance company keeps all of that person's money (unless the person designated a beneficiary to receive a portion of what he or she would have received, and the plan provides for that feature).

Other Employee-Benefit Plans

Following is a partial list of other retirement plans that you are likely to encounter in divorces: IRA, 401(k), SEP, ESOP, profit sharing, TSA (tax-sheltered annuity), and deferred compensation.

Become familiar with these terms and the basic operating concepts behind these plans. However, as mediator, you do not have to be an expert; no one can know the intricacies of every plan. Simply obtain the proper documents from your clients and, if necessary, have the clients ask their respective benefits directors at work to furnish the details of the plans. If necessary, the clients can also enlist the help of a neutral financial planner or pension expert in explaining the alternatives and choices that accompany each plan.

Dividing Retirement Accounts

Before the retirement assets can be divided, each client must first gather written information about all aspects of any retirement plan or employee-benefit account available through his or her employer. It can take some time to acquire this information, and for this reason the clients are asked to start the process as part of their first homework assignment (see Chapter Five in the client's workbook).

After the clients have received all necessary information, they should share it with each other so that they can both see the latest value for each account or plan. After the clients have agreed on the values of all retirement assets, they can work on dividing those assets. There are two ways to do this: (1) one person can be awarded the asset, and the other can take money or property of the same or equal value (assuming an equal division of all assets has been agreed to); or (2) the actual asset or entitlement can be divided into two accounts, just like slicing a pie in half. The most important part of your job at this point is to make sure that the clients understand their options and the implications of those options. They need to understand that pension accounts are non-liquid, pre-tax assets which cannot be cashed without being taxed and possibly incurring a penalty.

You need to find out whether the clients have pressing cash needs, worries about future retirement security, or other concerns. The average divorcing clients are worried about paying next month's bills, so it can be hard to get them to focus on retirement issues. Nevertheless, retirement planning is an important aspect of divorce mediation, and you need to encourage clients to address it.

Under federal law, a retirement account can be divided, provided that the division is done "incident to" (in connection with) the divorce decree. A pension can be divided in half (or in any other proportion, but usually half) so that the nonworking person or the person who has no pension can emerge with some pension assets, and neither person will be penalized or subject to any immediate tax consequences.

If your clients decide to divide a defined-benefit plan, a "Qualified Domestic Relations Order" (QDRO) drafted by the attorneys is necessary and will become part of the final divorce decree. In 1987 Congress permitted divorce courts to issue orders to pension plan administrators requiring them to create new accounts (or to send money out of the plan) for spouses who will receive a portion of the plan under the terms of a divorce decree. This method gives the couple another choice that can help solve many thorny property division problems.

The QDRO is essentially special language in the divorce decree that gives the nonemployee spouse (called an "alternative payee") an ownership account in the files of the pension plan administrator, even though that spouse has never worked for the company or contributed to the plan. It requires the alternate payee to be subject to the same restrictions and requirements that the employee is subject to. If the employee cannot start drawing on the plan until reaching age sixty-five, then the alternate payee also must wait until the employee reaches age sixty-five before becoming eligible to draw on the plan. The subject of QDRO's is highly technical and this is where the attorney and other experts can be helpful to the mediation process.

High-Conflict Issues Connected with Retirement Plans and Employee-Benefit Accounts

1. "I've been told what the law is, but I don't have to like the fact that she gets half of my retirement account and she never earned a penny of my retirement. I was the one who put up with all the garbage at work, just so she could stay home."
Your response: "Jeff, you might think of it this way: if the two of you had stayed married, you would have retired and bought that Winnebago and traveled around the country, living on your monthly pension. Now you have a chance to divide the pension at this time, and whatever you contribute to the plan after the divorce is entirely your own to keep. Gloria could argue that her staying home and raising the children allowed you to accumulate more retirement than you would have otherwise."

2. "Because I'm a woman and because I'm entering the job market later than he did, it's unlikely that I will ever be able to earn even half as much as he does. Why do I have to give him half of my meager pension earnings from all of my previous low-paying jobs?"
Your response: "Janice, you're not the first person ever to have asked that question, and I'm sure you won't be the last. In some courts, you are required to divide your property equally. In this room, you are certainly allowed to try to persuade Paul to agree to an unequal division of property in your favor. In fact, some mediated settlements I have drafted in the past call for the lower income spouse to get more than half of the marital assets on the theory that the higher income spouse will be able to more quickly acquire new assets due to the higher earnings. What amount did you have in mind?"

Tax Refunds
Ask the clients whether any tax refund or obligation is due and, if so, how much it is. List the tax refund or obligation and amount on the flip chart. At this time also

ask if they are current in their tax filings, and tax obligations. If not, ask them to provide information and decide who will be responsible for the potential liability.

Household Furnishings and Personal Property

This category of property assets is often difficult to divide due to the high emotions. The reason it may present problems for clients is because it often involves the memories of the marriage.

Household furnishings and personal property are usually be the last category of assets to be addressed, because by this time the clients will have had the opportunity to make some progress toward a settlement and will be more psychologically able to deal with personal items. It is usually more difficult for clients to reach agreement about dividing their personal property if this division is attempted early in the mediation process.

There are only two basic ways to approach dividing personal property: (1) either it will all be divided approximately in half, or (2) one client will receive more than the other sometimes requiring adjustments elsewhere or cash to be exchanged. First ask the clients to exchange their Household Furnishings Forms and to review each other's list, their preferences of retaining the various items, and notations about whether the items are separate non-property or marital property. It is important that the lists are exchanged simultaneously so that one client is not simply reacting to the demands of the other. By exchanging and reviewing lists at the same time, the clients will find this division easier to resolve.

Discourage the clients from hiring an estate-appraisal service to value their miscellaneous household property unless doing so is absolutely a last resort. Such a service can cost $500 to $1,000 and is rarely useful, because it is so difficult to know what approach to take in valuing the goods: do you use replacement value, depreciated value, garage-sale value, estate-sale value, or sentimental value? Consequently, it is best to see first whether the clients are able to divide their property on their own.

High-Conflict Issues Connected with Household Furnishings and Personal Property

1. "I'm quite sure that Barbara and I will have no trouble reaching agreement on dividing household property. Right, Barbara? Tell him that we should move on and not waste time on this, particularly at the hourly rate we're paying him."
Your response: "Barbara, I need to hear directly from you what you think. Will you and Leonard be able to reach agreement on this category of property?"

2. "It's only fair that I keep what's in the house. After all, it's not for me; it's for the children. I think it's unfair that you're telling him he should get some of the household goods. He abandoned us, and now he wants to take the children's furniture too."
Your response: "LeeAnn, I'm sorry that you think I'm trying to take some of your furniture from you. I happened to ask Jack first what his thoughts were about this category of property, and he said he still needed some things. Jack, will you prepare a list of the things you still need from the house? I think we should all take a five-minute break."

Debts and Liabilities

In dividing their debts, the clients have two basic options: (1) each client can assume responsibility for paying a portion of the indebtedness, or (2) one client can assume responsibility for all of the indebtedness and then get a credit for paying that debt in the property division calculation.

When the clients signed the Agreement to Mediate, they made a commitment to refrain from dissipating marital assets. However, some clients must spend money from their savings each month because their new expenses exceed their income. Most American couples (not just divorcing ones) tend to spend about 103 percent of what they make each month. Some couples are frugal, of course, but it is the exceptional or very wealthy couple that is able to save money each month.

Then, when a physical separation occurs, the cost of paying for two households can add an impossible burden. Therefore, it is normal for most couples to increase their debt load at the time of divorce. In fact, sometimes you will find that your clients have massive, unmanageable debts.

To assist your clients in determining how to address their debts, first ask them to identify all debts, and what those debts are incurred for. List the debts and amounts on the flip chart. If necessary, also ask the clients to provide each other with copies of old credit-card bills or other documentation so that both can know who incurred each debt and whether the money was used to benefit the family or to benefit only one of them after the separation.

Expenses incurred to benefit the family generally aren't sources of controversy. However, controversy often arises over nonfamily-related debts that one person incurred without the knowledge or approval of the other or after separation. Although couples often fight over whether one spouse or the other should restore money to the marital assets, in mediation they must first decide who is responsible for repayment of existing marital debt before they can think about restoration.

If your clients are seriously in debt, you might want to ask them to consider some type of consumer credit counseling or consulting with a financial planner or bankruptcy attorney. You also might want to remind them that only the federal government can engage in deficit financing forever.

High-Conflict Issues Connected with Debts and Liabilities

Following are some high-conflict problems that you might face:

1. "The Visa card debt was almost down to zero when I left, and now he's run it up to $2,000 again."
Your response: "Theresa, at this point let's just finish the listing. In a few minutes I'll want the two of you to talk about how all of this should be divided. By the way, Dan, would you be willing to provide an accounting of what the $2,000 debt is for?"

2. "I'm unable to continue to finance her spending addictions."
Your response: "One of the good things that happens when you get divorced is that the two of you are no longer responsible for each other's spending. The other person's behavior will not affect you—unless it affects the children, in which case it will also affect you."

Identifying Nonmarital Property

In most states divorce statutes and case law exempts nonmarital items from the division of property. Please learn about what your state's divorce practice is in regard to nonmarital or non-community property.

However, regardless of state law, you will need to assist the clients in determining whether they wish to designate any of their property assets as nonmarital. In general, marital property is that which is acquired during the marriage or that which is a product of marital effort; nonmarital property is that property which is seen as being acquired outside of or not connected to the marital partnership efforts.

Nonmarital property usually consists of (1) items that belonged to one of the clients before the marriage (sometimes referred to as premarital property) or (2) items received as gifts or inheritance—to one and not the other—during the marriage. Any property that the clients determine to be nonmarital becomes the separate property of the client who obtained it, and it is not subject to property division.

Defining Standards of Fairness

Before the clients can conclude their property division, you need to help them create standards of fairness for dividing their property (see "Defining Standards of Fairness" in Chapter Six.) Most couples decide that their standard of fairness is to divide their property fifty-fifty. (This concept of fifty-fifty equal division is also the law in most state courts.)

However, occasionally a couple chooses to divide the property unequally. In all cases where the clients decide on a standard of fairness that provides for an unequal division of property, because this usually means they are deviating from state law, it is a good idea to lead a discussion about why this approach is being taken so the reasons for the deviation can be explained in the Memorandum of Agreement.

Final Division and Distribution

Once all property has been listed and valued, nonmarital items have been dealt with, and a standard of fairness has been determined, the clients should be able to easily decide who gets what. A good place to start this discussion is with the family home, focusing always on their needs.

Compliment the clients if they cooperate effectively in dividing their property.

Be aware that you may have to develop several options before the clients make their final decisions. They need to see the numbers displayed on the flip chart, and they usually need to juggle those numbers so that the division reflects their own standard of fairness. Again, generally this means that the totals in the two client columns must be equalized, as clients usually agree to a fifty-fifty split.

If the property totals in the two columns are unequal, ask them what they intend to do about the difference. You might suggest alternatives, such as an exchange of cash or moving money from a retirement account to the other spouse. However, you will find that many couples do not insist on a precisely equal division.

Figure 14 shows a sample property division. (You can also use this figure as a template for creating your memo on this session.) Note that the property is divided approximately equally. However, in order to accomplish that result, Sylvia has to pay Doug $10,585 as an "equalizer" or equalizing amount.

Figure 14. Sample Property Division

Summary of Property Division

Doug and Sylvia agree to a standard of fairness consisting of an equitable division of all marital property.

Distribution	Value	To Doug	To Sylvia
First MN Chkg/#311-21207	150.	150.	
First Federal Sav/#2912-23604	8,312.		8,312.
Norwest Chkg/#77-258-2087	400.		400.
John Nyberg	500.	2	2
3M Stock 120 shs @ $83.25	9,990.*		X
Homestead Market Value	130,000.		130,000.
First Mortgage	(60,309.)		(60,309.)
Second Mortgage	(25,000.)	(25,000.)	
Cabin Market Value	78,000.	78,000.	
First Mortgage	(25,000.)	(25,000.)	
Conn. Mut. Life #22589431	0.	0.	
Lutheran Brotherhood #413210	895.*		X
Mutual of Omaha #37921-001	0.		0.
Sylvia's Piano Studio	0.		
Educational Consultants, Ltd.	10,000.	10,000.	
Radio Show Operetta	Future Royalties	To be divided among children.	
Dodge Caravan	18,000.		18,000.
Loan: Teacher's Credit Union	(14,000.)		(14,000.)
Chrysler	15,000.	15,000.	
Loan: Chrysler Credit	(8,000.)	(8,000.)	
16' Fishing Boat, 45hp	1,870.	1,870.	
TRA Def. Ben. #4189067	1,400./mo at 65	$1/2$	$1/2$
First Federal IRA #89207619	7,050.		7,050.
IDS Tax-Sheltered Annuity	19,431.	19,431.	
Steinway Piano	15,000.*		X
IBM Computer	500.	500.	
Mac Computer	500.		500.
Rest of Household Goods	Not Valued.	1/2	1/2
Dayton's	(432.)		(432.)
J.C. Penney	(90.)	Paid	
Sears	(75.)	Paid	
Visa	(1,400.)		(1,400.)
TOTALS:	155,072.	66,951.	88,121.
		+10,585.	−10,585.
		77,536.	77,536.

*Nonmarital property

A QDRO was used to divide Doug's Teacher's Retirement Association pension. The only other unusual item in Doug and Sylvia's property distribution is that Doug agreed to take over the second mortgage on the home, because that money was actually used to remodel the cabin. In the final Memorandum of Agreement, Doug agreed to refinance the cabin and include in the refinancing the $25,000 that was left on the house's second mortgage; he further agreed to pay off the house's second mortgage through the cabin refinancing within three months after the divorce is finalized. In this way, if something happened that made it impossible for him to make the payment on the cabin, that situation would not affect Sylvia.

After the Session

After the session, fold and file all flip-chart sheets and write a memo about the options and decisions the clients are considering. Send a copy of the memo to each client along with instructions to review the content and make notes about any questions or proposed changes.

9

Subject Area 4: Addressing Tax and Legal Issues and Reviewing Agreements

With this subject area, you and the clients address possible tax consequences and the legal details of the divorce and review all agreements made thus far (by referring to all memos from previous sessions plus any important decisions made during this session) in preparation for creating the Memorandum of Agreement.

Addressing Tax Issues

In addition to discussing tax information from this chapter, encourage the clients to have an accountant or their attorney review the draft of the Memorandum of Agreement (which is prepared and sent to them after this session) in order to address tax implications of their decisions. If the clients make or change any decisions as a result of the discussion about taxes, write the results on the flip chart. Figure 15 is a sample statement about taxes from a Memorandum of Agreement.

Cautionary Note: Because the mediator is not a CPA, you are helping them resolve conflict by understanding how taxes work; you should not be promising them certain tax results.

Claiming the Children as Exemptions

For each child, the IRS allows a parent to exempt a certain amount of their income from taxation. The exact amount of the exemption permitted increases each year. If the couple does not state in their Decree of Divorce who should claim the children as exemptions, the custodial parent is given the right to do so unless the custodial parent signs a form (IRS Form 8332) each year giving the non-custodial parent that right.

However, having the custodial parent claim the children as exemptions may not be a wise tax decision. Usually the custodial parent is also the lower-income parent. If it can be agreed that the higher-income parent claims the children as exemptions, that parent receives a greater tax advantage, and through their cooperation, they can divide the savings created by their cooperative effort.

Figure 15. Sample Statement on Taxes

REMAINING TAX CONSEQUENCES
OF THE SETTLEMENT

Doug and Sylvia agree to accept the recommendations of their accountant: Doug will have the right to claim the children as exemptions on his tax returns this year. Beginning next year and thereafter, they agree that Doug will claim the two older children and Sylvia will claim the youngest.

They will consult with their accountant or attorney about the remaining tax consequences of this agreement, particularly the liability that each has now and in the future for taxes as a result of the manner in which the homestead is being divided.

Doug and Sylvia will cooperate in correcting any errors or requests for information about the previous year's tax filings.

Encourage the clients to view this situation as an opportunity to cooperate in creating a larger pie to divide between them, particularly if they have children. Encourage the clients to see a tax adviser, who will help calculate the best way to cooperate and thereby reduce their combined taxes. You might also suggest that the clients have a neutral tax adviser prepare their taxes in the first year after the divorce and recommend an equitable way to balance the claiming of exemptions and how to share any resulting savings.

Let the clients know that if they decide to have the noncustodial parent with the higher income claim the children, the other parent has to sign a special tax form (IRS Form 8332) granting permission for this approach.

Claiming Head-of-Household Status

The person who claims head-of-household tax filing status is subject to a lower tax rate than the single filing status rate. The parent who cares for the children more than 50% of the time is eligible to claim Head of Household tax filing status. Even though it would probably create more of a tax savings, the lesser time parent may not claim Head of Household tax filing status. However, in cases where the couple has two or more children and are following a 50-50 equal time sharing schedule, it may be possible for both to claim Head of Household tax filing status. Suggest that the clients consult a neutral tax adviser, rather than as mediator telling them this is workable for their circumstances.

Understanding the Tax Effect of Spousal Support

Spousal support is taxable to the person receiving it, and a deduction for the person paying it. Child support is not taxable and it is not a deduction. Because spousal support is paid by the higher income spouse to the lower income spouse, the transfer payment has the effect of taking dollars taxed at a higher rate and giving them to a spouse who is taxed at a lower tax rate. This concept usually creates more combined income than during the marriage and it allows for solving some of the shortfall they may be experiencing as a result of higher expenses while living apart.

Selling the Family Home

Unless the couple's jointly owned home creates more than $500,000 of gain, they will not need to discuss capital gains tax upon a sale of the family home. (See Chapter 8 of *A Client's Workbook*.)

Equalizing the Bottom-Line Amounts in Property Division

Many couples incorrectly believe that there will be a tax consequence to dividing their property, particularly when they divide retirement accounts. There is no tax event created when a couple divides marital, or non-marital property in a divorce. If the couple decides to equalize their property division with payments over a period of time, the IRS could require some of the payments to be declared as taxable interest, even when they choose to make the payments interest free. Have them check this issue with an accountant or their attorney.

Addressing Legal Issues

Figure 16 presents a sample statement about legal isssues. Some of the final house-keeping matters related to legal implementation of their mediation agreements are:

- They agree on which attorney will prepare the legal documents necessary for the divorce.
- They agree on which client will appear in court, if court appearances are necessary.
- They agree on how to respond to any problems or concerns that the attorneys may have with the Memorandum of Agreement.
- They agree that they have both made full and complete disclosure of the information on which their Memorandum of Agreement is based.
- They agree on how they will share the attorneys' fees for reviewing the Memorandum of Agreement and preparing the legal document ending the marriage.
- They agree on returning to mediation if their circumstances change in the future and it becomes necessary to modify the Decree of Divorce.

Reviewing Agreements

After you have discussed tax issues with the clients, you and they should review all of the memos from previous sessions as well as any decisions made during this session. Explain that you will be combining the memos and decisions into a preliminary copy of the Memorandum of Agreement for their review. It is at this point that the clients discuss any unresolved issues and make any changes that they both want.

Assigning Homework for Next Session

Before the clients leave, review their homework for the next session (see "Homework" in Chapter Nine in the client's workbook). Also remind them to bring materials with them as indicated in the same "Homework" section.

The following is a sample statement about legal issues that we routinely include in all Memorandum of Agreements:

Figure 16.   Sample Statement About Legal Issues

LEGAL DIVORCE PROCESS

Doug and Sylvia agree that Sylvia's attorney will prepare the documents necessary to process the agreements they have reached in mediation. Sylvia will also appear in court. Both agree to retain attorneys who will respect the work they have completed in mediation. They will consult with their attorneys about all aspects of this memorandum; the attorneys will advise them about legal issues, property valuation issues, tax issues, and all other issues created by the decisions reached in mediation.

Should their attorneys find new or omitted issues, they agree to instruct their attorneys to resolve such issues cooperatively and efficiently, in an hour or less. If their attorneys are unable to resolve these in an hour or less, they agree to contact the mediator and return to mediation. Once they have received an independent judgment from their attorneys about their decisions reached in mediation, both agree to cooperate in producing documents or signing new documents to effectuate the terms of the agreements they reached in mediation. As both wish to have the dissolution entered as soon as possible, they will cooperate with each other and with their attorneys to achieve that end.

Doug and Sylvia agree that each of them has made a full and complete disclosure to the other regarding income and property assets and that each of them will sign such verifications under oath as an aid to final processing of their agreements. Remaining attorneys' fees incurred by both Doug and Sylvia in connection with the reviewing, processing, and implementing of the above agreements will be paid by each to his or her attorney.

AGREEMENT TO MEDIATE FUTURE ISSUES

Doug and Sylvia agree that if there are disagreements about the terms of their Decree or if there are substantial changes of circumstances that make the terms of their Decree unfair, they will first try to work out modifications on their own, returning to mediation and/or seeking the advice of legal counsel before seeking relief in court. Expenses incurred in using mediation in the future will be shared equally.

After the Session

After the session, use the clients' revised memos and decisions, including the decisions affecting tax and legal issues, to prepare the preliminary or draft copy of the Memorandum of Agreement. Figure 17 offers a list of all possible components of the Memorandum of Agreement; note that most of the agreements you create will not have all of these components, depending on the unique situations of your clients and what they want or need included. Figure 18 presents a sample of an entire Memorandum of Agreement. You will note that this sample reads like the samples of memos from individual sessions.

You also have the option of preparing a more legal-like document similar to the Marital-Termination Agreement (see Figure 19). Both formats—the Memorandum of Agreement and the Marital-Termination Agreement format—are effective, and neither is preferable in and of itself. If you prepare a Memorandum of Agreement, your clients will give copies of this document to their attorneys, who will then prepare the final legal documents for submitting to the court. If you follow a Marital-Termination Agreement format, their attorneys may more easily finish the legal work. Which format you follow usually depends on your profession of origin.

After you finish the draft, you will be sending a copy of it to each client. While you are preparing the draft, keep in mind that when your clients receive their copies, the reality of their divorce will set in. The implications for you are as follows:

- Understand the emotional impact of this document on the clients. The clients may feel shocked and saddened to see their marriage reduced to a few pieces of paper.
- Find ways of expressing their solutions that are clear and that respect their feelings.
- Describe their rationale for certain decisions clearly and thoroughly so that they, their attorneys, and the court will understand.
- Be willing to discuss the draft in detail in the next session.
- Be able to empathize with the clients' feelings about the dissolution of their marriage. This time can be difficult, regardless of how the clients originally felt about each other when they started mediation.

When spousal abuse exists in the relationship:

- In drafting the Memorandum of Agreement, explain the client's decisions more thoroughly than you would otherwise do. You might also want to provide more background.
- Contact the clients after they have received their copies of the preliminary Memorandum of Agreement to assist them in adjusting to the finality of the divorce and to answer any questions.
- Expect complaints and questions from each client. If there are a lot of unresolved issues, have the clients' attorneys attend the last mediation session to help finalize the Memorandum of Agreement.

Figure 17. Possible Components of the Memorandum of Agreement or the Marital-Termination Agreement

1. Introductory boilerplate language

2. Marriage date, clients' birth dates, and clients' Social Security numbers

3. Name change (if one party wishes to change the married name)

4. Parenting arrangements (child custody)
    a. Names and birth dates of children
    b. Legal custody statement
    c. Physical custody statement
    d. Parenting schedule(s)
    e. Holiday schedule
    f. Agreements about communicating as parents
    g. Special parenting rules and needs
    h. Statement of how clients have agreed to resolve future conflicts about parenting
    i. Children's higher education

5. Financial issues
    a. Budgets
    b. Explanation of each client's educational and employment background
    c. Discussion of recent past and present gross income as well as any necessary explanation

6. Child support
    a. Arrangements (including description of any deviation from state guidelines)
    b. Cost of living adjustment
    c. Child-care expenses

7. Spousal support
    a. Description of payment agreement and contingencies (or waiver or reservation)

8. Health insurance provisions
    a. Dependent spouse
    b. Dependent children, including payment of children's uncovered medical and dental expenses

9. Description of all assets and liabilities (identification and value)
    a. Bank accounts
    b. Loans to others
    c. Investments
    d. Real estate
    e. Cash value of life insurance

      f.   Business interests

      g.   Vehicles

      h.   Retirement plans and employee-benefit accounts

      i.   Tax refunds

      j.   Household furnishings and other personal property

      k.   Debts and liabilities (including any taxes owed)

10.   Summary of property distribution

11.   Special paragraphs

      a.   Nonmarital assets

      b.   Special details of property

      c.   Life insurance coverage and beneficiaries

12.   Tax issues and decisions

      a.   Children as exemptions

      b.   Filing status

      c.   Refunds or payments to IRS and state

      d.   Capital gains

13.   Agreement to mediate post-divorce issues

14.   Concluding boilerplate

      a.   Full disclosure

      b.   Attorneys

15.   Attachments (Documents that verify assets and values)

Figure 18. Sample Memorandum of Agreement

Memorandum of Agreement

Smith, Douglas (Doug) and Sylvia

Doug and Sylvia have made a decision to live separately and seek a dissolution of their marriage relationship. As a result of that decision, both have agreed to enter into mediation conducted by Erickson Mediation Institute for the purpose of settling all issues that might otherwise be the subject of contested litigation. Prior to entering mediation, they signed an agreement with each other and with Erickson Mediation Institute to be fair and equitable throughout the mediation process.

They understand that neither Erickson Mediation Institute nor the mediator legally represents either or both of them. Both agree to retain attorneys of their own choice to represent them legally and to provide each of them with an independent judgment about the decisions reached in mediation.

Mediation was conducted by Marilyn S. McKnight for Erickson Mediation Institute.

The following represents their intended decisions reached in mediation after careful review of all facts and options. Both have made a full disclosure to each other of the full nature and extent of their assets, and they wish their attorneys to incorporate the following into a legally binding settlement agreement. Both intend to incorporate this Memorandum of Agreement to the fullest extent possible in their legal documents of divorce. However, both understand that there may be some word changes based on their attorneys' reviews.

Doug and Sylvia were married twenty years ago in Robbinsdale, Minnesota. They separated six months ago.

Social Security Numbers: Doug: 999-99-9999; Sylvia: 999-99-9999.
Birth Dates: Doug: 2/10/XX (age 43); Sylvia: 7/17/XX (age 39)

Parenting Arrangements

Doug and Sylvia have three minor children from their marriage relationship: Heather L. Smith, age 17; Joshua M. Smith, age 12; and Susan F. Smith, age 5.

Doug and Sylvia agree to joint legal custody of their minor children. They agree that "joint legal custody" means that they will continue to cooperate in making important parenting decisions on such issues as education, medical treatment, and religious training. They also agree that "joint legal custody" means that each of them will continue to have equal access to all medical records, educational records, and any other important records concerning the children. If they have any disagreements concerning parenting, they agree first to try to resolve such differences between themselves and then to return to mediation if they are unsuccessful.

Doug and Sylvia agree that they will have *joint physical custody* of the children. They agree to a time-sharing arrangement in which the children live primarily in the family home with Sylvia and are with Doug every other weekend and one or two evenings each week, depending on their activities. Doug and Sylvia will talk with each other every Sunday evening at 9:00 p.m. to discuss the next week's schedule.

Doug and Sylvia agree that future exchanges of the children will be flexible and based on their travel and work schedules. However, they agree that they will always alternate having the children on the weekends and that Doug will always have the opportunity to have the children at least one evening per week. The weekends will begin after school on Friday and continue through Sunday night until Monday morning. Doug and Sylvia agree that the weekends with Doug will include his taking the children directly to school on Monday morning.

Doug and Sylvia agree to an initial weekly schedule as follows:

M–Mom; D–Dad

	MON	TUES	WED	THUR	FRI	SAT	SUN
WK 1	D/M	M	M/D/M	M	M	M	M
WK 2	M	M	M/D/M	M	M/D	D	D
WK 3	D/M	M	M/D/M	M	M	M	M
WK 4	M	M	M/D/M	M	M/D	D	D

Both are willing to experiment with different schedules to try to find one that does not unduly disrupt the children's daily schedules but still allows for significant parenting contact from both parents.

They also agree to a holiday schedule as follows:

HOLIDAYS	Even-Numbered Years	Odd-Numbered Years
Easter	Mom	Dad
Memorial Day	Dad	Dad
Fourth of July	Mom	Mom
Labor Day	Dad	Mom
Thanksgiving	Mom	Dad
Christmas Eve	Mom	Mom
Christmas Day	Dad	Dad
Childrens' Birthdays	(According to schedule and the other parent	
Parents' Birthdays	will have some contact, as requested)	
Mother's Day	Mom	Mom
Father's Day	Dad	Dad

Both will assist the children in remembering these days, and both agree that a deviation from the regular schedule can occur on these days.

They agree that next year and in subsequent years the schedule will alternate. In the event that it becomes necessary to deviate from the holiday schedule, they will try to give preference to the parent listed in the holiday schedule; in any event, it is their desire to share the holiday periods on an approximately equal basis. Both agree that there should be at least one month's planning for the holiday schedule. They agree that by February of each year they will have a preliminary discussion about summer plans for the children, with final plans being decided by May of each year.

Doug and Sylvia understand that the regular schedule as well as the holiday schedule may need to be revised due to special circumstances in the future. Each agrees to be flexible in responding to the needs of the other parent concerning parenting and scheduling, but they also agree not to use flexibility as a way of defeating the intent and purpose of the schedules.

Future Conflict Resolution

Doug and Sylvia agree that if they have disagreements in the future about scheduling exchanges or any other parenting disputes, they will first try to resolve such disagreements on their own, returning to mediation if they have difficulties in resolving these new issues on their own. The future costs of returning to mediation will be shared equally.

Principle of On-Duty and Off-Duty Parent

Doug and Sylvia agree to the concept of allowing each to provide parenting during the times that he or she is scheduled to care for the children. This means that if the children are ill or either Doug or Sylvia has other obligations during the scheduled time with the children, it will be the responsibility of the on-duty parent to make arrangements for the care of the children. Both welcome the on-duty parent to request assistance during his or her scheduled times with the children. However, both understand that if the off-duty parent is not able to assist the on-duty parent during the scheduled time, it will be the responsibility of the on-duty parent to make alternative arrangements for the children.

Binding Arbitration

If Doug and Sylvia have any major parenting disputes in the future that cannot be resolved after making a good-faith effort in mediation, they agree to submit the parenting dispute to binding arbitration. The arbitrators will be chosen from a panel maintained by Erickson Mediation Institute. The arbitrators will consist of two mental health professionals and a family-law professional who will have the right to interview the minor children as well as the parents.

The arbitration hearing will be subject to the terms and conditions of the Minnesota Arbitration Act and the Rules of Arbitration for Parenting Disputes published by Erickson Mediation Institute and in effect at the time the arbitration is commenced. Doug and Sylvia understand that by agreeing to binding arbitration, they may not have the issue heard in a District Court and that the ruling of the arbitrators is final and not subject to review except under certain narrow conditions.

Children's Health Insurance

Doug has health insurance through his employment. He agrees to continue to name the children as dependents of that policy and to be primarily responsible for providing health insurance coverage and dental insurance coverage for the benefit of the children until he no longer has an obligation to share in the cost of raising the children.

Uncovered medical and dental expenses will be shared equally by Doug and Sylvia. They agree to discuss nonemergency or elective medical or dental needs of the children before assuming the other parent will share in those costs. Doug agrees to ensure that Sylvia is supplied with current health insurance identification cards for the children.

Dependent Spouse Health Insurance

Sylvia does not have any health insurance and is currently carried as a dependent on Doug's policy available to him through his employment. Both agree to take advantage of the COBRA Law, which allows a spouse carried as a dependent on the family health insurance policy to continue to be insured under the same health insurance provider after the divorce. Therefore, Sylvia will be covered by Aetna Health Insurance under a separate policy established in the same group at a rate of $103 per month (not to exceed 102 percent of the cost of providing a single policy to other members of the group), for a period of thirty-six months from the date of decree.

Expenses

During the mediation process, Doug and Sylvia have examined their individual expenses as well as the expenses for the children. Their basic monthly expenses are as shown.

Education and Employment Status

Doug has an M.Ed. degree and is employed by the Robbinsdale Public Schools. His gross annual income from his employment is $52,000. In addition, Doug expects to earn $10,000 gross each year from his consulting. Sylvia has a B.A. degree and is self-employed as a music teacher. Beginning next fall she has a teaching position at the Robbinsdale Junior High School in the music department and will earn $22,000. She plans to continue teaching piano part-time, after school, and Saturday mornings. Their joint tax returns for the previous tax year will be attached for review by their attorneys.

Child Support

Doug agrees to pay child support to Sylvia in the amount of $1,250 per month, which is in line with the percentage required by the state guidelines. This amount is 35 percent of Doug's net monthly income. Child support will continue until each minor child reaches the age of eighteen years; enters the Armed Forces of the United States; is emancipated, self-supporting, or deceased; or reaches the age of twenty years if still attending secondary school; or until further Order of the Court.

Monthly Budgets

ITEM	Doug	Sylvia	CHILDREN—Paid by: DAD	CHILDREN—Paid by: MOM
Rent	650.			
Mortgage Payment (PITI)		628.		
Second mortgage		150.		
Utilities				
Electricity	35.	81.		
Heat		76.		
Water		18.		
Refuse disposal		25.		
Telephone	26.	37.		
Home Maintenance and Repair		65.		
Lawn care and snow removal		20.		
Other Property–Cabin				
Mortgage	185.			
Insurance and taxes	120.			
Food/Groceries/ Household Supplies	170.	225.	50.	150.
Lunches at work/school	40.			37.
Eating out	30.	30.	30.	25.
Clothing	50.	50.	10.	120.
Dry cleaning/laundry	30.	10.		
Medical Insurance	Thru Wk.	Included	60.	
Uncovered medical expenses	10.	10.		10.
Prescriptions	15.	5.		3.
Eye care	30.			
Dental Insurance	Thru Wk.	130.		
Uncovered dental expenses	20.	25.	15.	20.
Orthodontia			75.	

ITEM	Doug	Sylvia	CHILDREN—Paid by: DAD	MOM
Automobile Expenses/Payment	325.	350.		
Gas/oil	60.	75.		
Maintenance and repairs	20.	35.		
Auto insurance	50.	55.		60.
License	15.	12.		
Parking	10.			
Life/disability/insurance	28.	35.		
Recreation/entertainment	30.	20.	40.	40.
Vacations/travel	75.	30.	75.	50.
Newspapers/magazines	15.	10.		5.
Dues/clubs	10.	35.		
Personal Items/Incidentals	10.	15.		20.
Hair care	10.	20.		25.
Child Care				200.
Children's School Expenses				
Allowances				30.
Dance lessons				20.
Sports fees				25.
Clubs				20.
Contributions/Charities	30.	30.		
Gifts	40.	50.		
Monthly Expenses:	2,139.	2,357.	355.	860.
Children's Expenses	355.	860.		
TOTALS:	2,494.	3,217.		
TOTAL MONTHLY NET INCOME:				
SURPLUS/SHORTFALL:				

Cost of Living Adjustment (COLA)

In the future, Doug and Sylvia agree to include the standard cost of living adjustment (COLA) clause to be calculated every two years using $1,250. as the base amount for the calculations.

Each will be responsible for payment of all routine expenses of the children when the children are with him or her; these expenses include clothing costs, food costs, and all other normal costs. If extraordinary expenses related to the children come up, Doug and Sylvia will first meet and agree about whether to spend the money on behalf of the children; then they will decide on a method of sharing such extraordinary expenses.

Doug and Sylvia do not wish to pay their support through the Hennepin County support and collections services.

Post-Secondary Education Expenses

Doug and Sylvia agree to share in some way in the payment of a maximum of four years of post-secondary education (college) provided that the children are full-time students, in good academic standing, and unmarried.

Reservation of Spousal Support

Doug and Sylvia have consulted with their accountant for the purpose of reviewing several levels of spousal support. Their accountant has provided them with information; they have decided, on the basis of this information, that it is not necessary for Doug to pay Sylvia spousal support at this time. They further agree that Sylvia will reserve the right to request spousal support in the future only if it is necessary because of a major loss of income. This stipulation is particularly important in view of the fact that Sylvia will soon be starting her first teaching position and will not have tenure as a teacher for several years.

Doug and Sylvia further agree that this reservation of spousal support is necessary due to the fact that Sylvia is currently partially dependent on the marriage relationship for support. She is now teaching piano but does not make enough income to meet her expenses even with the child support. Nor does Doug's income, after paying child support, meet his needs and those of the children when they are with him. Both Doug and Sylvia are cutting back on their budgets so that they can make ends meet with the income each has.

Doug and Sylvia have been married almost twenty years, and they agree that Sylvia needs some time to build up her teaching income so that it will fully meet her needs in the future. Doug has a high-paying job with annual cost of living adjustments as well as merit increases. The spousal-support reservation will terminate on Sylvia's death or remarriage or on the expiration of six years from the date of entry of the Decree of Dissolution.

Property Identification and Division

The following is a complete listing of marital property as disclosed in mediation by Doug and Sylvia. Unless otherwise indicated, the date of valuation is December 31, last year. Items with an asterisk indicate nonmarital items.

Bank Accounts

Name of Bank	Type of Account/No.	Balance	Owner
First MN	Chkg #311-21207	150.	Doug
First Federal	Sav #2912-23604	8,312.	Joint
Norwest	Chkg #77-258-2087	400.	Joint

Doug and Sylvia will each be awarded one-half of the value of the First Federal joint account. Remaining bank accounts are nominal and vary with payment of living expenses and, therefore, will not count in the property division. However, the Norwest account will continue to be maintained by Sylvia, and Doug agrees to cooperate in removing his name from it.

Notes and Accounts Receivable

Due From	Amount Due
John Nyberg	500.

As Doug insists that this is a marital debt, he and Sylvia agree that he will be awarded the proceeds and will be responsible for collecting it.

Stocks and Bonds

Name of Stock	Number of Shares	Value	Owner
3M	120 shs @ $83.25 ea.	9,990.*	Sylvia

Both agree that the above stock will be awarded to Sylvia as her separate premarital property. (The stock was given to her by her grandfather prior to the marriage relationship and has not been changed since.)

Real Estate

Property	Value	Owner
Homestead	130,000.	Joint
First Mortgage	(60,309.)	Joint
Second Mortgage	(25,000.)	Doug
Net Equity	44,691.	

Doug and Sylvia are joint owners of the homestead located at 420 Orchard Lane, Minneapolis, Minnesota, which was purchased ten years ago for $95,000. The first mortgage is held by First Minnesota and has a current balance of approximately $60,309. There is a second mortgage in the amount of $25,000, which was taken out to fix up their cabin. Both agree that Doug will take steps immediately to move the second mortgage from the home. Until he is able to refinance the cabin, they agree that Doug will be responsible for the monthly principle and interest payments on the second mortgage. The home has been appraised by Edina Realty, and Doug and Sylvia agree that the present market value is approximately $130,000.

Doug and Sylvia agree that Sylvia will be awarded sole ownership of the home as a part of their property division. The property division summary calculates the net equity awarded to Sylvia. Doug will receive other assets or cash in exchange for relinquishing marital interest to the home.

Description	Value
Lake Mary Cabin	78,000.
Mortgage	(25,000.)
Net Equity	53,000.

Doug and Sylvia are also the owners of a cabin at Lake Mary purchased seven years ago for $42,500. A first mortgage is held by Home Federal Savings and Loan and has a principal amount of $25,000. The property has been appraised by Lake Land Realty, and Doug and Sylvia agree that the present market value is approximately $78,000. After subtracting the first mortgage, Doug and Sylvia agree that the estimated value of the property is $53,000.

Doug and Sylvia agree that the cabin will be awarded to Doug in the distribution of assets. Doug realizes that if he cannot afford to pay for it he may sell it. Because the $25,000 home equity loan on their homestead is related to cabin fix-up costs, Doug agrees to take steps to refinance the cabin and remove the $25,000 home equity loan as an encumbrance on the home awarded to Sylvia.

Life Insurance

Company	Face Value	Value	Owner/Insured
Connecticut Mut #22589431	90,000.	0.	Doug/Sylvia
Lutheran Brotherhd. #413210	1,000.	895.*	Sylvia/Doug
Mutual of Omaha #37921-001	30,000.	0.	Sylvia/Doug

Doug agrees to designate Sylvia and the children as beneficiaries of an amount of life insurance benefits that will fund his future child- and spousal-support obligations in the event of his death.

Doug and Sylvia agree that the Lutheran Brotherhood policy is a policy that Sylvia's parents gave her after college and that it was paid up at the time. Therefore, it is Sylvia's separate, nonmarital policy.

Business Interests

Description	Value	Owner
Sylvia's Piano Studio	0.	Sylvia

Sylvia runs this piano-teaching business out of her home. She has been providing children piano lessons since shortly after she and Doug were married. They built a special addition to the house with a separate entrance for her studio. After discussing with their accountant and each with their attorneys, Doug and Sylvia agree that it has no value as a business except for the income that Sylvia earns, which is approximately $1,200 per month.

Description	Value	Owner
Educational Consultants, Ltd.		
50 percent ownership	10,000.	Doug

Doug formed a business with a colleague several years ago. It is a consulting business based on Doug's expertise in learning disabilities. He and his partner each invested $10,000 to develop marketing materials and advertising. Doug and Sylvia agree that it is not appropriate to spend money to obtain a professional valuation and, therefore, have agreed to value the business at $10,000, which is the amount of the marital investment.

Description	Value	Owner
Radio Show Operetta	Future Royalties	Joint

Sylvia wrote this operetta for a radio show fifteen years ago. It has been published, but no copies have ever been sold. Both Sylvia and Doug agree that it is a marital asset and that if there are ever any royalties from it, those royalties will be divided equally among the children.

Automobiles

Vehicle Make and Model	NADA Value	Listed Owner
Dodge Caravan	18,000.	Joint
Loan: Chrysler Credit	(14,000.)	Doug
Chrysler	15,000.	Doug
Loan: Teacher's Credit Union	(8,000.)	Doug
16' Fishing Boat, 45hp	1,870.	Doug

Doug and Sylvia agree that Doug will be awarded the Chrysler and the boat, as listed above in his name. Sylvia will be awarded the Dodge Caravan. Doug will be responsible for repayment of the loan to Chrysler Credit after the divorce. Sylvia will be responsible for repayment of the Teacher's Credit Union loan.

Pension, Profit Sharing, and IRA Accounts

Description	Value	Owner
TRA Def. Benef. #4189067	1,400./mo. at 65	Doug
First Federal IRA #89207619	7,050.	Sylvia
IDS Tax-Sheltered Annuity	19,431.	Doug

Doug and Sylvia agree that the Teacher's Retirement Defined-Benefit in the amount of approximately $1,400 per month (when Doug reaches the age of sixty-five) will be divided equally as of the date of entry of Decree of Dissolution by using a Qualified Domestic Relations Order (QDRO), which will be drafted by their attorneys. The First Federal IRA will be awarded to Sylvia.

Household Furnishings and Other Personal Property

Doug and Sylvia have already made an equitable division of this category of property. They agree that each will be awarded the miscellaneous household goods and other personal property of the marriage that is in his or her possession as of the date of decree.

Other Property	Value
Piano*	15,000.*
IBM Computer	500.
Mac Computer	500.

Doug and Sylvia agree that each will own one of the computers and that they will divide the programs, printers, and other equipment related to the computers equitably.

Tax Refund

Doug and Sylvia agree that they will divide equally any tax refund or tax obligation arising from their joint tax filing for the previous tax year.

Liabilities

Doug and Sylvia agree that all debts and obligations incurred in their individual names since the date of separation will be the responsibility of the person incurring the debt. There are no other unpaid debts and obligations of the marriage.

Description	Amount Owed	In Name of
Dayton's	(432.)	Sylvia
J.C. Penney	(90.) Paid	Doug
Sears	(75.) Paid	Doug
Visa	(1,400.)	Sylvia

Summary of Property Division

Doug and Sylvia agree to a standard of fairness consisting of an equitable division of all marital property.

Distribution	Value	To Doug	To Sylvia
First MN Chkg/#311-21207	150.	150.	
First Federal Sav/#2912-23604	8,312.		8,312.
Norwest Chkg/#77-258-2087	400.		400.
John Nyberg	500.	$1/2$	$1/2$
3M Stock 120 shs @ $83.25	9,990.*		X
Homestead Market Value	130,000.		130,000.
First Mortgage	(60,309.)		(60,309.)
Second Mortgage	(25,000.)	(25,000.)	
Cabin Market Value	78,000.	78,000.	
First Mortgage	(25,000.)	(25,000.)	
Conn. Mut. Life #22589431	0.	0.	
Lutheran Brotherhood #413210	895.*		X
Mutual of Omaha #37921-001	0.		0.
Sylvia's Piano Studio	0.		
Educational Consultants, Ltd.	10,000.	10,000.	
Radio Show Operetta	Future Royalties.	To be divided among children.	
Dodge Caravan	18,000.		18,000.
Loan: Teacher's Credit Union	(14,000.)		(14,000.)
Chrysler	15,000.	15,000.	
Loan: Chrysler Credit	(8,000.)	(8,000.)	
16' Fishing Boat, 45hp	1,870.	1,870.	
TRA Def. Ben. #4189067	1,400./mo at 65	$1/2$	$1/2$

Distribution	Value	To Doug	To Sylvia
First Federal IRA #89207619	7,050.		7,050.
IDS Tax-Sheltered Annuity	19,431.	19,431.	
Steinway Piano	15,000.*		X
IBM Computer	500.	500.	
Mac Computer	500.		500.
Rest of Household Goods	Not Valued.	$1/2$	$1/2$
Dayton's	(432.)		(432.)
J.C. Penney	(90.)	Paid	
Sears	(75.)	Paid	
Visa	(1,400.)		(1,400.)
TOTALS:	155,072.	66,951.	88,121.
		+10,585.	−10,585.
		77,536.	77,536.

The above distribution of assets represents an division of property that is acceptable to Doug and Sylvia. Both agree that the division is fair. They further agree that the division should be equal and that Sylvia will pay Doug the sum of $10,585 when the divorce decree is signed and entered by the Court and on exchange of quit-claim deeds.

Remaining Tax Consequences of the Settlement

Doug and Sylvia agree to accept the recommendations of their accountant: Doug will have the right to claim the children as exemptions on his tax returns this year. Beginning next year and thereafter, they agree that Doug will claim the two older children and Sylvia will claim the youngest.

They will consult with their accountant or attorney about the remaining tax consequences of this agreement, particularly the liability that each has now and in the future for taxes as a result of the manner in which the homestead is being divided.

Doug and Sylvia will cooperate in correcting any errors or requests for information about the previous year's tax filings.

Legal Divorce Process

Doug and Sylvia agree that Sylvia's attorney will prepare the documents necessary to process the agreements they have reached in mediation. Sylvia will also appear in court. Both agree to retain attorneys who will respect the work they have completed in mediation. They will consult with their attorneys about all aspects of this memorandum; the attorneys will advise them about legal issues, property valuation issues, tax issues, and all other issues created by the decisions reached in mediation.

Should their attorneys find new or omitted issues, they agree to instruct their attorneys to resolve such issues cooperatively and efficiently, in an hour or less. If their attorneys are unable to resolve these issues in an hour or less, the clients agree to contact the mediator and return to mediation. Once they have received an independent judgment from their attorneys about their decisions reached in mediation, both agree to cooperate in producing documents or signing new documents to effectuate the terms of the agreements they reached in mediation. As both wish to have the dissolution entered as soon as possible, they will cooperate with each other and with their attorneys to achieve that end.

Doug and Sylvia agree that each of them has made a full and complete disclosure to the other regarding income and property assets and that each of them will sign such verifications under oath as an aid to final processing of their agreements. Remaining attorneys' fees incurred by both Doug and Sylvia in connection with the reviewing, processing, and implementing of the above agreements will be paid by each to his or her attorney.

Agreement to Mediate Future Issues

Doug and Sylvia agree that if there are disagreements about the terms of their decree or if there are substantial changes of circumstances that make the terms of their decree unfair, they will first try to work out modifications on their own, returning to mediation and/or seeking the advice of legal counsel before seeking relief in court. Expenses incurred in using mediation in the future will be shared equally.

Figure 19. Memorandum of Agreement
Smith, Doug, and Sylvia Smith

MEMORANDUM OF AGREEMENT

REASON FOR SEEKING MEDIATION: Doug Smith and Sylvia Smith have made a decision to live separately and seek a dissolution of their marriage relationship. As a result of that decision, both have agreed to enter into mediation conducted by Erickson Mediation Institute for the purpose of settling all issues which might otherwise be the subject of contested litigation. Prior to entering mediation, they signed an agreement with each other and with Erickson Mediation Institute to be fair and equitable throughout the mediation process.

EACH AGREE TO LEGAL REPRESENTATION: Both understand that neither Erickson Mediation Institute nor the mediator legally represents either or both of them. Both agree to retain attorneys of their own choice to legally represent them and to provide each of them with an independent judgment about the decisions reached in mediation.

MEMORANDUM REFLECTS THEIR AGREEMENTS REACHED IN MEDIATION: Mediation was conducted by Marilyn S. McKnight for Erickson Mediation Institute. The following represents their intended decisions reached in mediation after careful review of all facts and options. Both have made a full disclosure to each other of the full nature and extent of their assets, and they wish their attorneys to incorporate the following into a legally binding settlement agreement. Both intend to incorporate this mediation agreement to the fullest extent possible in their legal documents of divorce. However, both understand that there may be some word changes based upon review by their attorneys.

The full names of the Co-Petitioners are Doug Smith, born on the 10th day of February, 19XX, is presently 43 years of age, and resides at 12360 Nicollet Ave. #810, Minnespolis, MN 55419; and Sylvia Smith, born on the 17th day of July, 19XX, is presently 39 years of age and resides at 420 Orchard Lane, Minneapolis, MN 55419. Co-Petitioner Sylvia Smith's maiden name is Anderson. Both parties have resided in Hennepin County in the State of Minnesota for more than 180 days prior to the commencement of this proceeding. Co-Petitioner Doug Smith's social security number is 999-99-9999. Co-Petitioner Sylvia Smith's social security number is 999-99-9999.

I.

Co-Petitioner Sylvia Smith is represented in this proceeding by S. O. Tuff, Esq., attorney registration number 563478. Co-Petitioner Doug Smith is represented in this proceeding by Joseph Bloh, Esq., attorney registration number 984576.

II.

The parties were duly married each to the other on the 7th day of June, 19XX, in Robbinsdale, Minnesota and ever since said date have been and now are Wife and Husband.

III.

There are three children born as issue of the parties' marriage. Namely, Heather L. Smith, born June 15, 19XX, age 17; Joshua M. Smith, born October 12, 19XX, age 12, Susan F. Smith, born November 14, 19XX, age 5.

IV.

There has been an irretrievable breakdown of the parties' marriage relationship.

V.

This proceeding is brought in good faith for purposes of obtaining a decree of dissolution of the marriage relationship existing between the parties. Neither party has commenced a separate proceeding for dissolution, or custody in this state or elsewhere and no such separate proceeding is pending.

VI.

Neither party is now and neither party has been in the military service of the United States at any time relevant herein.

VII.

Doug has an M.A. degree and is employed by the Eagan Public Schools. His gross annual income is $55,000. In addition, Doug receives approximately $10,000 per year from independent consulting. Sylvia has a B.A. degree and is self-employed as a music teacher. Her gross annual income is approximately $14,400. Beginning in the fall of 19XX she has a teaching position at the Eagan Junior High school in the music department and she will earn $22,000. She will continue teaching piano part time, after school and Saturday mornings while she teaches school.

Their joint tax returns for the 19XX tax year will be attached for review by their attorneys.

EXPENSES: During the mediation process, the parties have examined their expenses individually as well as for Heather, Josh and Susan. Their basic monthly expenses are as follows (see next page):

VIII.

The parties are owners of various personal savings and checking accounts as follows:

Name of Bank	Type of Account/#	Balance	Owner
1.01) First Federal	Sav #2912-23604	8,312.	Joint
1.02) Norwest	Chg #77-258-2087	400.	Joint
1.03) First MN	Chg #311-21207	150.	Doug

Of the above accounts, each will be awarded one half the value of the First Federal (1.01) joint account. Remaining bank accounts are nominal and vary with payment of living expenses, and therefore, will not count in the property division. However, the Norwest (1.02) account will continue to be maintained by Sylvia, and Doug shall cooperate in removing his name from it.

IX.

The parties are owners of various notes and accounts receivable as follows:

Due From	Amount Due
2.01) John Nyberg	500.

Doug will be awarded from the proceeds and will be responsible for collecting the above debt.

X.

The parties are owners of various stocks and mutual fund accounts as follows:

Name of Stock	Number of Shares	Value	Owner
3.01) 3M *	120 shares @ $83.25 ea.	9,990. *	Sylvia

The above stock shall be awarded to Sylvia as her separate pre-marital property. The stock was gifted to Sylvia by her grandfather prior to the marriage relationship.

XI.

The parties hereto are the owners of the following real property, held in the following manner:
(a) <u>Homestead.</u> The parties are the owners in joint tenancy of their homestead located at 420 Orchard Lane, Minneapolis, MN 55419, Hennepin County, Minnesota, which is legally described as follows:

Lot 7, Block 5, Suburban Park, Hennepin County, Minnesota.

Property	Value	Owner
4.01) Homestead	130,000.	Joint
First Mortgage	(60,309.)	Joint
Second Mortgage	(25,000.)	Doug
Net Equity	44,691.	

Said homestead was purchased in 19XX for $95,000. A first mortgage is held by Fourth Minnesota Bank, account #777-888893 with a current balance of approximately $60,309. A second mortgage is held by Mortgage Managers, Inc. with a current balance of approximately $25,000. The parties have obtained a market analysis from a realtor and they agree that market value for purposes of their

ITEM	Doug	Sylvia	DAD	MOM
Rent	650.			
Mortgage Payment (PITI)		628.		
Second mortgage		150.		
Utilities				
Electricity	35.	81.		
Heat		76.		
Water		18.		
Refuse disposal		25.		
Telephone	26.	37.		
Home Maintenance and Repair		65.		
Lawn care and snow removal		20.		
Other Property–Cabin				
Mortgage	185.			
Insurance and taxes	120.			
Food/Groceries/Household Supplies	170.	225.	50.	150.
Lunches at work/school	40.			37.
Eating out	30.	30.	30.	25.
Clothing	50.	50.	10.	120.
Dry cleaning/laundry	30.	10.		
Medical Insurance	Thru Wk.	Included	60.	
Uncovered medical expenses	10.	10.		10.
Prescriptions	15.	5.		3.
Eye care	30.			
Dental Insurance	Thru Wk.	130.		
Uncovered dental expenses	20.	25.	15.	20.
Orthodontia			75.	

ITEM	Doug	Sylvia	DAD	MOM
Automobile Expenses/Payment	325.	350.		
Gas/oil	60.	75.		
Maintenance and repairs	20.	35.		
Auto insurance	50.	55.		60.
License	15.	12.		
Parking	10.			
Life/disability/insurance	28.	35.		
Recreation/entertainment	30.	20.	40.	40.
Vacations/travel	75.	30.	75.	50.
Newspapers/magazines	15.	10.		5.
Dues/clubs	10.	35.		
Personal Items/Incidentals	10.	15.		20.
Hair care	10.	20.		25.
Child Care				200.
Children's School Expenses				
Allowances				30.
Dance lessons				20.
Sports fees				25.
Clubs				20.
Contributions/Charities	30.	30.		
Gifts	40.	50.		
Monthly Expenses:	2,139.	2,357.	355.	860.
Children's Expenses	355.	860.		
TOTALS:	2,494.	3,217.		
TOTAL MONTHLY NET INCOME:				
SURPLUS/SHORTFALL:				

marriage dissolution proceeding is approximately $130,000. Without subtracting selling costs, the net equity of their house is approximately $44,691, which will be awarded to Sylvia in the distribution of assets. The parties hereto are owners of normal household goods, furnishings and other personal property situated in and about the homestead of the parties.

(b) Cabin. The parties are the owners in joint tenancy of a cabin located at 817 Hwy 17, Lake Mary, MN 55812, which is legally described as follows:

Lot 8, Block 42, Lake Mary, Minnesota.

Property	Value
4.02) Lake Mary Cabin	78,000.
Contract for Deed	(25,000.)
Net Equity	53,000.

The Lake Mary cabin was purchased in 1984 for $42,500. A first mortgage is held by Home and Farm Savings and Loan with a principal amount of $25,000. The property has been appraised by Lake Land Realty and both agree that the present market value is approximately $78,000. Subtracting the first mortgage, the estimated value of the property is $53,000.

Doug will be awarded this property in the distribution of assets. Because the $25,000 home equity loan on their homestead is related to cabin fix-up costs, Doug shall immediately make application to re-finance the cabin and remove the $25,000 home equity loan as an encumbrance on the home awarded to Sylvia.

XII.

The parties have various term life insurance policies as follows:

Company	Cash Value	Face Value	Owner/ Insured
5.01) Connecticut Mut, #22589431	90,000.	0.	Doug/Sylvia
5.02) Lutheran Brotherhood, #413210	1,000.	895. *	Sylvia/Doug
5.03) Mutual of Omaha, #37921-001	30,000.	0.	Sylvia/Doug

Doug will designate Sylvia and the children as beneficiaries of an amount of life insurance benefits that will fund his future child and spousal support obligations in the event of his death.

XIII.

The parties have various business interests as follows:

Description	Value	Owner
6.01) Sylvia's Piano Studio	0.	Sylvia

Sylvia operates a piano teaching business out of her home. She has been teaching children piano lessons since shortly after they were married. During the marriage, Doug and Sylvia built a special addition to the house with a separate entrance for her studio. Bases upon discussions with their accountant and with each of their attorneys, Doug and Sylvia have valued the business at zero value.

Description	Value	Owner
6.02) Educational Consultants, Ltd. 50% ownership	10,000.	Doug

Doug formed a business with a colleague in 19XX, five years ago. It is a consulting business that takes advantage of Doug's expertise in learning disabilities. Doug and his partner invested $10,000 to develop marketing materials and advertising. Doug and Sylvia do not wish to incur the cost to obtain a professional valuation of the business and therefore, will value the business at $10,000 which is the amount of the marital money invested in the business.

---

*The Lutheran Brotherhood policy (item 5.02) is a policy that Sylvia's parents gave her after college, and was paid up at the time. It therefore is Sylvia's separate, non-marital policy.

Description	Value	Owner
6.03) Lake Land Operetta	Future Royalties.	Joint

Sylvia wrote this operetta for a radio show fifteen years ago. It has been published but no copies have ever sold. The operetta is a marital asset, and if there are ever any royalties from it, the royalties will be divided equally among the children.

XIV.

The parties are the owners of the following motor vehicles and boats:

Vehicle Make & Model	N.A.D.A. Value	Owner
7.01) Dodge Caravan	18,000.	Joint
Loan: Teachers Credit Union	(14,000.)	Doug
7.2) Chrysler	15,000.	Doug
Loan: Chrysler Credit	(8,000.)	Doug
7.3) 16' Fishing Boat, 45hp	1,870.	Doug

Doug will be awarded the Chrysler and the boat (items 7.02 and 7.03) as listed above in his name. Sylvia will be awarded the Dodge Caravan. Doug will be responsible for repayment of the loan to Chrysler Credit after the divorce. Sylvia will be responsible for repayment of the Teachers Credit Union loan.

The parties are owners of various retirement and IRA accounts with values as follows:

Description	Value	Owner
8.01) TRA #4189067	1,400./mo. at 65	Doug
8.02) First Fed IRA #89207619	7,050.	Sylvia
8.03) IDS Tax Sheltered Annuity	19,431.	Doug

The Teacher's Retirement Defined Benefit (item 8.01) projecting a monthly entitlement in the amount of approximately $1,400 per month at Doug's 65 shall be divided equally between them using a Qualified Domestic Relations Order which will be drafted by their attorneys. The First Federal IRA (item 8.02) will be awarded to Sylvia. The IDS Tax Sheltered Annuity (item 8.03) will be awarded to Doug.

XVI.

Doug and Sylvia have already made an equitable division of miscellaneous household goods and other personal property and each will be awarded the miscellaneous household goods and other personal property of the marriage that is in their possession as of the date of decree.

Other Property	Value
9.01) Piano *	15,000. *
9.02) IBM Computer	500.
9.03) Mac Computer	500.

Each will own one of the computers and they will divide equitably the programs, printers, and other equipment related to the computers.

XVII.

They will divide equally any tax refund or tax obligation arising from their joint tax filings for the previous year.

XVIII.

The parties have incurred either jointly or individually debt as follows:

Description	Debt	Owner
10.01) Mastercard	(432.)	Sylvia
10.02) Retail Credit	(90.) Paid	Doug
10.03) Discover	(75.) Paid	Doug
10.04) Visa	(1,400.)	Sylvia

XIX.

There are no arrearages in voluntary child support or maintenance as of the date of the signing of this Agreement. Since there has been prompt payment of voluntary child support payments in the past and would not be in the best interests of the minor children to require wage withholding.

XX.

The parties hereto have entered into mediation with Marilyn S. McKnight of Erickson Mediation Institute and have signed and adopted rules of mediation wherein they promise to obtain legal representation of their own choice to represent each of them in reviewing and implementing the decisions reached in mediation. The parties have entered into this Stipulation and Marital Termination Agreement and the Court has read and approved the Stipulation and the Stipulation is incorporated into these Findings of fact. The parties understand that they have legal rights in addition to the interests they have adjusted in mediation and both have thoroughly consulted with their respective attorneys about these legal rights.

WHEREFORE, the parties pray for the Judgment and Decree of this Court granting the following relief:

1. <u>Dissolution.</u> Dissolving the bonds of matrimony existing by and between the parties administratively, pursuant to Section 518.13, subd. 5. Both parties acknowledge that the marriage relationship is irretrievably broken and waive any right under Section 518.145, subd. 1, to appeal a finding of irretrievable breakdown of the marriage relationship.

2. <u>Custody/Visitation.</u> The parties will share joint legal custody and they will share joint physical custody of their two minor children: Namely, Heather L. Smith, born June 15, 19XX, age 17; Joshua M. Smith, born October 12, 19XX, age 12, Susan F. Smith, born November 14, XXXX, age 5. The parties represent and understand that their agreement to share joint legal custody is intended as a means of sharing joint decision making in the future regarding the parties' minor children. Both parties agree that they will continue to cooperate in making decisions regarding education, medical treatment, religious training and other significant parenting decisions in the children's lives. Both parties also agree that they will have equal access to all medical, educational and other records relating to the children. Should they have disagreements concerning parenting of the children, they agree to first try to resolve such differences and return to mediation if they are unsuccessful. The future costs of returning to mediation, if needed, will be shared equally between the parties.

The parties shall exercise their rights of joint legal and joint physical custody in accordance with the following provisions:

a) The parties shall confer with each other before making a decision on a matter involving a major concern in the lives of their children, such as religious training, education or health care. The parties shall make sincere efforts to cooperate and shall put the best interests of the children first.

b) Neither party shall do anything that would estrange the children from the other parent or behave in any way that would hamper the natural development of the relationship of the children for each parent.

c) In the event that the on-duty parent (with whom the children are residing or scheduled to reside) has other obligations at the time, it is the responsibility of that parent to make arrangements for the care of the children. If the off-duty parent is not available to assist in providing such care, then the on-duty parent (with whom the children are residing or scheduled to reside at that time) will have ultimate responsibility for making alternative arrangements for the care of the children.

3. <u>Parenting Plan Agreement:</u> Doug and Sylvia have three minor children of the marriage relationship: Namely, Heather L. Smith, born June 15, 19XX, age 17; Joshua M. Smith, born October 12, 19XX, age 12, Susan F. Smith, born November 14, 19XX, age 5.

a.) GENERAL—As parents, they share a concern for the well being and interest of Heather, Josh and Susan. They agree that both parents are very important to Heather, Josh and Susan and they need each parent to be significantly involved in his or her life after divorce. They agree to respect the other parent's individual role with Heather, Josh and Susan. Each understands that sending messages to the other parent through the children, and demeaning the other parent is harmful to Heather, Josh and Susan's sense of self and so they each agree not to do these things. They will give encourage Heather, Josh and Susan to love, and be proud of, the other parent.

Heather, Josh and Susan will each be legally and publicly known under the surname (last name) of Smith.

b.) RESIDENTIAL ARRANGEMENTS—They realize **Heather, Josh and Susan's needs** are the most important people to consider as they plan their living arrangements, and also that the children's needs will change as they grow older. They know that Heather, Josh and Susan are individuals and they will continue to be sensitive to each child's adjustment during this time of restructuring their family. They recognize that children of all ages adjust to changes better when they know what will be happening to them and what the schedule will be for them to be with each other and with the other parent.

Although Heather, Josh and Susan need living arrangements that are **predictable, specific, and routine,** sometimes there may be exceptions to the normal schedule. They will consider a request from the other parent for a change in schedule when an unexpected event occurs. They will give each other as much advance notice as possible of the need to make changes for special circumstances.

Both parties will from time to time, experiment with different schedules in order to try to find an exchange schedule that does not unduly disrupt the children's daily schedules, but still allows for significant parenting contact by both parties. They will follow an initial time sharing arrangement as follows:

M–Mom; D–Dad

	MON	TUES	WED	THUR	FRI	SAT	SUN
WK 1	D/M	M	M/D/M	M	M	M	M
WK 2	M	M	M/D/M	M	M/D	D	D
WK 3	D/M	M	M/D/M	M	M	M	M
WK 4	M	M	M/D/M	M	M/D	D	D

They will follow a time sharing arrangement in which the children are home-based with Sylvia, with Doug having the children with him every other weekend and one or two evenings each week depending on their activities. Doug and Sylvia will talk with each other each Sunday evening at 9:00 p.m. to discuss the next week's schedule.

Future exchanges of the children will be flexible based upon each of their travel and work schedules, but they will always alternate the weekends and provide for Doug to have the children at least one evening per week. The weekends will begin after school on Fridays and continue overnight Sunday until Monday morning. They agree that the weekend times with Doug will also include taking the children directly to school on Monday morning.

During the **SUMMER** Heather, Josh and Susan will be with each parent the same way as listed on the schedule above.

c.) HOLIDAY SCHEDULE—The parties shall abide the following holiday schedule. The holidays will be treated as an exception to the regular weekly schedule of exchanges without the need to have makeup time.

For summer vacation, they shall have a preliminary discussion about summer plans for the minor children by February of each year with final plans being decided upon by May of each year.

If the parties disagree in the future about scheduling changes or have disputes about the holiday schedule, they shall first try to resolve such disagreements on their own, and shall return to mediation should they have difficulties in resolving these new issues on their own. The future costs of returning to mediation if needed shall be shared equally.

Heather, Josh and Susan will spend **HOLIDAYS** as follows:

When **Mondays are a legal holiday,** Heather, Josh and Susan will be with the parent they spend the preceding Sunday with until 5:00 p.m. on Monday.

Thanksgiving: For purposes of this agreement, Thanksgiving is considered to begin at 5:00 p.m. Wednesday, and end at 5:00 p.m. on Friday.

Christmas: For purposes of this agreement, Christmas Eve is considered to begin at noon on December 24th and end at 11:00 p.m. on December 24th. Christmas Day is considered to begin at 11:00 p.m. on December 24th and end at 5:00 p.m. December 25th.

Mother's Day will be with mother and **Father's Day** will be with father each year.

Heather, Josh and Susan will spend **Spring Break** with Sylvia in odd numbered years and with Doug in even numbered years.

HOLIDAYS	Even-Numbered Years	Odd-Numbered Years
Easter	Mom	Dad
Memorial Day	Dad	Dad
Fourth of July	Mom	Mom
Labor Day	Dad	Mom
Thanksgiving	Mom	Dad
Christmas Eve	Mom	Mom
Christmas Day	Dad	Dad
Childrens' Birthdays and Parents' Birthdays	(According to schedule and the other parent will have some contact, as requested by that parent)	
Mother's Day	Mom	Mom
Father's Day	Dad	Dad

d.) RELATIONSHIPS IMPORTANT TO HEATHER, JOSH AND SUSAN—Doug and Sylvia recognize Heather, Josh and Susan will benefit from maintaining ties with grandparents, relatives and people important to them and will help Heather, Josh and Susan continue to be with these people from time to time.

e.) DAY TO DAY DECISIONS AND MAJOR DECISIONS—They recognize decision making is an important part of parenting and agree that the parent Heather, Josh and Susan are with (the "on-duty" parent) will make decisions about their **day to day care and control**.

They agree to the concept that each of them will provide parenting during the times they are scheduled to care for Heather, Josh and Susan. This means that if Heather, Josh or Susan is ill or either of them have other obligations during the scheduled time with the children, it will be the responsibility of the on-duty parent to make arrangements for the care of Heather, Josh and Susan. They each welcome the on-duty parent to request assistance during their scheduled times with Heather, Josh and Susan, but they both understand that if the off-duty parent is not able to assist the on-duty parent during the scheduled time, it will be the responsibility of the on-duty parent to make alternative arrangements for Heather, Josh and Susan.

1.) Education: Each of them will communicate with Heather, Josh and Susan's schools to remain informed about the children's needs, progress and special events including parent-teacher conferences. They also agree to share information about Heather, Josh and Susan's school progress, behavior and events with each other. They realize college or technical training is important and will encourage and support Heather, Josh and Susan's efforts for further education. Major decisions about Heather, Josh and Susan's education will be made by both Doug and Sylvia together.

2.) Health Care: In emergencies each parent can consent to emergency medical treatment for Heather, Josh and Susan as needed. Their intent is to take care of the medical emergency first and communicate with the other parent as soon as possible. They each have the right to Heather, Josh and Susan's medical information and records, and will communicate with each other on major health care for Heather, Josh and Susan. Major decisions about health care will be made by both mother and father together.

3.) Religion: They will communicate with each other on major religious ceremonies involving Heather, Josh and Susan, and will decide together about any religious upbringing issues.

4.) Child Care: If child care is needed by one parent, when practical, they agree to offer the other parent the opportunity to provide this care before seeking someone else to care for Heather, Josh and Susan. Major decisions about child care will be made by both mother and father together.

f.) COMMUNICATION—During separation from Heather, Josh and Susan, each parent will maintain frequent contact with them by phone, letter, post cards, video or audio tapes. They will also encourage and help the children communicate frequently with the other parent by phone, letter, etc. They agree to give the other parent the address and phone number where each child can be reached anytime they are away from home for more than 48 hours.

g.) SAFETY—They each agree not to compromise the safety of Heather, Josh or Susan. They will not leave Susan unattended until she is 12 years old. They agree not to operate a vehicle when under the influence of alcohol or non-prescription drugs when the children are in the vehicle, or use these substances carelessly when Heather, Josh or Susan is in their care.

h.) TRANSPORTATION—They each agree the parent who is receiving the children will transport them. They will bring Heather, Josh and Susan's belongings at the same time they drive Heather, Josh and Susan. Remembering is difficult for children, so they will cooperate and help their children (who are old enough) to remember to take belongings with them, so they will have with them the personal belongings and school supplies they need.

i.) MOVE FROM CURRENT RESIDENCE—If a move from a current residence makes it impossible to continue the schedules in the Plan, they each agree to renegotiate the Parenting Plan Agreement prior to a move. They will focus on how they can still be involved as parents in a way that would meet the needs of Heather, Josh and Susan.

j.) DURATION—They understand this Plan will be in effect until the court issues a new court order regarding their shared parenting arrangements. They agree any changes to this Plan will be made in writing, dated and signed by each of them. Until such a written change is approved by the Court, they realize agreements made in this Plan will govern any dispute.

As Heather, Josh and Susan grow and their life situations change, Sylvia and Doug agree to be flexible and cooperative, and communicate so they can meet the changing needs of Heather, Josh and Susan. If one parent does not follow a part of this Plan, they understand the other parent's obligations under the Plan are not affected. When they cannot agree about what a part of this agreement means, or if a significant change (such as a move or remarriage) causes conflict, they will make a good faith effort to resolve our differences through mediation and counseling.

k.) OTHER—They will not remove Heather, Josh and Susan from the State of Minnesota without permission of the other parent. They will be reasonable when the other parent requests to take Heather, Josh and Susan out of Minnesota.

They understand this is not a binding agreement until issued as a court order, and that their signatures are a reflection of our good faith efforts to make arrangements that are in the best interest of Heather, Josh and Susan.

4. Child Support. Doug will pay child support to Sylvia for the support of the minor children the sum of $1,250 per month payable in two equal installments on the first and fifteenth days of each month, commencing in the month of the entry of the judgment and decree herein. A child shall remain entitled to support until the child reaches eighteen (18) years of age, marries, is emancipated, self-supporting, deceased, or in the armed forces of the United States of America, whichever shall occur first, or until further order of the Court. In the event a minor child is attending high school at the time of his eighteenth (18) birthday, the child support obligation shall continue so long as the child is attending high school, but in no event after the child becomes twenty (20) years of age. There will be no reduction in child support as each child is no longer eligible. In the future, they agree to include the standard cost of living adjustment clause to be calculated every two years using $1,250. as the base amount for the calculations.

Each will be responsible for payment of all routine expenses of the children such as clothing, food when the children are with them and all other normal costs of the children. Should there be extraordinary expenses related to the children that are unusual or extra, they will first meet and agree as to whether or not to spend the money on behalf of the children and then they will decide upon a method of sharing such extraordinary expenses.

The facts of this case establish a waiver of the mandatory wage withholding and the monthly child support payments shall be paid directly from Doug to Sylvia. Should child support payments be in arrears by more than 30 days, Sylvia may make application for income withholding under Minnesota Statutes 518.661 subd. 7.

5. Spousal Maintenance. Doug and Sylvia have consulted with their accountant for the purpose of reviewing several levels of spousal support. Based upon this information, it is not necessary for Doug to pay Sylvia Spousal Support at this time. However, spousal support is reserved for a period of six (6) years from the date of entry of Judgment and Decree. Sylvia will have the right to request spousal support if she has not maintained her full time employment earning at least $22,000 per year gross. This reservation is granted based upon the following facts:

a.) Sylvia has not worked full time outside the home during the marriage.

b.) Sylvia must complete a twelve (12) month probation status, during which time she may be terminated at any time without cause.

c.) At the end of six years, she is automatically granted tenure as a teacher.

The spousal support reservation will terminate upon Sylvia's death or remarriage or upon the expiration of six years from the date of entry of Decree of Dissolution.

6. Post Secondary Education Expenses. The parties shall share in the payment of the children's post secondary education expenses while the children are full-time students, in good standing and unmarried for up to four years of their post high school education at an institution similar to the University of Minnesota. Two years from the date of decree, they will meet and establish a method of jointly contributing to a college education fund.

7. Life Insurance to Insure Child Support Obligation. Each party shall maintain sufficient life insurance naming the other as beneficiary of the same to secure anticipated child support payments under this agreement. In addition, each shall continue to carry such insurance until each minor child completes a four year course of college education or reaches the age of twenty-two (22) , whichever first occurs. In order to meet these obligation, each shall maintain a minimum of life insurance with a face value in the amount of $_____ per child until child support is no longer required under this agreement and shall provide verification to the other of the same upon request. In the event of the death of either parent, the surviving parent will be designated as the recipient of the life insurance funds to be used for child support and college education expenses.

8. Health Insurance for the Parties. Sylvia is currently covered as a dependent on Doug's health insurance policy available to him through his employment. Doug shall cooperate with Sylvia to ensure that she is able to take advantage of C.O.B.R.A. extension or continuation of health insurance coverage under Minnesota State Statutes. Any monthly premium for such continued coverage for Sylvia will be her responsibility.

9. Dependent Health Coverage. Doug shall provide health coverage for the benefit of the minor children of the parties as is available to him through his employment until such time as each minor child is emancipated, reaches the age of majority, or graduates from high school, unless otherwise mutually agreed. The parties shall be equally responsible for all unreimbursed medical and/or dental expenses relating to the minor children. Both parties shall discuss non-emergency or elective medical or dental needs of the minor children before assuming the other parent will share in those costs.

10. Dependency Exemptions. Based upon the recommendations of their accountant, Doug will have the right to claim the children as exemptions on his tax returns in 19XX. However, beginning in 19XX and thereafter, they agree that Doug will claim the two older children (Heather and Josh) and Sylvia will claim the youngest (Susan).

They will consult with their accountant or attorney about the remaining tax effects of this agreement, particularly the liability that each of them have now and in the future for taxes as a result of the manner in which they are dividing the marital property. Both will cooperate in correcting any errors or requests for information about previous year's tax filings.

When two children may no longer be claimed as an exemption by either party, Doug shall claim the remaining exemption during the even years, and Sylvia shall claim the exemption during the odd years. The parties each agree to execute IRS Form 8332, Release of Claim to Exemption for Child of Divorced or Separated Parents, in accordance with present and future Internal Revenue Code provisions and/or corollary state income tax forms, as required to fully implement the foregoing agreement. If either party fails or refuses to execute IRS Form 8332 and there is no valid reason for their failure to execute the form, then the party not in compliance shall be obligated to reimburse the other party for any additional taxes, penalties, accountant fees or attorneys' fees incurred, if any, by the party entitled to the exemption under this section.

11. Resolution of Conflict. Any claim or controversy arising under this agreement involving support or property division which cannot be resolved by the parties through direct communication without mediation, shall be promptly submitted to mediation.

A. Definition of Mediation. Mediation is a voluntary process entered into by the parties. In this process, the parties continue direct communication but with the assistance of a neutral person who is the mediator, which mediator has no authority to require any concession or agreements. A good faith effort shall be made to resolve any claim or controversy arising between the parties.

B. Selection of Mediator. The mediator shall be named by mutual agreement of the parties.

C. Duties and Responsibilities of Mediator. The mediator shall have the duty and responsibility to assist the parties in resolving all issues submitted for mediation.

D. Duty to Cooperate and Complete. Both parties agree to cooperate and operate in good faith to resolve the matters in dispute with or without the assistance of the mediator.

E. Payment of Costs. The parties shall equally share the fees and disbursements of mediation.

F. Confidentiality and Privilege. Within the limits of the law, the mediator will accord confidentiality and privilege to all communications with the parties.

G. The mediator shall not participate as a witness, collateral contact or attorney in a custody or visitation study or inquiry involving either party. Further, neither party may ever call the mediator as a witness to testify at any proceeding involving their children or the subject matter of the mediation.

H. <u>Compromise or Offers to Compromise During Mediation or Arbitration.</u> State statutes shall be applicable throughout the entire process of mediation.

I. <u>Applicability of Dispute Settlement Procedures.</u> The above procedure shall apply to any claims or controversies regarding the spousal support and the property division.

J. <u>Exhaustion of Remedies.</u> The above procedure shall be followed before either party may apply to the Court for relief.

12. <u>Binding Arbitration:</u> Should they have any major parenting disputes in the future that cannot be resolved after making a good faith effort in mediation, they agree to submit the parenting dispute to binding arbitration. The arbitrators will be chosen from a panel maintained by Erickson Mediation Institute. The arbitrators will consist of two mental health professionals and a family law professional who will have the right to interview the minor children as well as the parents.

The arbitration hearing will be subject to the terms and conditions of the Minnesota Arbitration Act and the Rules of Arbitration for Parenting Disputes published by Erickson Mediation Institute and in effect at the time the arbitration is commenced. Husband and wife understand that by agreeing to binding arbitration, they may not have the issue heard in a District Court and the ruling of the arbitrators is final and not subject to review except under certain narrow conditions.

13. <u>Homestead.</u> Co-Petitioner Sylvia is awarded all right, title and interest to the homestead of the parties located at 420 Orchard Lane, Minneapolis, MN 55419, Hennepin County, Minnesota, which is legally described as follows:

Lot 7, Block 5, Suburban Park, Hennepin County, Minnesota.

Co-Petitioner Doug Smith's attorney shall prepare and deliver a quit claim deed to be executed by Doug Smith. Co-Petitioner Sylvia shall be responsible for encumbrances of record as well as monthly payments of principle, interest, taxes and insurance and shall hold Doug harmless and indemnify her for any liability thereon.

14. <u>Cabin.</u> Co-Petitioner Doug is awarded all right, title and interest to the cabin of the parties located at 817 Hwy 17, Lake Mary, MN 55812, which is legally described as follows:

Lot 8, Block 42, Lake Mary, Minnesota.

Co-Petitioner Sylvia Smith's attorney shall prepare and deliver a quit claim deed to be executed by Sylvia Smith. Co-Petitioner Doug shall be responsible for encumbrances of record as well as monthly payments of principle, interest, taxes and insurance and shall hold Sylvia harmless and indemnify her for any liability thereon.

15. <u>Household Goods and other Miscellaneous Property of the marriage:</u> Each party is awarded the household goods and furnishings in the possession of each at the time of entry of Judgment and Decree of dissolution.

16. <u>Summary of Property Division.</u> Each party is awarded, free and clear of claims on the part of the other, the remaining items of property assets as follows:

Distribution	Value	To Doug	To Sylvia
BANK ACCOUNTS			
1.01) First Federal, Sav #2912-23604	8,312.		8,312.
1.02) Norwest, Chg #77-258-2087	400.		400.
1.03) First MN, Chg #311-21207	150.	150.	
ACCOUNTS RECEIVABLE			
2.01) John Nyberg	500.	–	–
STOCKS & BONDS			
3.01) 3M Stock, 120 shares @ $83.25 ea.	9,990. *		X
REAL ESTATE			
4.01) Homestead market Value	130,000.		130,000.
First Mortgage	(60,309.)	(60,309.)	
Second Mortgage	(25,000.)	(25,000.)	
4.02) Cabin - Market Value	78,000.	78,000.	
First Mortgage	(25,000.)	(25,000.)	
LIFE INSURANCE			
5.01) Connecticut Mut, #22589431	0.	0.	
5.02) Lutheran Brotherhood, #413210	895. *		X
5.03) Mutual of Omaha, #37921-001	0.		0.

Distribution	Value	To Doug	To Sylvia
BUSINESS INTERESTS			
6.01) Sylvia's Piano Studio	0.		0.
6.02) Educational Consultants, Ltd.	10,000.	10,000.	
6.03) Lake Land Operetta	Future Royalties.	To be divided among children	
AUTOMOBILES			
7.01) Dodge Caravan	18,000.		18,000.
Loan: Teachers Credit Union	(14,000.)		(14,000.)
7.2) Chrysler	15,000.	15,000.	
Loan: Chrysler Credit	(8,000.)	(8,000.)	
7.3) 16' Fishing Boat, 45hp	1,870.	1,870.	
RETIREMENT ACCOUNTS			
8.01) TRA #4189067	1,400./mo. at 65	–	–
8.02) First Fed IRA #89207619	7,050.		7,050.
8.03) IDS Tax Sheltered Annuity	19,431.	19,431.	
MISCELLANEOUS			
HOUSEHOLD ITEMS			
9.01) Piano *	15,000. *		X
9.02) IBM Computer	500.	500.	
9.03) Mac Computer	500.		500.
TAX ASSETS AND LIABILITIES		–	–
DEBTS			
10.01) Mastercard	(432.)		(432.)
10.02) Retail Credit	(90.)	Paid	
10.03) Discover	(75.)	Paid	
10.04) Visa	(1,400.)		(1,400.)
TOTALS:	155,072.	66,951.	88,212.
		+10,585.	-10,585.
		77,536.	77,536.

The above distribution of assets represents an acceptable and fair division of property as viewed by Doug and Sylvia. Both agree that the above division is fair and equitable. They further agree that the division be equal, and that Sylvia will pay to Doug the sum of $10,585, no latter than 30 days after the divorce decree is signed and entered by the Court and upon exchange of quit claim deeds

17. <u>Debt.</u> Except as set forth herein, the parties each shall be solely liable for any and all debts incurred by them in their own name from and after the date they separated. The debts incurred either separately or jointly during the marriage shall be allocated between the parties as listed above in the property distribution summary. Each shall hold the other party harmless from responsibility for the above stated unsecured debts, and indemnify the other. The parties are not acknowledging the legality or enforceability of the above debts and each are responsible only for the debts assumed by each as outlined above.

18. <u>Attorney's Fees.</u> Each shall be one half responsible for payment of both attorney's fees and costs associated with this dissolution of marriage proceeding. The sharing will be accomplished by adjusting the above property distribution.

19. <u>Service by Mail.</u> The Judgment and Decree of Dissolution to herein be served by the United States mail by counsel for Co-Petitioner Doug Smith mailing a copy thereof to counsel for Co-Petitioner Sylvia Smith and furnishing to the Court Administrator an Affidavit of such service for attachment to the original Judgment and Decree, as proof thereof for all purposes.

20. <u>Transfer.</u> Both parties shall execute any and all documents and transfers necessary to effectuate the terms of the Judgment and Decree entered herein. In the event that either party fails to execute the necessary documents, a certified copy of the Judgment and Decree shall serve to transfer ownership.

21. <u>Warranty.</u> Each party shall warranty to the other that there has been an accurate, complete and current disclosure of all income, assets, debts and liabilities. The property which either party has an interest in or a right to, whether legal or equitable, owned in full or in part by either party, separately or by the parties jointly has been fully disclosed. In the event that additional assets of value are determined to exist, those assets may be the subject of future Court proceedings pursuant to Rule 60 of

the Minnesota Rules of Civil Procedure and the party having failed to disclose assets of value shall be responsible for all reasonable attorney's fees and costs ordered by the Court.

22. <u>Withdrawal of Counsel.</u> Ordering, adjudging and decreeing that ninety-one (91) days after entry of Judgment and Decree of Dissolution herein, that Joseph Bloh, Esq. be discharged as counsel of record for Co-Petitioner Doug Smith. S. O. Tuff, Esq. be discharged as counsel of record for Co-Petitioner Sylvia Smith herein.

23. For such other and further relief as the Court may deem just, fair and equitable.

24. Appendix A is attached hereto and incorporated by reference.

SUBJECT TO THE FOREGOING and subject to the full compliance therewith, each of the parties does otherwise in all respects, manners and things release and fully discharge the other from any liability, claims or obligations of any kind or character, whether arising out of the marriage relationship or otherwise and the foregoing shall be deemed to constitute a full, final and complete property settlement between said parties in lieu of any other provisions for spousal maintenance and other claims or any other claims of any kind or character which otherwise might subsist and extend between said parties hereto. (*Signature lines and verifications follow*).

> File # XX1234-HDVO6
> Start date: June 26, 19XX / MSM
> First draft: June 26, 19XX / cgd
> Erickson Mediation Institute
> Northland Plaza, Suite 850
> 3800 West 80th Street
> Minneapolis, MN 55431
> 612-835-3688
> FAX 612-835-3689

---

*The attachment is not included in this figure.

10 Subject Area 5: Finalizing the Memorandum of Agreement

Between sessions, the clients will have reviewed the preliminary or draft copy of the Memorandum of Agreement. During this session, you and the clients carefully read the draft together, paying special attention to wording, making any necessary changes, and ensuring that decisions are recorded to the clients' satisfaction.

At the conclusion of the session, let the clients know that you will be sending them copies of the revised Memorandum of Agreement. They may then take their copies to their attorneys and have the attorneys review the copies and either approve the document as is or discuss the changes they desire. If there are proposed changes, ask the clients to have their attorneys attempt to resolve any differences; suggest that if the attorneys are unable to resolve the situation efficiently on their own, you will be glad to meet with the clients one more time to iron out the details-with the attorneys present if they wish.

Before the clients leave, express your appreciation for their hard work and their cooperation. Remember to be sensitive because the divorce may still be new to them, and they may be experiencing some pain. Let them know that you will be available to them in the future if any further mediation needs arise.

11 Mediator Strategies

This chapter offers many strategies to use during the mediation process. The first section offers *basic mediator strategies* that you will use with all couples throughout the mediation process. The second section presents *strategies for mediating special situations* that may arise only sporadically. The third and final section offers *strategies for avoiding an impasse*. In addition to recommended actions, some of the strategies include comments you may choose to make, as a way of helping you see how to implement a particular strategy.

Some separate strategies also include ways to mediate with relationships in which abuse exists. Note that these strategies assume that the husband is the abuser and the wife is the abused person. As mentioned elsewhere in this book, most studies show that this situation is far more common than the reverse.

Basic Mediator Strategies

Basic mediator strategies include the following:

- Creating an atmosphere of cooperation
- Influencing communication
- Influencing attitudes
- Influencing the process of bargaining and negotiating
- Managing the discussion of issues

Creating an Atmosphere of Cooperation
To generate an atmosphere of cooperation for mediation, you need to build the right physical setting, emotional setting, and procedural setting.

The Physical Setting
Ways to build the right physical setting are as follows:

- Arrange the table and chairs in the room to promote a comfortable, businesslike atmosphere. We recommend a round table.
- Sit equidistant from the clients. (Being closer to one than the other can appear to be a sign of favoritism.)

- Focus on mutual problem solving. For each session, have a flip chart to list and illustrate information and agreements.

When there is spousal abuse:

- Have one of the clients arrive early, seat her in a different room until the session begins.
- During mediation, have the clients sit apart from each other and give each as much space as possible.
- Offer frequent breaks to lower the tension and make sure that the clients are not together during breaks. Do not leave them alone together in the room at any time.

The Emotional Setting

Ways to build the right emotional setting are as follows:

- Ensure and encourage mutuality and cooperation.
- Contrast the emotional setting of mediation to the setting of an adversarial divorce. For example, you might say, "The adversarial system encourages you to believe that you can only achieve a fair result for yourself at the expense of the other person. In mediation, I want you to understand that in order to achieve a good, fair result for yourself, you must also help the other achieve a fair result."
- In orienting clients to the mediation process, emphasize the benefits of cooperative behavior. Challenge them to obtain a better result in mediation than they could ever achieve through competitive behavior.

When there is spousal abuse:

- Schedule the initial consultation so that the wife arrives fifteen to thirty minutes before the husband. Screen the clients separately; then, if the wife is comfortable, meet with both clients and discuss the mediation process and any special conditions necessary to mediate their case (see "Mediating with Clients in an Abusive Relationship" in this chapter). Have the wife leave fifteen minutes before the husband. It is advisable to escort her to her automobile to make sure that she leaves before her husband does.
- Inform the clients that mediation is a choice and that you will decide whether to mediate based on the separate meetings with each. Assure them that neither of them will bear the responsibility if you do not accept their case for mediation.
- Inform the clients that although mediation is an excellent process for most couples, an abused wife's choice not to mediate must not be construed as a decision against the best interest of her children. That is, the wife's choice is not to be used against her in court as evidence of uncooperative behavior.

The Procedural Setting

Ways to establish rules to ensure the integrity of the mediation process:

- Provide rules or guidelines for the mediation process. Client-centered mediators operate within a set of formal written rules, and also use informal, unwritten rules of conduct. Be sure to provide the clients with the written rules and explain the informal rules you may impose to keep the session productive and safe.

- Explain rules about payment of fees, communication within the session, confidentiality, full disclosure, the selection and prioritizing of issues, and any other procedures that relate to your management of the process.
- Assure the clients that all mediation discussions are confidential and that they can work on a settlement without fearing that what they say might be used against them later if they ended up in litigation. However, point out any limits on confidentiality that your rules create (such as reporting physical or sexual abuse of minor children).
- Create any ground rules that you feel are appropriate for encouraging cooperative behavior.

The following are examples of some ground rules:

- A client is encouraged to speak only for himself or herself, not for the other client.
- A client is discouraged from saying what he or she thinks the other person is thinking or feeling. (Unless, of course, a client has clairvoyant powers.)
- The mediator will intervene in discussions to prevent any victimization, to keep the process emotionally and physically safe.

The rules should be imposed with restraint and clients need to always be asked if they understand and agree with the rules. The reason for these rules is to create a safe environment and advance the process of mutuality and cooperative decision making. Therefore, always be prepared to explain the underlying reason for any rules offered.

When there is spousal abuse:

- Manage the process even more carefully than usual and use the rules as a strategy to maintain safety and integrity.
- To ensure safety, consider creating special rules as a condition of mediation, such as different arrival and departure times for the clients; no communication or only limited communication between sessions; and discussion about one or both spouses entering counseling or chemical dependency treatment (or both).

Influencing Communication
Strategies that enable you to influence productive communication are the following:

- Encouraging open and honest communication
- Encouraging persuasion rather than coercion
- Encouraging blameless communication rather than investigation of the past to determine blame or fault
- Encouraging neutral language rather than inflammatory words, phrases and concepts.

Encouraging Open Communication
Ways to encourage open, honest communication:

- Set the tone by asking for open, honest communication and then expect it will happen (even if it doesn't at first).
- Assure the clients that their discussions during mediation are confidential.

- Keep the focus on problem solving; discourage blaming and delving into what happened in the past. (Avoid dissecting custody studies.)
- Verify information with documents.
- Recognize when the clients exhibit good communication, by commenting about it.

To counter secretive and deceptive communication, try the following:

- Change the game: "This is not the courthouse. Because no one is attacking you, it isn't necessary to act defensively in the mediation room to be understood. I ask that each of you try to bargain and negotiate from a point of view that allows you to get what you want for yourself while helping the other to achieve a good, just result. Would you agree to that?"
- Caucus separately with each: "I need to talk privately with each of you so that I can understand why you feel you can't talk openly about this."
- Discourage mind-reading statements: "Tom, would you agree not to speak for Denise? After all, isn't she really the only person who knows what she is thinking? Denise, would you also agree not to speak for Tom?"

Encouraging Persuasion Rather Than Coercion
Ways to encourage persuasive rather than coercive communication include the following:

- Try to learn the client's motiviation to make a threat.
- When a person's concerns, fears and needs are resolved and met, there is no reason to make a threat.
- Ask what each client needs and wants, then assure them that in mediation they may work hard to find a way to meet their needs.
- Because threats often arise when one client feels overpowered, discounted, or insecure, initiate and manage a discussion of their feelings and ask if each understands and recognizes the other's motivation for making the threat.

To counter threatening communication:

- Discourage "if . . . then" sequences: "Cathy, you sound desperate. You certainly can hire an aggressive attorney and fight Bob in court, but let's see if it is possible to get at what your true needs are. Are you agreeble to that?"
- Reframe the threat as a need: "Doug, when you threaten to fight for custody, it suggests that you want Sylvia to understand that you are more than a visitor. Speak to Sylvia about your desire to be a good, loving parent instead of a noncustodial visitor, and then you won't feel the need to threaten a custody contest in order to get your needs met."
- Eliminate the need to make threats; encourage the clients to make sure that each obtains a good result: "When both of you work hard to build a parenting plan that allows each of you to be loving, significant parents, there is then no need to make threats. When it becomes a win-lose contest, people make threats. In this room, you don't have to feel powerless or make threats."

Encouraging Blameless Communication

Ways to encourage blameless communication are as follows:

- Refer the clients to marriage-closure counseling to help them understand their own and each other's feelings about what caused the divorce.
- Stay on task all of the time by using the flip chart to list the clients' budgets, parenting schedules, property, and other information.
- Emphasize the present and future. Avoid investigations of past harm and litanies of complaints about the past.
- Remind the clients that they are getting divorced to make things better, not worse.

To counter communication that focuses on blaming and fault-finding, try the following:

- Continually remind the clients that the past cannot be changed: "Pete, I need to remind you that none of us has the power to change the past."
- Ask a different question: "Phyllis, do you want to determine who has been the more unfit parent in the past, as a custody investigator would? Instead, perhaps you'd rather decide what future parenting arrangements the two of you can agree to so that you can both be the parents you want to be."
- Establish a rule for the clients to follow when they fall into blaming and fault finding: "Mary, Steve, would both of you be willing to follow a rule that says, `Either of you may complain about anything you want. But you must follow each complaint with a positive, constructive suggestion about what can be done differently in the future so that the behavior you don't like doesn't happen again.'"

Encouraging Neutral Language

Ways to encourage neutral language are as follows:

- Use words and labels that are different from the ones used in an adversarial divorce.
- Do not determine "custody"; instead, build a "parenting plan."
- Visitors are not part of the family. Talk about "exchange schedules" rather than "visitation privileges."
- First talk about how the clients will share the cost of raising the children; then look at child support based on disparate incomes and unequal expenditures.
- Avoid dwelling on any previous custody study conerning which one of you is less `unfit' as a parent." Instead, change the focus by asking a different question: "What future parenting arrangements are the two of you willing to consider?"
- Reframe and clarify to create understanding. Instead of talking about the "primary parent" and "residential parent" or about the "managing conservator" and "possessory conservator," talk about "parenting" (which connotes behavior and activity). Until all decisions have been made about the parenting arrangements, avoid using the term "custody" (which connotes ownership).

To counter judgmental language, try the following:

- Change the game by pointing out that the clients have shared interests and, therefore, do not need to judge each other's behavior: "You know, Russell, I think that if you were in court, you would be trying to show that Angela was unwilling to work full-time just so that she could win big alimony payments. However, in this room, both of you can work together on figuring out how Angela is going to increase her income. Isn't the real problem the fact that the two of you need to create a way for her to have the money to do that?"

- Ask both clients to refrain from determining who is at fault: "Julia, I'm not really sure why Mark wants to be divorced, but isn't it possible that the reason for the divorce is much more complex than the fact that he has been unfaithful? After all, both of you have said that the marriage has been in trouble for years, and Mark has said he only began dating two months ago."

- Reframe the question and focus on the future: "Charles, instead of calling Sheila a bad parent, could you tell her what it is that you want her to do differently so that you can appreciate her as a good parent?"

Influencing Attitudes

Strategies for influencing cooperative attitudes include the following:

- Creating a positive attitude
- Building trust
- Promoting mutuality
- Creating a problem-solving attitude
- Encouraging a future focus

Creating a Positive Attitude

Ways to create a positive attitude are as follows:

- Give hope that things will work out.
- Portray conflict as an opportunity to make good decisions: "You can choose to do this yourself and create a settlement that each of you is satisfied with, or a judge and two attorneys can do it for you. If you are unsure about whether this agreement will work for you, why not simply experiment for some period of time and then reevaluate the agreement?"

To counter a negative attitude, try the following:

- Remind the clients that a custody trial might be only the beginning of their problems: "If you can't find a way to make the exchanges of the children work, you may doom yourselves and your children to legal motions and court appearances for years. You're the experts about your children, the people in the legal system are not. Do you want to try to work this out together for your children's sake?"

- Acknowledge the clients when they have cooperated well: "I know that this has been difficult for both of you, but you've done a good job of creating a temporary schedule of exchanges through the rest of the month."

- Offer the clients an opportunity to see each other in a more positive light: "Are you disregarding all of the years of your marriage as a dismal failure, or can you acknowledge to each other that you once had an intimate, caring relationship? Can you still hold on to the good memories and what you appreciated about each other?"

Building Trust

Ways to build trust are as follows:

- Conduct an orientation session and assist both clients to understand mediation, even if they have been ordered to mediation by the court. When clients understand mediation, they usually commit to it. That commitment is based on trust.
- Encourage small agreements and joint tasks that have a high likelihood of success.
- Help the clients to achieve some early successes; then point out these successes to them.
- Encourage them to take responsibility to complete any homework regarding unresolved tasks of the present session. Also, after each session show progress by writing a memo about the agreements made and send it to the clients.
- Help the clients to create a businesslike trust. Help them understand that this trust will never be as deep as it was in the early years of the marriage but that it will help them feel comfortable about their new businesslike relationship. Explain that this new trust is operating when one of them says to the other, "I'll be over to pick up the kids at four," the other knows that this will happen.

To counter mistrust and suspicion, try the following:

- Help the clients to trade assurances: "Sarah and Martin, will each of you agree to tell the other your worst fears about this agreement and then try to find a way to assure the other that those fears will not be realized?"
- Ask the clients to create new rules about their conduct in the future and then help them follow those rules: "Larry, if you and Karen have an agreement about when the children will be exchanged, then Karen won't have to say the kids are busy and you can't see them. The agreement—not Karen—controls the parenting. Do you want to talk about creating a schedule that the two of you can agree on?"
- Separate the marriage issues from the parenting issues: "Lisa, do you think it's possible for you to trust David to care for the children properly, despite your belief that he's broken the marriage vows?"

Promoting Mutuality

Ways to promote mutuality include the following:

- Emphasize the connectedness between the two clients.
- Let the clients know that a win-win result is possible.
- Remind the clients that they are "in the soup together".
- Avoid a rights-based approach; instead, focus on shared interests.
- Ask mutual questions; use phrases like "the two of you," "you both," and "you two."
- When one client always makes the proposals and the other always simply responds or reacts, say that you would like to hear proposals from both.

To counter an individualistic attitude, try the following:

- Point out that each client must be satisfied with the outcome before a settlement can be agreed to: "If the two of you choose to mediate, you are choosing to meet your own needs while helping the other to obtain a just, fair result."

- Use concerns for the children's best interests to help the clients adopt some measure of cooperation: "Research shows that children are harmed by the intensity and duration of their parents' conflict."
- Ask future-oriented questions:
  "How will the two of you share the costs of raising your children?
  How will you parent your children in the future?
  What is your plan for reducing Adrienne's dependence on the marriage relationship?
  How can each of you be satisfied that you have an adequate home for the children when they are with you?"

Creating a Problem-Solving Attitude
Ways to create a problem-solving attitude include the following:

- Ask the clients to use "I" statements and to speak only for themselves, not for each other.
- Encourage ideas rather than complaints.
- Ask the clients to state what they need.
- Ask them to suggest what will work rather than what will not work.
- Offer the idea that they can do better for themselves at the mediation table than they could in a courtroom.

To counter avoidance or aggression, try the following:

- Help the clients define their needs and interests: "Alex, when you say that you don't really care what happens, it makes it very difficult to get your needs met in this room. Would you talk about why you don't care? Then perhaps it will be easier for you to identify what you need."
- Help the clients attack the problem instead of each other: "It's much easier to work with people who are fighting to be with their children than with parents who don't want to spend time with their kids. However, what I want you to understand is that you could be fighting the real enemy rather than each other. The real enemy is the problem of trying to raise your children in two separate homes instead of in the same house. The real enemy is the problem that's created when children try to manipulate their parents because they are feeling so much pain and frustration; and now that the two of you are divorcing, they have an even greater opportunity to manipulate you."

Encouraging a Future Focus
Ways to encourage clients to focus on the future are as follows:

- Ask each client to write their script for the future.
- Remind the clients that they are getting divorced to make things better, not worse.
- Focus on the task at hand and keep the clients so centered on creating their separate futures that they begin to concentrate on the tasks to do so.
- Remind the clients that they can do nothing about the fact that the past did not turn out the way they planned but that with your help them plan their future so it turns out better than the past.

To counter a focus on the past, try the following:

- Discourage blame and fault: "I'm not sure that this is getting you anywhere. I bet if I sat here and listened for another three hours—no, make that three days—I would still not be able to help the two of you figure out who was more at fault in the past. Fortunately, that's not my job. What about the future? What do you want?"
- Disallow opening statements: "Don, I appreciate the fact that you've taken the time to write down your positions. However, I didn't know that you were going to make opening statements at this point. And, quite frankly, most opening statements tend to be based on a journey through a person's perception of the past. Even if your positions turn out to be close to what the two of you finally agree to, in this room it is more beneficial to both of you to build your settlement together. Perhaps it would be more helpful for the two of you to journey into the future to address the issues that you raise together."
- Continually try to reframe the issue in a future direction: "Charlotte, instead of having a court-ordered custody investigator determine who was the more unfit parent in the past, wouldn't it be more useful to hire a therapist as a neutral expert to advise you about a parenting plan that will work best for both of you? Is that something you'd like to learn more about?"

Influencing the Process of Bargaining and Negotiating

Strategies for influencing the process of bargaining and negotiating are as follows:

- Encouraging bargaining from interests, not positions
- Encouraging clients to attack the problem, not each other
- Fostering the development of standards of fairness
- Building creative options

Encouraging Bargaining from Interests, Not Positions

A client who begins discussing an issue by stating his or her position on that issue is, in effect, declaring a premature (and unilateral) solution. Essentially the client limits himself or herself to only one option for resolving the issue. As a mediator you need to encourage clients to bargain on the basis of their interests rather than positions. You can do so in the following ways:

- Encourage clients to explore their needs, interests, concerns, standards of fairness, and creative options instead of their positional demands.
- Help the clients to avoid the feeling of having given up something—the feeling that arises when two people have compromised and each has settled midway between two opposite positions. You can do this by opening up more possibilities for settlement. For example, you might ask each client to state what else might be done to meet his or her needs. Or, if you are dealing with the custody issue, you might ask each client what protections he or she would need in order to give up the "joint custody" label and award physical custody of the children to the other.
- Suggest that bargaining from positions forces the clients to concentrate on winning rather than on a full exploration of information, ideas, and possibilities.

- Suggest that the best negotiators are not those people who state the most extreme claims, yell the loudest, and cave in at the last minute to avoid impasse. In fact, the best negotiators are those who try to ensure that everyone's underlying needs and interests are met.
- Ask the clients if they are willing to listen to each other's point of view, think in terms of possibilities, and adopt a standard that says, "Whatever we decide, it has to satisfy both of us to the greatest extent possible."

To counter positional bargaining, try the following:

- Convert a positional statement into an interest-based statement: "Walt, you want joint physical custody and fifty-fifty sharing of the children. Nancy wants physical custody. However, she says that she needs you to be much more than a visiting parent who comes every other weekend and Wednesday evening. Not only is she saying that she needs your involvement; she's also saying that the children need you to be actively involved in their lives. Do you see that both of you believe you are just as important to the children as Nancy is? So will you talk with Nancy about a schedule that will work for everyone? And will both of you stop counting the days you spend with the children?" With this approach, the positional demand of "I want custody" is converted to "I want to be a an active, involved parent in the future." The task then is to help the clients make that happen by creating an effective schedule for parenting.
- Discourage clients from making premature statements about the solution: "Bob, the reason I'd like you to wait on presenting your ten-page settlement proposal is that you've only been in session for fifteen minutes. Rachel, do you have enough factual information in order to evaluate his proposal? Would the two of you agree to build a property settlement together, piece by piece? Is it possible that when you do this, your settlement will be stronger because you'll both be contributing your best ideas and because you'll be well informed about the facts and your options?"

When there is spousal abuse:

- You may have to take "baby steps" to get the husband to understand the concept of bargaining from needs and interests rather than positions, and you may have to repeat the rationale several times as different issues are addressed. The husband is probably a positional bargainer by nature and will have a difficult time considering his wife's needs and interests.
- When the clients state their positions, work with both of them to help them understand their underlying needs and interests.
- Be careful not to impose your own biases. For example, you may believe that the battered woman should have custody of the children. Or perhaps because the battered woman seems helpless and her husband seems so together you believe the children would be best living with him. Focus instead on what is in the children's best interests and suggest the services of a neutral expert who understands the dynamics of the battering relationship and its impact on children to offer some advice to both parents.

Encouraging Clients to Attack the Problem, Not Each Other

Ways to encourage clients to attack the problem rather than each other include the following:

- Focus on the process.
- Focus on having the clients jointly establish rules about their present and future conduct. Discourage them from getting caught up in past failures.
- Ask each client to describe what he or she wants the other to do differently in the future so that their complaint about the other will be satisfied.
- Let the clients know that everyone has trouble solving problems like the ones involved in divorce. Acknowledge them when they try to solve problems rather than engage in blaming or fault finding.

To counter personal attacks, try the following:

- Reframe a personal attack: "Judy, you said that Richard has been `irresponsible' when he picks up and drops off the children. Do you mean that he has not picked them up and dropped them off when you expected? Richard, when Judy states the problem that way, how do you respond to her concerns? Judy, what do you need Richard to do differently?"
- Keep the mediation room a safe environment: "Mitch, would you refrain from shaking your finger and jabbing it close to Rita's face each time you get angry? When you do that, I notice that Rita withdraws and shuts down. Then it takes the two of you about a half-hour to get back on track. Can each of you describe what just happened? What would work better?"
- Move beyond global fault-finding statements by narrowing the issue: "Janet, when you say Tim is a bad parent, would you go a bit further and tell what specifically he's doing that causes you to view him as a bad parent? Then you can ask him to change a specific behavior."

Fostering the Development of Standards of Fairness

Ways to foster the development of objective standards of fairness that can be used to judge the outcomes of the mediation process are as follows:

- Be willing to explore what each client means by "fairness."
- Encourage the clients to try to meet their own and each other's needs before making specific decisions about issues.
- Let the numbers do the talking. For example, instead of explaining state law to the clients, suggest that the budget numbers and the property values will answer the question of whether it is possible for one of the clients to stay in the family home.
- Ask each client what he or she thinks is necessary in order to be treated fairly by the other. **Be willing to allow them to deviate from State law if that is what both want.**

To counter one client's reliance on state law to the detriment of the other client, try the following:

- Point out that "he who lives by the law dies by the law": "Fred, it may be true that the state child-support guidelines would have you pay less than Betty wants at this time.

But how does that fit with your desire for Betty to relinquish her claim to your recent inheritance? If you two lived in Grand Forks, North Dakota, rather than in East Grand Forks, Minnesota, you might choose to be flexible about adhering to state law, because North Dakota is one of the few states in the country that has not passed laws about non-marital property claims and rather allows judges wide discretion to decide this issue. You need to decide if you can agree on what will work best in your situation and what each of you feels is fair, or if you want to have the state laws make decisions for you."

- Be willing to deviate from state law: "Marge, I can't help you mediate an agreement that as closely as possible conforms to what a judge would do in your case. No one can really accurately predict what any judge will do with regard to financial issues in a divorce. I suggest that the two of you do what you believe is fair."
- Be willing to challenge the clients' thinking on fairness issues: "Walt, the reason that spousal maintenance questions are so tough is that neither of you had a crystal ball ten years ago. Had both of you known you'd be sitting here in my office, you surely would have made very different decisions, and Juanita might have gotten that teaching certificate. And, Juanita, most of the time I find that the independent spouse is waiting for the dependent spouse to give some clear indication of when the spousal maintenance should stop. But what you both really need to figure out is what makes sense for you based on your plans and projections."

Build Creative Options

Just because a solution has not been found does not mean that a solution does not exist; it simply means that the clients have not looked hard enough or long enough or that the timing is not right. Ways to encourage creative options include the following:

- Spend time brainstorming and building options.
- Focus on needs.
- Seek the advice and consultation of an experienced expert.
- Ask the clients if they would consider options that have some measure of benefit to both of them. If the option benefits only one client, encourage them to look for another part of the settlement agreement that might be adjusted in favor of the other person, so that some measure of balance is created.

To counter solutions that benefit only one client to the other's disadvantage, attempt the following:

- Ask the clients if they might need to consider options that work for both of them rather than for purely legal solutions that turn the problem into a win-lose outcome: "You've been told by your attorneys that based on past history, each of you stands a good chance of winning custody of the children. What if I told you that one option is really quite simple? Both of you can have custody of the children. It's just that each of you will have custody of the children at certain times according to the parenting schedule you create."
- Be willing to deviate from your state's law to help the clients create a divorce settlement that meets their own standard of fairness: "George, I know your attorney will raise some question about why you've agreed to pay higher spousal maintenance

than he advised you to pay. But please remind him that Liz is agreeing to a fifty-fifty sharing of the children, which, in turn, allows her more time to finish school and get a well-paying job sooner."

Managing the Discussion of Issues

Strategies that you can use to manage the discussion of issues are as follows:

- Defining issues
- Narrowing issues
- Managing the process issues
- Time and timing
- Promoting reality
- Defining interests and needs
- Reaching agreements based on facts
- Finding mutual solutions

Defining Issues

It is easier for clients to resolve conflict when they have a clear understanding of the issue or problem that is causing the conflict. Mediators understand that the person who defines the problem has a great deal of power over the outcome. Your task is to help the couple define the typical divorce problems in easier, client-oriented rather than law-centered ways.

- Suggest to the clients that a conflict is easier to manage if the clients first agree on the definition of the issue.
- Help define the problem in a way that requires a future focus and a mutual effort to solve. A solution is easier to obtain when the typical adversarial questions are reframed. For example: Not who will have custody, but rather what parenting plan will work for both of you. Not how much child support can you pay, but rather how will the two of you share the cost of raising the chilren in the future. For example, the issue is not why the wife finds herself dependent on the husband's income but rather what plan will work to decrease or elminate the dependancy.
- Elicit discussion concerning what the dispute is about. (One of the most common mistakes made by beginning mediators is that they forge ahead with the mediation before obtaining agreement about the definition of the problem or issue.)
- Suggest that there are many ways to define the issue.

Consider the following example: Alice says, "I don't want Eric to see the children because he's a bad parent." The mediation is lost if the discussion concentrates on whether Eric is a bad parent. That issue cannot be mediated. However, the issue of what Eric is doing that makes Alice conclude he is a bad parent can be mediated. Once it is determined what exactly Alice objects to, then it is possible to see if both clients can agree to certain remedies.

In order to maintain balance, ask the client who is making the complaint what changes need to be made by the other client. If this approach is successful, you will have moved the definition of the issue from "Eric is a bad parent" to "What specific things must each of you do to make you better parents in the eyes of the other and in the eyes of the children?"

When there is spousal abuse:

- Be especially cognizant of the "control agenda" of the husband. Display extra confidence and strength in leading the discussion so that the husband does not usurp control.
- Take charge of defining the issue; make sure that each client is able to express his or her perspective and thoughts.
- Listen even more carefully than in any other type of session. Try to get the husband's message without buying into his rationale and without minimizing the risk of the wife when she talks.

Narrowing Issues

Issues that are stated in broad, global terms are much more difficult to resolve than those that are narrowly defined. Ways to narrow issues include the following:

- Break the problem into smaller components.
- Settle for a short period of time with a review later. Settle part of the issue for a short period and agreeing to return to the rest of the issue later. For example, if you are dealing with property division, you might help the clients settle only what will happen to the family home; then leave the rest of the property division until later.

When there is spousal abuse:

- You need to caucus with both clients so that you can investigate the issue more thoroughly. For example, if the wife says that the husband is a "bad parent," you need to find out exactly what that means, as children are more at risk for abuse when spousal abuse exists in the relationship.
- Be careful not to narrow the issue in such a way that it is minimized.

Managing the Order and Discussion of Issues

In mediation you must continually monitor whether the course of the negotiations is helpful to the resolution of the clients' issues. You may need to intervene to assure progress. Ways to intervene to manage the discussion effectively include the following:

- Manage the agenda of the discussion and the order in which subject areas are discussed.
- Control emotional outbursts, sharp statements, and other forms of blaming or non-productive communication.
- Monitor the clients' behaviors to ensure that each is emotionally protected.
- Listen objectively to the negotiations to determine whether the clients are staying on task.
- Direct the flow of communication such that it proceeds through all of the subject areas from smaller to larger agreements and then to fine-tune and balance the entire package.

- Balance the control of the discussion. If you are overly controlling, the clients may begin to feel that the solution arrived at is yours rather than theirs. An indicator of a successful discussion is full involvement and participation on the part of the clients and relatively less involvement on the part of the mediator. Some mediators maintain that a session is not progressing well if they are doing more talking than their clients.
- Leave the more difficult issues until last so that the clients will develop earlier successes. This approach allows clients to build upon their successes in agreeing on smaller, more workable issues, and be encouraged as they confront the more difficult issues.

When there is spousal abuse:

- You may need to encourage the wife to talk.
- You need to reframe carefully in order to manage productive discussions. When you reframe a message without the emotional intensity and tone of the abusive person, the other client is able to hear and respond to the message itself instead of the emotion behind it.

Time and Timing
Ways to manage time, and the timing of issues are as follows:

- Use time limits as a means of keeping the clients on task.
- Assist the clients in setting deadlines for completing homework, producing documents, and finishing mediation.
- Understand that some discussions will be more productive and will progress more rapidly than others.
- Consider whether the timing of addressing a particular issue might be more of a problem than the issue itself. It may simply be the wrong time for the clients to address the issue at hand; you may want to save that issue until later and proceed with another.

Promoting Reality
Ways to promote reality are as follows:

- Help the clients discuss what is possible and what is not possible.
- During the initial consultation, ask the clients whether they are, in fact, actually getting a divorce.
- Clarify euphemisms.
- Talk about difficult issues straightforwardly but with care.
- Always complete budgets so each sees what it costs to live.
- Verify values of assets and liabilities.
- Use a flip chart to display information.
- Educate the clients about what children need when trying to cope with their parents' divorce.
- Ask questions about what will work when a client takes an extreme position.
- Discuss norms and standards.
- Lead a discussion of the clients' needs and interests.
- Assist in creating realistic options.

- Question whether a client is realistic in his or her thinking.
- Offer statistics and research to clarify global statements or criticism.

Following are two examples of countering an unrealistic position:

- "Joyce, most mothers I have worked with in the past have said it's unrealistic to continue to be a full-time mother, become a full-time student, and earn a part-time income in order to contribute to strained finances. How do you plan to do all of this?"
- "Jeff, how do you plan to maintain a close, involved, significant relationship with the children when the parenting schedule calls for you to visit the children only on alternate weekends and two Wednesday evenings per month? Do you think the parenting schedule is realistic if Joyce plans to have 90 percent of the responsibility for raising the children?"

When there is spousal abuse:

- Repeatedly emphasize the reality that the clients are getting a divorce. In abuse cases the husband seldom wants the divorce and will even attempt in mediation to get his wife to come back to him.
- You need to be comfortable in promoting the reality that even though children need both parents, the husband's abuse in the past may have harmed the children psychologically. The harm that has already occurred may preclude a shared parenting arrangement after the divorce; in fact, sometimes the children's relationship with their father may need to be limited or even supervised.

Defining Interests and Needs

Many people have a great deal of difficulty formulating a statement of what they hold dear (their needs, concerns, values, fears, and beliefs). Ways to help your clients as they try to express their real interests are as follows:

- Help clients understand that a position is often a premature solution being pushed by one person.
- Help clients understand that a position may be formulated out of a client's fear of losing. Such a position may be offered as a starting point in negotiating, under the client's assumption that it will be whittled down in the bargaining process.
- Before addressing solutions, try to learn about clients' needs and interests that underlie a position.
- Ask "What do you need?" in response to a positional demand.
- Ask questions or inquire about a position to learn what will satisfy the client's needs.
- Expand the realm of possibilities by showing that a client's position or demand may limit that person's creativity in creating options.

Suppose, for example, that a client says "I absolutely have to get ten years of alimony at $800 a month." This statement limits the discussion by presenting only two factors, a period of ten years and an $800 monthly alimony payment.

Here are some questions you might ask the person requesting alimony:

- Why ten years?
- What if you get a job that pays more than your spouse makes?
- What is the $800 based on?
- Is the $800 a tax deduction for you, or is it a net amount?
- How do you know that the $800 is enough?
- How do you know it isn't too much?

You might also ask one client what he or she thinks about the other client's proposal. All of these questions expand the discussion and encourage creative thinking. The answers might reveal deeply held feelings about alimony, fear, fault, responsibility, and so on. You might then follow with this mutual question which opens the position to many more possibilities: "Would the two of you consider delaying a discussion of this proposal until you have completed your monthly budgets and seen how the proposal might affect each of your incomes and living expenses in the future?"

When there is spousal abuse:

- The wife may not know what she needs or may be afraid to state her needs in front of the husband. You may need to caucus with her to assist her in considering her own needs as separate from his.
- Do not allow the husband to speak for his wife or to discount her; this behavior may be a repetition of the abuse she experienced during the marriage.

Reaching Agreements Based on Facts

Ways to help clients to reach agreements based on all necessary factual information are as follows:

- Intervene to assist the clients in gathering, understanding, and agreeing on the facts.
- Insist on complete documentation of assets and income.
- After the clients have gathered information, make copies of that information for each.
- If they wish to negotiate property division without having firm, agreed-upon values, suggest that they can give away anything they want as long as they know the value of the item and the consequence of giving it away.
- Educate the clients about the difference between facts and perception.
- Distinguish between fault finding and any necessary discussions about past facts. For example, it is not as useful to spend time on some past disagreement between the clients as it is to have them discuss what they wish to do differently in the future so the pain of the past does not continue to repeat itself.

As you gain experience in mediating, you will find it easier to determine which facts are essential for resolution of the issues and which facts are nonessential and related to blame and fault finding.

When there is spousal abuse:

- The facts may be manipulated by the husband as a way to prolong the divorce or to ensure that he gets what he wants. For example, he may give mixed messages about the facts or "forget" to bring in or obtain necessary information.

Finding Mutual Options

Creative, mutual options are those that benefit both clients. Mutual options should not be confused with compromise, which often means that both clients must give up something. Ways to help clients find mutual options are as follows:

- Ask mutual questions that contain phrases such as "the two of you," "both of you," "you two," and "both of you parents."
- Ask both clients to respond to questions or ask each to discuss the option.
- Suggest that the clients are "in the soup together" and that it will take a joint effort for both to emerge from the divorce in a satisfactory way.
- Ask the client who raises a one-sided option to consider changing that option in such a way that it meets both clients' needs to the greatest extent possible.
- Offer a "What if the shoe were on the other foot?" test that determines whether the option would work equally well for each person.
- Become familiar with some creative forms of property and support settlements as well as innovative parenting arrangements. (See "Strategies for Avoiding Impasse" in this chapter.)

For example, if one parent attends school several evenings per week, and the other parent, who wants more time with the children, agrees to have the children on those evenings, the clients have found a mutual option that advances both people's needs.

When there is spousal abuse:

- Be patient in assisting the husband and wife in developing mutual options. They may not ever fully agree on options; therefore, they may have to create a settlement consisting of the least disagreeable options.
- Be sure that the clients participate equally in the discussions of options. Do not allow the abuser to dominate.
- Be aware that both clients may use putdowns to get what they want. Sometimes through the mediation process the wife actually becomes stronger and angrier at her husband; she may even become abusive toward him. If either uses a mediation session as a forum to "get" the other, stop this behavior immediately, ask the clients to do some positive brainstorming, focus on the process, and then help them to discuss the options.

Strategies for Mediating Special Situations

Strategies for mediating special situations include the following:

- Mediating with clients in a destructive relationship
- Discouraging clients' misuse of power
- Managing the audience effect
- Normalizing divorce-related behaviors and emotions

- Responding to clients' concerns about gender bias
- Using humor as a tension reliever

Mediating with Clients in an Abusive Relationship

The following are some special ways to mediate with clients when abuse exists in their relationship:

- Make sure that the abused client leaves fifteen minutes before the abuser.
- Be more directive than you would when abuse is not involved.
- Exert greater control in the process.
- Frequently check on the comfort levels of each client; offer breaks.
- Caucus separately as necessary to ensure safety, relieve tension, and learn important information.
- If clients are not making progress due to abuse dynamics, ask both clients to have their attorneys present at sessions as a condition for continuing the mediation.

Discouraging Clients' Misuse of Power

Client-centered mediation views both clients as capable. However, occasionally a client will misuse his or her power by

- Intentionally using skill, intimidation, knowledge, information, or verbal acumen to influence or manipulate a situation to his or her own advantage
- Attempting to control the process or the other client by taking advantage of the other's fear, misunderstanding, mistrust, or insecurity

Ways to discourage a client's misuse of power are as follows:

- Negotiate rules or agreements that meet the needs of both clients.
- Point out that conflict in the family can be resolved by using power, rights, or needs. But when each person's needs are met, the misuse of power and rights becomes unnecessary.
- Educate the clients about better communication strategies.
- Ask them what they need to agree to not make any more threats.
- Encourage them to share knowledge or information.
- Help them to identify instances of power imbalance in their dealings with each other by describing your observations and asking them if they understand.
- Help them to alter the power imbalance through a process of identifying their underlying needs and interests.
- Offer to caucus separately with each client so that you can discover each person's underlying or unmet concerns or needs.

Audience Effect

It seems that people are always willing to give divorcing clients information and advice, often based on their own situations or the latest talk show. Very often this advice is bad and is not even pertinent to the clients' situation. Ways to counter bad advice are as follows:

- When you suspect from a client's brief or vague comments that he or she has

---

received some bad advice, ask for more information.

- Make the problem of bad advice a mutual one by asking the other client if he or she has had the same experience.
- Explain that giving advice is not an unusual behavior; friends are just trying to help.
- Ascertain whether the advice has any merit without alienating the client.
- Ask the clients if they are willing to keep the received advice out of the negotiations.

For example, suppose Alicia says, "My friend Mary said I should get at least $1,000 per month alimony because Bob earns a good income and I don't."

You respond by saying, "Alicia, does Mary know your financial situation and that you and Bob are working very hard to figure out a fair support amount? Bob, have you had similar advice from anyone?"

Bob might respond with "Yes, a friend of mine at work says I shouldn't pay any alimony because Alicia has a college degree and several credits toward her teaching certificate."

You then say, "Those are good examples of what I call the `audience effect.' Your well-meaning friends and acquaintances, your audience, can impact your negotiations by offering unsolicited advice to you. Although your friends mean well, of course, this kind of advice usually isn't helpful. Do the two of you agree?"

Normalizing Divorce-Related Behavior and Emotions

It is important to keep clients from feeling that they are the only ones ever to have experienced such a difficult divorce or that they are "crazy." Ways to assure them that they are "normal" are as follows:

- Use such phrases as "most divorcing parents," "many divorcing couples," "that's not unusual," "that issue frequently comes up in divorce," "I've heard many divorcing people say that," "that's normal during divorce."
- Let the clients know that research shows it is normal, for example, for their children to "feel abandoned," "be angry," and "act out" as a reaction to their parents' divorce.

Responding to Clients' Concerns About Gender Bias

Ways to respond to a client's suggestion that you are biased because of your gender are as follows:

- Clarify the criticism and then respond as straightforwardly as possible.
- Do not become defensive.
- Acknowledge the criticism if you understand it; ask a clarifying question if you do not.
- Request feedback from the other client.
- Offer the option of changing mediators or adding an opposite-gender mediator to resolve the concern.
- Err in the other direction without favoring the opposite-gender client.
- Prove yourself by demonstrating competence in the area in which the criticizing client may perceive you as most weak.

If you are concerned that the charge may have some merit, consult with a colleague or supervisor.

Using Humor as a Tension Reliever

Using humor in mediation takes great skill and is not recommended when there is little trust between the two clients or between you and the clients. However, the use of humor in mediation can be a great tension reliever and can be greatly appreciated by clients. Ways to use humor effectively are as follows:

- Use humor intuitively and spontaneously.
- Be willing to take a chance with a humorous comment to alleviate tension.
- See the humor in things and decide whether or not to use it.
- Make an example of yourself.
- Be cautious about laughing at clients' comments; sometimes clients disguise "cheap shots" in humorous remarks.

Here is an example of using humor during mediation: "Beverly, you still iron Mac's shirts? And, Mac, you just put the child support check in a shirt pocket for Beverly when you give it to her to iron? That's one of the most unusual ways to transfer child support that I've ever heard! But I suppose, Beverly, that you'll be assured of getting the child support every other Monday as long as you continue to iron Mac's shirts. And, Mac, you will continue as long as you want Beverly to iron your shirts. What happens when one of you remarries? Do you really want this in your Memorandum of Agreement?"

Strategies for Avoiding Impasse

The course of bargaining and negotiating differs for every couple. Some couples are able to reach cooperative agreements quite easily, whereas others constantly appear on the brink of disaster or impasse. There are many strategies that you can employ to avoid impasse. Most are used when the clients are well into the mediation process.

Cases often settle more easily when everyone in the room clearly knows what is causing the disagreement. In some instances, therefore, an impasse strategy is used as a method of identifying the roadblock to settlement. In other instances, such a strategy is used to create a turning point in the discussion, allowing the clients to develop a better understanding of the nature of their dispute and what must be done to achieve settlement.

A number of strategies are discussed in the following paragraphs:

1. Restarting the mediation process
2. Delaying further discussion of the issue until later
3. Using an expert
4. Caucusing
5. Shaking up the game board
6. Introducing the concept of experimentation

7. Referring clients to a therapist
8. Discussing fairness
9. Encouraging a decision
10. Requesting that the children attend a mediation session
11. Requesting a second opinion from an attorney
12. Conducting a meeting with the clients' attorneys
13. Commenting on the give-and-take
14. Discussing the "sanity factor"
15. Refocusing on the future
16. Suggesting advisory nonbinding arbitration
17. Settling for a short length of time with a review later.
18. Suggesting alternative parenting arrangements
19. Suggesting alternative approaches to spousal maintenance
20. Asking a judge a hypothetical question
21. Pointing out the cost of continued litigation
22. Drafting contingency clauses
23. Identifying and discussing roadblocks
24. Giving the disputed item to the children
25. Asking a financial planner to help with future income
26. Using four-square analysis

1. Restarting

Often it helps to repeat all of the previous process subject areas in an abbreviated fashion. Restarting is most useful when you cannot determine exactly what is causing the clients to be at the brink of impasse. This technique is analogous to what a pilot does when the airplane will not start: the pilot goes back to the beginning and runs through the preflight checklist again. Remember that it is always the process—and not the mediator—that works to solve the conflict. Repeating the steps often allows you and the clients to identify and resolve what is causing impasse.

Reviewing the Contract to Mediate

In this step, the clients re-examine their initial commitment to the mediation process. The goal is to strengthen cooperative attitudes and to uncover any negative attitudes, such as suspicion or mistrust, that may be delaying progress. Remember that one of the most crucial elements of success in any cooperative conflict-resolution process is the attitudes held by the clients.

During the later stages of a mediation discussion, in particular, reviewing the clients' commitment can strengthen that commitment. Most mediation contracts state that each client agrees to be fair throughout the mediation process. Ask if each feels that the other has been fair. This question can help determine whether one client feels that the other is using mediation for a different purpose. Also ask if the clients feel that you have been fair; the problem may be something in your behavior that you can correct.

Obtaining Necessary Facts

Early in any mediation session, the clients collect and exchange factual information.

If impasse occurs during the negotiations that take place after the sharing of information, ask whether more facts are needed. As all agreements and decisions are based on factual information, the importance of this aspect of the process should not be overlooked. Frequently you will find that clients in conflict disagree about some factual aspect of the case, but the disagreement is not apparent to them or you. Rechecking facts gives you an opportunity to learn why they are having difficulty.

Defining Issues

The next step in the process is to determine whether or not the issues have been correctly defined. Any unresolved issue should be reviewed to see if a different definition of that issue will move the process forward. A good technique is to ask each client these questions: "What is the single most important issue or problem standing in the way of settlement? If that issue or problem could be solved, would the case move toward agreement?"

Compare whether the issues stated at this point are the same as they were when the step was completed the first time. Also, if the clients are still defining the parenting issue, for example, in win-lose terms ("who will have the children"), raise with *them* again that the issue is not *who* will own the children but *when* each parent will be with the children. Attempting to state issues in a way that lends itself to a mutual solution will usually help clients make progress.

Addressing Needs and Interests

Frequently clients are either unwilling or unable to state clearly what they need or have an interest in. Each may state personal needs in a way that keeps the other from meeting those needs. A useful strategy is to ask each client to state very clearly what is needed today to enable the clients to settle the case. By listening to the answer, you may learn a more clear idea of the roadblock to settlement.

There are universal needs basic to all divorcing clients that, when met, seem to make the case less likely to stall:

- The need to continue to be active, involved parents to the children in the future
- The need to have some measure of financial security, even though the process of terminating the marriage may leave them both in a precarious financial position
- The need to feel that the accumulated assets of the marriage have been divided in a fair manner consistent with the clients' own agreed-on standards of fairness

Refocusing on the clients' needs has the effect of encouraging them to state clearly what will settle the case. When you understand what need is not being met, you will be able to help them find a way to address their mutual needs.

Brainstorming About Options

This step is often very useful in the process of settlement negotiations. It involves not only generating new options but also reviewing how previously proposed options will work. Frequently an option presented by one side may be rejected even before the person has finished describing that option.

A technique used to prevent the premature dismissal of a useful option is to ask the clients to examine in detail how the option will work. For example, the clients may be asked not to reject any option until it has been completely described.

2. Delaying Discussion

Experienced mediators know that sometimes an issue cannot be settled because the time is not right for it to settle. As facilitator of the sequence of when issues are discussed, you can decide whether it is wise to skip a particular issue for the time being. If the issue cannot be resolved when it is being discussed the first time, that does not mean that the issue will never be settled; it just means that the issue will have to be deferred. Timing is more important to the mediation process than most people realize.

3. Using an Expert

This impasse strategy attempts to ensure that decisions are based on the best possible facts. Experts are used throughout the adversarial divorce process such as: to appraise property, to determine tax consequences, and create options. Skilled mediators also make use of experts to assist in situations in which reaching a resolution is particularly difficult, such as when working out parenting arrangements. The use of a child psychologist or skilled family therapist can be just what is necessary to help the clients reach agreement on parenting.

4. Caucusing

As mentioned previously, caucusing or meeting with each client separately must be used sparingly, as it can cause mistrust and concern about what is being discussed in the separate rooms. However, it can be an effective approach to use when you have already gained the trust of the clients and when you need to find out why the settlement process is near impasse. It can reveal information that the clients do not want to share with each other, thereby reducing tension. In the caucus session, you can ask each person about their opinion of why mediation is not working and what must be done to make the process work for each of them.

If it appears that the discussion is at a stalemate and you are considering caucusing, first ask permission from the clients to do so. Also make an agreement with them about whether the information disclosed to you will be shared with the other client.

5. Shaking Up the Game Board

This impasse strategy is best described as throwing the game pieces in the air and starting over again. Sometimes it is necessary to ask the clients if it is possible to attack the issue or problem from a completely different perspective. Doing so means that you will have to keep track of all approaches previously tried and then suggest another route.

Essentially, this strategy tries to get the clients to look at an issue in a different way. You might ask them whether they have considered doing something that has not yet been discussed, such as selling the home or experimenting with a different parenting exchange schedule. One recent case in which this technique was successful involved two clients who could not agree on who would move out of the family home in order to accomplish a physical separation. After listening to them argue for over an hour about all of the reasons each had for staying in the home, the mediator asked, "Why don't both of you move out?" This question then led to a discussion about the concept of "birdnesting," in which the children live full-time in the house and the parents move in and out. Many couples rent a small efficiency apartment nearby and use it as the place where each parent lives when not at the house with the children.

On this occasion, both of our clients liked the idea. It meant that neither of them was given an advantage, and both were able to experience what it was like living somewhere other than the family home. By shaking up the pieces with these types of questions, the mediator is able to create what Deutsch describes as a key element in the creating thinking process: "Approaching" the problem from a different perspective and its reformulation in a way that permits new orientations to a solution to emerge. (Deutsch, 1973, p.360)

6. Introducing the Concept of Experimentation
Experimentation is based on the theory that settlement will occur more easily if there is an opportunity to change the decision later should one of the clients not be satisfied. This strategy is used more in the early stages of the mediation process, and it encourages the clients not put pressure on themselves to make permanent agreements but rather practice them before they are made final and binding.

This strategy works well in the area of parenting schedules. For example, clients may not be able to decide whether the children should live primarily in one home or alternate living in both parents' homes for approximately equal amounts of time. In a case like this you might offer an option that the clients try each of these proposed arrangements for one month and return to mediation in two months after experimenting with them. After this length of time, the children's reactions to both schedules can also be appraised. For support disputes, this allows an amount to be exchanged with a review later after the financial turmoil of the immediate divorce has settled down.

7. Referring Clients to a Therapist
The process of divorce occurs on two levels, the concrete things of the marriage and the intense emotional feelings and behaviors of the divorce. You can help your clients negotiate about the concrete aspects of the marriage (children, money, property), and usually these negotiations can be emotionally therapeutic. However, some clients have great difficulty in mediation because they have not yet resolved the emotional pain of the divorce. The most common example of this is when one spouse refuses to accept the separation or divorce. A skilled family therapist can take the couple through a process of marriage-closure counseling, which helps to reduce the likelihood of impasse in mediation. (Remember that when a couple engages in mediation, one way for the less-accepting spouse to resist divorce is to sabotage the mediation process by making outrageous demands or by engaging in blaming and fault finding.)

8. Discussing Fairness

This strategy helps to determine whether the clients are using the same definition of fairness. If they are not, this might be the source of their difficulty in reaching agreement on the issue in question.

For example, suppose the wife's idea of fairness is that she should receive spousal support for the rest of her life because she was faithful and the husband was not. Also suppose the husband's idea of fairness is that he should pay rehabilitative spousal support only until his wife completes retraining. If this is the case, the clients will have some difficulty resolving the issue of duration of spousal support.

To mediate this, you need to help the clients determine a mutual concept of fairness. Urge the wife to let go of blaming and fault finding. Foster the husband's understanding that women tend to earn much less than men and that he may need to share his income for a longer period than he wants in order for the wife to become more self sufficient. Impasse may be avoided if they both agree to a new standard of fairness such as this: "Each spouse has the right to basic economic security after the divorce, provided each is devoting similar efforts to achieve the level of support needed by both. Or each of us will have similar, but reduced life styles in the future."

Although the ensuing discussion may be time-consuming as the clients attempt to define what is meant by "basic economic security," at least you will have given clients the opportunity to expand their original ideas so that they can proceed with mediation.

9. Encouraging a Decision Because a Decision is Needed

This technique allows you to help clients realize that it is not necessary to agree on everything. For example, if one spouse is Catholic and the other is Methodist, both still need to decide on the direction of the children's future religious instruction. This is the type of issue that can cause clients a great deal of trouble unless they realize that the same problem would have surfaced even if they had stayed married.

For the sake of the children, what is most important is that they simply make the decision. Stress that neither choice is "wrong." The only wrong choice is the continued conflict of no decision at all that results in harm to the children.

10. Requesting the Presence of the Children

In high conflict custody disputes, you may suggest that the children attend a mediation session. Although it is not the children's responsibility to decide whom they will live with, their ideas and concerns can serve a useful purpose and can prevent the case from reaching impasse.

When the children come to the session, arrange with the parents about whether or not to meet with them privately about their concerns. Generally children will express the fact that they care deeply about both parents. When the parents are assured of this, they may be able to proceed more comfortably. By giving the children an opportunity for input, the children feel respected and recognized, and that their parents care about them. When the mediator is able to share some of the children's thoughts, the parents are given an opportunity to adopt a different perspective.

11. Requesting a Second Opinion from an Attorney

A frequent cause of difficulty in a session is the advice given to one of the clients by his or her attorney. If the attorney has made an unrealistic prediction about the potential outcome of litigation, this will cause that client to make unreasonable demands in mediation.

With tongue in cheek, it is sometimes possible to ask the client who has made the demands to obtain a written guarantee that the outcome in court will be as predicted. As such a guarantee cannot, of course, be given, this request presents an opportunity to suggest that a second opinion be requested from another attorney concerning the likelihood of such an outcome. Note: This strategy poses some risks and should be used sparingly. It works best in cases where one of the clients is using a non-family-law specialist such as a corporate attorney who knows nothing about divorce. Encourage this client to seek the advice of a family law specialist.

12. Conducting a Five-Way Meeting with Both Attorneys Present in the Mediation Room.

The presence of both clients' attorneys at a mediation session can help to facilitate a settlement, even if one or both of the attorneys are zealous litigators. Use their presence to show the ineffectiveness of the litigation process. As neither attorney can predict with certainty what the outcome in court will be, the clients have an opportunity to assess each attorney's competence.

Ask the attorneys to tell the clients what it would cost to litigate all of the issues. Upon learning the costs of litigation, most clients ask their attorneys to assist them in settling the case in mediation.

If both attorneys are supportive of the mediation process, such a session can actually save time in the final processing of the case. For example, you will find that it is much easier to impose reality when an attorney leans over toward one of the spouses and says, "I think you have some likelihood of not achieving your goals in court on this issue, and perhaps the settlement should be seriously considered." Although you may have wanted to say the same thing, the comment is much more effective when it comes from an attorney.

13. Commenting on the Give-and-Take Score

Sometimes you can prevent impasse by reminding the couple that they have made considerable progress and have been very successful in the give-and-take process of mediation. Often clients become so consumed by the conflict that they forget to observe the progress each has made. However, you will have been recording their decisions on the flip chart, so you can actually point out the progress they have made toward settlement. This strategy can also be effective in encouraging one client to reconsider a strongly held position.

14. Discussing the "Sanity Factor"

Sometimes it helps to explain to the clients that in divorce mediation, as in most complicated negotiations, it is not possible to achieve perfection. For example, you can help the clients see that if their marital estate exceeds $400,000 and each will receive approximately $200,000 of value, it makes little sense to fight over a $50 lamp.

This strategy can also be used in the case of impasse over the duration or amount of spousal support. Suppose, in the preceding example, the client with the higher income agrees to pay the other client spousal support of $1,500 a month for four years, but the other client wants that amount per month for seven years. The two positions are really not that far apart considering the couple's net worth of $400,000, because the value of the extra alimony is considerably less when two facts are taken into account: taxes are owed on that money, and the inflation over a period of seven years would reduce the present-day dollar value.

Therefore, suppose an accountant tells the clients that the present value of $18,000 per year for the sixth and seventh year is really $14,000 today. (That is, $14,000, deposited today at average interest rates, would earn enough to fund the after tax monthly payments in years six and seven.) The $14,000 amount disputed would represent less than 4 percent of the entire marital estate to be divided; it would be unfortunate to come to an impasse when the clients are so close to settling the case.

If, in this example, you intervened to point out the "sanity factor," the clients might decide to have a slightly unequal division of property allowing the spouse with less income to receive 54 percent of the $400,000 and the spouse with more income to receive 46 percent. Viewed in this way, the issue becomes easily resolvable.

15. Refocusing on the Future

When clients focus on future solutions—rather than on the past, blaming, and fault finding—they can begin to forgive each other and to see beyond the pain and suffering of yesterday. Sometimes an apology is needed in order for the mediation to proceed. But in most cases, the more you keep refocusing on the future, the less likely impasse will result.

For example, consider a situation in which the clients cannot resolve the issue of custody because one does not trust the other's parenting. You can refocus the discussion on the future by asking, "What do you want done differently so that the problem doesn't occur again?" Of course, it is more difficult to move some couples from the blame and fault of the past than others, but continually reframing everything you hear into a question about how it will work in the future lessens the difficulty.

If the case you are mediating involves affidavits used in previous court motions, avoid reading them, as well as any custody studies that have been prepared: Ask the clients not to give you a lengthy history of all of their problems. Simply keep refocusing on the future so that the clients make decisions that create a better future.

This strategy can be used again and again. Some clients do not assimilate the message until they have heard it repeatedly.

16. Suggesting Advisory, Nonbinding Arbitration

This strategy can take many forms. The basic concept is that when the clients are close to throwing in the towel and going to divorce court, you can ask them and their attorneys for the names of three other attorneys whose understanding of family law is respected by everyone in the room. You then offer to present the case to the three attorneys and videotape their discussion of the case.

If the clients agree to this approach, consult with the three chosen attorneys, who form an advisory arbitration panel. To provide background for the attorneys, you need to summarize the agreed-on facts, the claims made by each client, and the efforts that have been made to settle the case. Then ask them to agree unanimously on the answers to two questions: (1) Based on your experience in the court system, what would you consider to be the most likely ruling of a family-court judge concerning this case? and (2) What would be a reasonable solution to the case, even if that solution were to deviate from the law?

The names of the clients and their attorneys are not revealed to the panel. When the panel has completed its work and that work has been videotaped (a process that usually takes less than an hour), you provide the clients and their attorneys with a copy of the videotape to review. Generally you will find that the clients change at least some of their former opinions after reviewing the tape.

17. Making a Short-Term Decision and Reviewing Later

Clients frequently fight over certain positions that have not yet been experienced. Even though each holds strong opinions about the way things should be, neither has had a chance to see if his or her way will actually work. At this point you might suggest that the clients make a short-term decision, try it, and then later review the results.

This strategy is based on the belief that a problem faced by two people is easier to resolve if both can give up the notion that they must settle 100 percent of that problem forever. Instead of trying to decide on the exact amount of spousal maintenance for the next ten years, for example, the clients can determine an agreed-on amount for the next twelve months and then review the results.

Similarly, if the clients are fighting over who should be the primary parent, ask them if they will agree to a four-month trial period during which one parent has primary responsibility for the children for two months and the other parent has primary responsibility for the next two months. At the end of the four-month period, they can return to mediation and determine whether either approach has worked for the children. (It is also useful to predetermine that during the four-month period the children will be seen by a neutral therapist, who can then attend the follow-up mediation session and report on the children's reactions.)

Clients who understand that issues like custody and support are never truly final appreciate this strategy. They see the advantages of ending a fight over custody and support that are often modified in the future, anyway.

18. Changing Traditional Custody Labels

When clients are fighting over who is the better parent, or who was most unfit in the past, keep bringing them back to a different question: "What future parenting arrangements can the two of you agree on that will allow each of you to have a significant parenting relationship with your children?" Suggest options that allow the clients to mediate a parenting relationship that is not limited by the custody labels, such as the following:

- Diminish the importance of the "custody" label by mediating agreements about all of the issues the label controls. (Schedules, child support, move out of state, day-to-day decision-making.)
- Suggest that they make no "custody" finding.

- Have them award "custody" to each during the scheduled time with the children. Save the discussion of the custody label until after the parenting plan is decided.

19. Suggesting Alternative Approaches to Spousal Maintenance

In jurisdictions that have alimony statutes, making the decision about spousal maintenance is always difficult for clients. The following are some options:

- Reservation
- Modified reservation
- Mutual waiver of spousal support
- Waiver of the court's jurisdiction to modify spousal support in the future
- Lump-sum "buyout" of the alimony obligation by an unequal division of assets
- Partial lump-sum "buyout" of the alimony obligation
- Variable maintenance with floor and ceiling amounts
- Establishment of standards for future review and modification

20. Asking a Retired Family Law Judge a Hypothetical Question

Between sessions, call a retired Family Court Judge and pose a "hypothetical" question about the issue that is causing impasse, ask for an opinion on resolving that issue, and then share the judge's opinion with the clients. There could be ethical prohibitions in your jurisdiction regarding this strategy, so be sure to find out local custom and practice rules before implementing it. This strategy works well for the following reasons:

- You receive instant feedback.
- The fact that the opinion comes from a judge lends validity to that opinion.
- This strategy links the mediation process with the judicial process in a constructive manner.
- A judge can render an expert opinion that takes less time and money to obtain than opinions from other experts.

21. Pointing Out the Cost of Continued Litigation

When the clients are stuck on a particular issue, you may ask each of them to discuss with his or her attorney the cost of litigating that issue. Once they have their answers, compare the cost of litigation with that of continued mediation. When confronted with the discrepancy in cost, the clients usually become highly motivated to settle in mediation, even if doing so means additional sessions or sessions with their attorneys present (or both).

22. Drafting Contingency Clauses That will Meet Clients' Needs

When one client objects to a particular option because it does not meet his or her needs, suggest that the client state how the needs might be drafted as a contingency to the decision.

23. Identifying and Discussing Roadblocks

When the clients are unable to make progress, and their difficulty does not seem to make sense, ask yourself, What is really going on here? The difficulty is probably attributable to something that is not obvious: a mistaken assumption, a previous communication or discussion that one of the clients is stuck on, or something else that is bothering one of the clients. Ask questions to identify the underlying issue that is blocking progress, lead a discussion of that issue and help the clients to resolve it, and then focus the clients on the original issue.

24. Giving the Disputed Item to the Children

During the division of property, the clients may fixate on the disposition of a particular item. Often the item is something that evokes sentiment, such as the wife's engagement ring or the family cabin. In this case, try suggesting that the clients give the item to their children in some way. An engagement ring can be given to one of the children, for instance, and a cabin can be gifted to the children. Future royalties may be placed in a college fund for the children.

25. Asking a Financial Planner to Help

The mediation process is often blocked by fear, especially the fear of financial instability after divorce. This is especially true with older couples who are looking toward retirement. Engaging the services of a financial planner can be very helpful in showing the clients how each will fare financially in the future according to various options concerning spousal support and the division of the marital estate.

26. Using Four-Square Analysis

To use this strategy, you first draw a large box on the flip chart and divide it into four boxes or squares. In each of the two top-row boxes you ask each client's position on the issue causing difficulty. In each of the two bottom-row boxes, you ask them to argue against their position stated in the box above.

Figure 20, for example, presents a situation in which the clients are having trouble deciding which of them stays in the family home. A statement of the husband's position ("Husband stays in the house") is written in the top-left box, and a statement of the wife's position ("Wife stays in the house") is written in the top-right box. Each client is asked to cite reasons in support of (or advantages that would be realized from) both positions. In each case, the supporting reasons are written below the position statement.

Figure 20. Example of Four-Square Analysis

Assumption: Children reside primarily in the family home

<table>
<tr>
<td valign="top">

HUSBAND STAYS IN THE HOUSE

1. *Husband's reasons in support*
   a. Finish remodeling
   b. Less expense on house mainte-nance
   c. More day-to-day contact with children
   d. Emotional attachment

2. *Wife's reasons in support*
   a. He helps kids with homework
   b. He's not afraid to stay alone
   c. Growth experience for him
   d. He could experience primary responsibility for children

</td>
<td valign="top">

WIFE STAYS IN THE HOUSE

1. *Wife's reasons in support*
   a. Primary parent home after school; no need for afternoon day care
   b. Opportunity to manage home as a separate parent without hus-band's comments
   c. Religious instruction
   d. More frequent interaction with children

2. *Husband's reasons in support*
   a. Nurturing by wife recognized
   b. Agree with a through d above

</td>
</tr>
<tr>
<td valign="top">

WIFE LEAVES THE HOUSE

1. *Wife's reasons in support*
   a. Emotionally removed from the situation
   b. More time to spend on personal goals
   c. No maintenance problems in apartment

2. *Husband's reasons in support*
   a. Husband's personal preference
   b. Family routine less affected
   c. Children would get more help with their homework

</td>
<td valign="top">

HUSBAND LEAVES THE HOUSE

1. *Husband's reasons in support*
   a. Nurturing of children probably better from wife
   b. Outside child care not needed
   c. Can't think of any other reasons

2. *Wife's reasons in support*
   a. Her personal preference
   b. Emotional reasons (control)
   c. Family routine less affected if husband leaves

</td>
</tr>
</table>

Then, in each of the two bottom boxes, the mediator writes each person's argu-ment against their own position shown in the box above. In Figure 20, the top-left box is labeled "Husband stays in the house." The result of that position, from the wife's point of view, would be "Wife leaves the house," so that result is written in the bottom-left box. The same process is followed for the bottom-right box, which then reads "Husband leaves the house." Again the mediator asks each client to cite reasons in support of each opposing position, and the supporting reasons are written below the position statement.

This strategy requires each client to state reasons in support and against their own alternative. It has several advantages:

- It concentrates on the effects of each choice.
- It tends to minimize negative discussion of the issue.
- It forces each client to see the issue from the other client's point of view.
- It allows the clients to focus on the most important factors and to discuss each factor separately.

In the example cited, which comes from our practice, the clients decided that the two most important issues for each were (1) close contact with the children in the home environment and (2) the need for each to be independent of the other. They made a temporary agreement to obtain a small efficiency apartment and trade places with each other weekly. In this way each parent was with the children in the family home for a week and alone in the apartment the next week.

The four-square analysis has a strong theoretical base in the theory of cognitive dissonance (Cohen, 1964). Numerous studies have indicated that a "person induced to argue against his private attitude will tend to change his attitude toward the position for which he has argued" (Cohen, 1964, p. 85). In finding reasons to support another's position, a person begins to change his or her own attitude. Consequently, the gap between the two positions is reduced

When you reach this point with your own clients, you can introduce options not previously discussed. Because both clients have altered their attitudes, both will be more receptive to those options than they would have been if four-square analysis had not been used.

Reference

Cohen, A. (1964). Attitude change and social influence. Out of Print. Library of Congress #ASIN 0465005659.

Part III
Appendixes

A   Forms

INTAKE FORM

CONFIDENTIAL—Not to Be Shared with Other Party
(The mediator needs to assess the level and potential of any abuse in the marital relationship
and establish boundaries about safety before issues can be mediated.)

Name_____ Date_____

Address_____ City_____ Zip Code_____

Home Phone_____ Work Phone_____

Name of Employer_____ Position_____

Full-time ❑   Part-Time ❑   Number of Years Employed_____

Date of Marriage_____ Date of Separation_____

Names and Ages of Children_____

With whom are the children living?_____

Was abuse present in the marriage relationship?   ❑ Yes   ❑ No

       Type: ❑ Physical   ❑ Emotional   ❑ Chemical   Other:_____

Is there an Order for Protection or Restraining Order?_____

Have you had or are you now in counseling?_____

       If yes, with whom?_____ How Long?_____

A treatment program?   ❑ Yes   ❑ No   If Yes, what type?_____

       Successful completion? ❑ Yes   ❑ No   Date Completed_____

Do you have an attorney?   ❑ Yes   ❑ No

       If yes, who?_____

Who referred you to mediation?_____

May we send a thank-you note to the above-named referral source?   ❑ Yes   ❑ No

Area of greatest concern about the divorce_____

FOR OFFICE USE ONLY

Mediator_____ Outcome_____
Comments _____
_____

Intake Form, p. 2

<table>
<tr><td colspan="2">

CONFIDENTIAL—Not to Be Shared with Other Party
(The mediator needs to assess the level and potential of any abuse in the marital relationship and establish boundaries about safety before issues can be mediated.)

</td></tr>
</table>

Please mark whether you ("Self") or your spouse has done any of the following to the other:

	Self	Spouse
A. Emotionally/Psychologically Abusive Behaviors		
1. Joked about your habits or faults	____	____
2. Refused to talk; withheld approval, affection, or sex to punish	____	____
3. Yelled, shouted, or invaded the other's personal space	____	____
4. Used insults, name calling, labels, swearing against the other	____	____
5. Verbally pressured the other to have sex or to act against his or her will	____	____
6. Threatened to leave the marriage or relationship	____	____
7. Threatened to take away cildren, money, home	____	____
8. Manipulated with lies and contradictions (played mind games)	____	____
9. Blamed the other for his or her own faults, abuse, or behavior	____	____
B. Indirect Threats of Violence		
1. Restricted physical movement or social contact	____	____
2. Intentionally interrupted the other's sleeping or eating	____	____
3. Followed the other or harassed the other by phone	____	____
4. Refused to meet physical needs of the other	____	____
C. Direct Threats of Violence		
1. Threatened to hit or throw something at the other	____	____
2. Slammed doors, hit walls, broke objects	____	____
3. Drove recklessly to frighten the other	____	____
4. Thretened to hurt or kill the children or pets	____	____
5. Threatened to get custody or to abuse or kidnap the children	____	____
6. Threatened or attempted suicide	____	____
7. Forced unwanted touching or viewing	____	____
D. Direct Violence		
1. Threw something at the other or broke meaningful possessions	____	____
2. Pushed, pulled, carried, restrained, grabbed, shoved, wrestled the other	____	____
3. Slapped, bit, scratched, backhanded, or spanked the other	____	____
4. Forced the other to watch sex	____	____
5. Threw the other bodily	____	____
E. Severe Violence		
1. Choked or strangled the other	____	____
2. Forced sex on the other	____	____
3. Engaged in incestuous behavior with the children	____	____
4. Burned, punched, or kicked the other	____	____
5. Kicked or punched the other in the stomach when pregnant	____	____
6. Beat the other unconscious	____	____
7. Threatened the other with weapon such as knife or gun	____	____
8. Used any weapon against the other	____	____
9. Caused injuries that required medical attention	____	____

AGREEMENT TO MEDIATE

This AGREEMENT TO MEDIATE is signed by the clients and [**Your Name or Your Business Name Here**] to create and clarify the mediation relationship. The clients desire to mediate all issues that might be involved in contested litigation. The clients herein agree to abide by the rules set forth by the mediator. This agreement reflects the clients' and the mediator's sincere intention to be fair during mediation.

IN CONSIDERATION OF THE ABOVE:

1) _____ will conduct the mediation and will be compensated at the rate of $_____ per hour for mediation sessions. Payment for each mediation session will be made at the conclusion of the session.

2) [**Your Name or Your Business Name Here**] has provided the parties with the Rules of Mediation and a description of the fees for mediation services.

All parties agree that legal advice and legal representation are not part of the mediation services and will not be provided by [**Your Name or Your Business Name Here**]. The clients agree that legal issues created by the decisions they reach in mediation will be referred to their attorneys. Each client agrees to retain legal counsel prior to implementing the decisions reached in mediation.

By signing this agreement, each client acknowledges receipt of a copy of the Rules of Mediation. Each also acknowledges and agrees to abide by the agreements stated within the Rules, both as between themselves and as between clients and [**Your Name or Your Business Name Here**]. The Rules herein are incorporated as part of this Agreement to Mediate and are attached to this Agreement.

This CONTRACT TO MEDIATE is signed by the clients and by [**Your Name or Your Business Name Here**], this _____ day of _____, _____.

By _____   _____

   _____   _____

RULES OF MEDIATION

The purpose of these rules is to assist the parties in reaching a settlement of the issues submitted for mediation. The rules are necessary to protect the integrity and confidentiality of the mediation process. The guidelines that follow the rules are designed to assist each party in examining relevant factors necessary for a full and fair discussion of the issues.

AGREEMENT TO BEGIN MEDIATION: These rules are a part of your signed Contract to Mediate. All parties will be asked to sign such a contract prior to the commencement of mediation with [**Your Name or Your Business Name Here**], mediator.

CONDUCT OF THE MEDIATION SESSIONS: The mediation process will be conducted in a manner that the mediator believes will most expeditiously permit full discussion and resolution of the issues. The mediator will assist the parties in fully discussing and understanding each issue before agreements are made so that both parties arrive at solutions that they believe are fair and equitable.

CONCERNS OF THE MEDIATOR: The mediator may indicate verbally or in writing his or her concerns regarding any final decisions that the parties make when the mediator is concerned about or does not understand the parties' standard of fairness. The mediator's comments may appear in the preliminary and/or final Memorandum of Agreement.

CONFIDENTIALITY OF MEDIATION SESSIONS: Although some State Statutes and Rules of Court say that all communications, documents, and work notes made or used in mediation are privileged (that is, confidential), the parties contract with each other and with [**Your Name or Your Business Name Here**] to keep the mediation discussions and documents confidential. By signing the Contract to Mediate incorporating these rules and the following guidelines, the parties agree as follows:

1. Through the adoption of these rules, the parties agree that they will not call either the mediator or any officer or agent of [Your Name or Your Business Name Here] as a witness in any litigation of any kind regarding the mediation sessions conducted by [**Your Name or Your Business Name Here**]; and, in like manner, the parties shall be stopped from requiring the production of any records or documents or any other notes or papers made by the mediator of [**Your Name or Your Business Name Here**] for any purpose(s) associated with the litigation of any issue(s) dealt with in mediation.

2. The foregoing exclusions from evidence and exemptions of the mediator and parties from giving testimony or being called on to produce documents shall apply also to the use of neutral experts and other professionals called on by the parties in mediation.

3. Mediation conducted by a professional mediator shall come within the purview of his or her professional privilege as established by the Academy of Family Mediators and any other statutory protection enacted either before or after the commencement of mediation by the parties.

FULL DISCLOSURE: The parties agree that they will fully disclose to the other party and to the mediator all information and writings as requested by the mediator, including financial statements, income tax returns, and so on, and all information requested by the other party if the mediator finds that such other disclosure is appropriate to the mediation process and may aid the parties in reaching a settlement. At the conclusion of the mediation process, the parties may find that their attorneys request further verification and disclosure in order to review and implement the decisions reached in mediation, and the parties agree that they will provide such information at the request of the other party. Likewise, at the conclusion of mediation, the parties agree that they will sign a verified (notarized) statement declaring that they have fully and truthfully disclosed all information concerning assets, liabilities, and income if so requested by the mediator or the other party.

PREPARATION OF BUDGETS: The preparation of a budget by each party is an essential part of the mediation process. If either party fails or refuses to prepare a budget adequately reflecting his or her needs, the mediator shall have the option of suspending mediation of this issue or, at the parties' discretion, declare an impasse.

PARTICIPATION OF CHILDREN AND OTHERS: Children of sufficient age or other persons having a direct interest in the mediation may participate in mediation sessions related to issues concerning them, with the consent of the parties and the mediator.

PROHIBITION AGAINST TRANSFERS OF PROPERTY, CHANGE OR CANCELLATION OF INSURANCE, OR ANY OTHER ACTION THAT CHANGES THE MARITAL ESTATE: On beginning mediation, the parties agree that they will not engage in any transactions that materially affect the status quo of the existing marital estate. They agree that transfers or sales of property without the written agreement of both parties and their attorneys are prohibited, except in the usual course of meeting ordinary monthly obligations. Likewise, they agree that cancellation or change of health insurance, life insurance, or other benefits shall not occur while the parties are meeting in mediation.

DRAFTING OF MEMORANDUM OF AGREEMENT: NO DECISIONS REACHED IN MEDIATION BECOME FINAL AND BINDING UNTIL THEY ARE APPROVED BY THE PARTIES' ATTORNEYS AND IMPLEMENTED THROUGH A COURT ORDER OR BINDING STIPULATION OF THE PARTIES AND THEIR ATTORNEYS.
At the conclusion of the mediation sessions, the mediator will draft a detailed memorandum setting forth the decisions agreed on by the parties in mediation. The Memorandum of Agreement will contain background information about the parties

and will set forth the factual information relied on by the parties in reaching settlement. The Memorandum of Agreement will be submitted by each of the parties to his or her attorney for review and implementation of the decisions as reflected in the memorandum. Any new or omitted issues raised by the attorneys will be returned to mediation if the parties and their attorneys are unable to efficiently and cooperatively resolve such new or omitted issues.

LEGAL REPRESENTATION:

The mediator does not legally represent either of the parties. Effective legal representation is required, and it is strongly recommended that each party retain legal counsel of his or her choice no later than at the conclusion of the mediation process. [Your Name or Your Business Name Here] recommends that the parties retain legal representation at the beginning of the mediation process. By doing this, each party will have a better understanding of his or her legal rights and responsibilities and will less likely be surprised by legal issues or concerns raised by his or her attorney after thinking that all decisions have been finalized.

ALTHOUGH [Your Name or Your Business Name Here] RECOMMENDS THAT EACH PARTY EDUCATE HIMSELF OR HERSELF ABOUT THE LEGAL APPROACH TO DIVORCE, THE MEDIATOR WILL ENCOURAGE BOTH PARTIES TO DISCUSS AND NEGOTIATE A SETTLEMENT BASED ON THEIR OWN STANDARDS OF FAIRNESS AND THEIR OWN DECISIONS ABOUT WHAT IS BEST FOR THEMSELVES AND THEIR FAMILY.

[Your Name or Your Business Name Here] maintains a panel of attorneys who specialize in family law and are familiar with the divorce mediation process. This list is available to [Your Name or Your Business Name Here] clients on request. Each party is encouraged to choose and interview an attorney who will respect the decisions that the parties have made in mediation and who will provide him or her with an independent judgment of those decisions.

SCHEDULING OF SESSIONS AND STARTING TIMES:

If any party needs to change a scheduled appointment, he or she is requested to do so at least 24 hours in advance. Failure to do this will result in a charge of $100 for the canceled session. In-session mediation time will be billed commencing with the time that the session is scheduled to begin, unless the delay in starting time is attributable to [Your Name or Your Business Name Here].

HOURLY FEES AND ADMINISTRATIVE CHARGES:

In addition to hourly charges for the mediation sessions, the parties will be charged for the mediator's work outside the mediation sessions, whether for the preparation of the mediated settlement agreement or for discussions with parties, their counsel, or with other persons concerning matters related to the mediation. A detailed fee schedule is given to the parties when they begin mediation.

DISAGREEMENTS: Should any disagreements arise between either party and **[Your Name or Your Business Name Here]** concerning fees or charges, the parties agree that they will use the services of a mediator to resolve the disagreement (after first trying to resolve it themselves), and should they not resolve the disagreement through mediation, they agree to submit the matter for binding arbitration pursuant to the terms of the [your state's arbitration statutes].

PHONE CALLS AND SPECIAL SAFETY CONCERNS: **[Your Name or Your Business Name Here]** has a general policy of not caucusing separately with either party unless the mediator believes it is necessary to do so to avoid possible impasse or to reduce the intensity of the conflict. For this reason, the parties are asked not to communicate with their mediator outside the working session about any issues of substance associated with a dispute. Procedural questions are permitted. **However, parties are encouraged and permitted to discuss with the mediator, either in sessions or in private, any concerns related to either their physical or emotional safety and well-being as it relates to the mediation process.**

If any party feels that separate (private) communications with the mediator are imperative, he or she may call the mediator and present his or her concern(s) and reason(s) for discussing the matter outside the scheduled mediation sessions.

CHILD ABUSE: Although mediators are not mandated by Minnesota Law to report child-abuse allegations, the mediator may encourage self-reporting of any such allegation disclosed during the mediation process. In circumstances in which the mediator believes the safety of a child to be in question, the mediator may report such information to the local child protection agency.

WITHDRAWING FROM MEDIATION: These rules assume that because mediation is voluntary, either party may withdraw from the mediation process at any time. However, by adopting these rules, you agree to return to mediation to discuss a withdrawal from mediation. (A phone call stating that you are not attending the next session is not sufficient to comply with this provision.)

[Your Name or Your Business Name Here] reserves the right to amend these rules at any time; however, any such amendments will not apply to existing cases in mediation on the date of such amendments.

INFORMAL RULES FOR PARTICIPATING
IN MEDIATION

1. Speak only for yourself and in the first person. (Make "I" statements.)

2. Use language that does not blame or find fault with others.

3. Do not interrupt while another person is speaking.

4. Use noninflammatory words.

5. If stating a complaint, raise it as your own concern and follow it with a constructive suggestion about how it might be resolved.

6. Attack the problems and concerns at hand; do not attack other persons.

7. Make statements about your interests and needs, not your position.

8. Be respectful of others.

9. Listen to and understand what each person is saying without being judgmental about that person or the message.

10. Do not point or make any other gestures toward another person in the room.

Mediation Questionnaire

INSTRUCTIONS: Please provide all of the following information to the best of your ability, even though it may duplicate what the other party may provide. Please use ink to fill out this questionnaire.

1. Your Name_____ (Maiden Name)_____

   Birth Date_____ Place of Birth_____

   Street Address_____Home Phone_____

   City_____ State_____ Country_____ Zip_____

   Workplace_____ Work Address_____

   City_____ State_____ Zip_____ Phone_____

   Continuous Residence in [STATE] since_____ Social Sec. #_____

2. Marriage Date_____ Place_____

3. CHILDREN (list full names)   Birth Date: Age: Living With:

   _____ _____ _____ _____

   _____ _____ _____ _____

   _____ _____ _____ _____

   _____ _____ _____ _____

4. Are you and the other party living together?   ❑ No   ❑ Yes

   If not, please give the date of separation:_____

5. Are you employed? ❑ No   ❑ Yes Employer_____ Position_____

   Employed since_____ Salary_____ H.S. Diploma_____

   College Degrees/   Continuous
   Certificates_____ Major/Year_____ employment since_____

6. Is your spouse employed? ❑ No   ❑ Yes Employer_____

   Position_____ Employed since_____ Salary_____

   Educational status_____ Continuous employment since_____

7. List all prior marriages (include name of prior spouse, and when and where marriage was terminated)

_____

8. List names and ages of any children from prior marriges and state with whom these children live

_____

_____

9. Do you have an interest in reconciliation?   ❑ Yes   ❑ No

10. Is there a dispute involving the children?   ❑ Yes   ❑ No

11. Have you had marriage or family counseling?   ❑ Yes   ❑ No

    If yes, with whom?_____

12. Are you presently in therapy or counseling?   ❑ Yes   ❑ No

    If yes, with whom?_____

13. Attorney's Name_____ Phone_____

    Address_____ Fax_____

14. Are there joint bank accounts to which your spouse has access?   ❑ Yes   ❑ No

15. Does your spouse have credit cards for which you are responsible?   ❑ Yes ❑ No

    If yes, specify_____

16. Who referred you?_____

    Address_____

    Do you have any objection to our acknowledging this referral?   ❑ Yes   ❑ No

17. Date you completed this form _____

Assets and Liabilities: Please list the value of each of the following items of property. If you are unable to obtain the exact present value, estimate what you think the value may be. If any item is located in a state other than that in which you live, indicate where such item is located; if necessary, give details on a separate sheet. Please indicate items acquired by gift, inheritance, or prior marriage by marking with an asterisk (*). Bring the statement or other document that verifies the value so that copies can be made for your spouse and the mediation file.

Be sure to list the names and account numbers of all of the items and the legal descriptions of real estate. This information is important in identifying the items and is necessary for inclusion in your legal papers.

List Appropriate Information as Completely as Possible

ASSETS:

A. Bank Accounts

Bank Name:	Account No.	Balance:	Owner:
_____	_____	_____	_____
_____	_____	_____	_____
_____	_____	_____	_____
_____	_____	_____	_____
_____	_____	_____	_____

B. Accounts Receivable, Notes, Loans Made to Others, Etc.

Due From:	Balance Due:	Owner:
_____	_____	_____
_____	_____	_____
_____	_____	_____
_____	_____	_____

C. Stocks and Bonds
(List company, number of shares, value per share today, total value of stock, and owner)

Company Name:	Number of Shares:	Value/Share:	Total Value:	Owner:
_____	_____	_____	_____	_____
_____	_____	_____	_____	_____
_____	_____	_____	_____	_____
_____	_____	_____	_____	_____

D. Real Estate
Homestead:

Address_____

Legal Description:_____

Date of Purchase:_____ Purchase Price:_____

Mortgage through:_____ Account No.:_____

Appraised Value:_____ Appraised By:_____

Special Information:_____

Other Real Estate:

Address_____

Legal Description:_____

Date of Purchase:_____ Purchase Price:_____

Mortgage through:_____ Account No.:_____

Appraised Value:_____ Appraised By:_____

Special Information:_____

Other Real Estate:

Address_____

Legal Description:_____

Date of Purchase:_____ Purchase Price:_____

Mortgage through:_____ Account No.:_____

Appraised Value:_____ Appraised By:_____

Special Information:_____

E. Life Insurance

Company:	Account No.:	Face Value:	Cash Value:	Insured/Beneficiary:
_____	_____	_____	_____	_____
_____	_____	_____	_____	_____
_____	_____	_____	_____	_____
_____	_____	_____	_____	_____
_____	_____	_____	_____	_____
_____	_____	_____	_____	_____

Where are the policies located?_____

F. Business Interests

Please furnish last balance sheet, P & L statement, tax return, buy-sell agreements, etc.

Name of Business:_____ Location:_____

Owned Since:_____ % Ownership:_____

Appraised By:_____ Appraised Value:_____

Special Information:_____

Name of Business:_____ Location:_____

Owned Since:_____ % Ownership:_____

Appraised By:_____ Appraised Value:_____

Special Information:_____

G. Miscellaneous Property
(Patents, trademarks, copyrights, royalties—Please furnish last statement and descriptive booklet):

Description:	Value:	Owner:
_____	_____	_____
_____	_____	_____

H. Automobiles and Other Vehicles

Vehicle Make & Year:_____ NADA Value:_____

Loan With:_____ Acct. #:_____ Amount:_____

Vehicle Make & Year:_____ NADA Value:_____

Loan With:_____ Acct. #:_____ Amount:_____

Vehicle Make & Year:_____ NADA Value:_____

Loan With:_____ Acct. #:_____ Amount:_____

I. Pension, Profit Sharing, IRA, and Other Retirement Plans

Plan Name: Acct. # :   Value: Owner:

_____   _____   _____   _____

_____   _____   _____   _____

_____   _____   _____   _____

_____   _____   _____   _____

_____   _____   _____   _____

_____   _____   _____   _____

J. Personal Property, Furnishings, Etc. (Attach lists if necessary)

Specific Items: Value: Disposition:

_____   _____   _____

_____   _____   _____

_____   _____   _____

_____   _____   _____

_____   _____   _____

_____   _____   _____

_____   _____   _____

K. Income Tax Refunds/Amounts Due

                                                Refund Due: Amount Owed:

State:_____ Year:_____ _____ _____

Federal:_____ Year:_____ _____ _____

Special Information:_____

_____

L. Liabilities: (Add lists if necessary)

Loans Owed to:	Acct. #:	Amount Due:	Whose Account:
_____	_____	_____	_____
_____	_____	_____	_____
_____	_____	_____	_____
_____	_____	_____	_____

Other Debts: (Medical, Dental, Charge Accounts, etc.)	Acct. #:	Amount Due:	Whose Account:
_____	_____	_____	_____
_____	_____	_____	_____
_____	_____	_____	_____
_____	_____	_____	_____

Monthly Income

Income: (Please supply most recent pay stub)
1. **How often do you receive paychecks?**

   Every other week?   ❑ Yes   ❑ No

   Twice a month?   ❑ Yes   ❑ No

   How many exemptions do you claim?_____

2. **Earned income:**
   Gross salary per paycheck   _____

   Federal tax deduction   _____

   State tax deduction   _____

   FICA deduction   _____

   Mandatory pension deduction   _____

   Medical insurance deduction   _____

   Life insurance deduction   _____

   Other deductions   _____

3. **Net income per paycheck**   _____

4. **Net income figured on a
   monthly basis:**
   If paid twice a month,
   multiply #3 by two: _____

   If paid every other week, multiply #3
   by 26 and divide by twelve   _____

5. **Other income amortized by month:**
   Dividend income   _____

   Interest income   _____

   Income from trusts   _____

   Rental income   _____

   Pension   _____

   Social Security   _____

   Other income (describe)   _____

   Total Other Income   _____

   **Total Monthly Income
   (Net Pay Plus Other Income):**   _____

Monthly Expenses

Item	Self	Children
Rent		
Rental Insurance		
Mortgage Payment		
(Principle) _____ (if known)		
(Interest) _____ (if known)		
Real Estate Taxes		
Homeowner's Insurance		
Second Mortgage/Home Equity Line		
Contract for Deed		
Association Fee		
Electricity		
Heat		
Water		
Garbage		
Telephone		
Cable TV		
Cellular Phone		
Home Maintenance and Repair		
House Cleaning		
Lawn Care		
Snow Removal		
Other Property		
Contract for Deed		
Insurance and Taxes		
Maintenance		
Utilities		
Food/Groceries		
Lunches		
Eating Out		
Other Household Supplies		
Clothing		
Dry Cleaning/Laundry		
Medical Insurance		
Uncovered Medical Expenses		

Item	Self	Children
Prescriptions		
Dental Insurance		
Uncovered Dental Costs		
Orthodontia		
Eye Care		
Automobile Payment		
Gas/Oil		
Maintenance/Repairs		
Auto Insurance		
License		
Parking		
Life/Disability Insurance Premiums		
Recreation/Entertainment		
Vacations/Travel		
Newspapers/Magazines		
Dues/Clubs		
Personal Items/Incidentals		
Hair Care		
Child Care—Day Care		
Babysitting		
Children's School Expenses		
Books/Supplies		
Activity Fees		
Allowances		
Nonschool Classes		
Sports Fees		
Clubs		
Pet Expenses		
Contributions/Religious/Charity		
Gifts		
Other Miscellaneous		
Monthly Debt Reduction		
TOTAL MONTHLY NEED		
TOTAL MONTHLY NET INCOME		
SURPLUS/SHORTFALL		

Household Furnishings and Personal Property Form

List of Items by Room/Location	Value*	Who Gets	Sep/Mar**

*What you believe the item is worth.
**"Sep" means separate, nonmarital property
 "Mar" means marital property

List of Items by Room/Location	Value*	Who Gets	Sep/Mar**

B Recommended Readings

Those marked with an asterisk (*) are highly recommended by the authors.

*Ahrons, C. (1994). The good divorce. New York: HarperCollins.

Ahrons, C., & Rodgers, R. H. (1987). Divorced families. New York: Norton.

Bautz, B. J., & Hall, R. M.. (1989, Fall). Divorce mediation in New Hampshire. Mediation Quarterly, 7.

Bush, R. A. Baruch (1989, Fall). "Mediation and adjudication, dispute resolution and ideology: An imaginary conversation" Vol. 3, No. 1, University of San Diego School of Law.

Braver, S. H., Wolchik, L., Sandler, S. A., Fogas, N., & Zvetina, D. (1991). "Frequency of visitation by divorced fathers: Differences in reports by fathers and mothers" American Journal of Orthopsychiatry, 61, 448–454.

*Coogler, O. J. (1978). Structured mediation in divorce settlement. Lexington, MA: Heath.

*Deutsch, M. (1973). The resolution of conflict: Constructive and destructive processes. New Haven, CT: Yale University Press.

Ellis, D., & Stuckless, M. (1996). Mediating and negotiating marital conflicts. Thousand Oaks, CA: Sage.

Erickson, S. K. (1984, March). A practicing mediator answers the questions most often asked about divorce mediation. Mediation Quarterly.

Erickson, S. K. (1985). Comparison between the legal process of divorce and the mediation process. In J. Folberg & A. Milne (Eds.), Divorce mediation: Theory and practice. New York: Guilford Press.

Erickson, S. K., & McKnight, M. S. (1988). Family mediation casebook: Theory and process. New York: Brunner/Mazel.

Erickson, S. K., & McKnight, M. S. (1992). The children's book: A separate parenting handbook. West Concord, MN: CPI Publishing.

Folberg, J. (1984). Joint custody and shared parenting. City: Bureau of National Affairs, Inc., and the Association of Family and Conciliation Courts.

Folberg, J., & Taylor, A. (1984). *Mediation: A comprehensive guide to resolving conflicts without litigation*. San Francisco: Jossey-Bass.

*Kaslow, F. W., & Schwartz, L. L. (1987). The dynamics of divorce. New York: Brunner/Mazel.

Kressel, K. (1985). *The process of divorce*. New York: Basic Books.

Kressel, K. (1989). *Mediation research: The process and effectiveness of third-party intervention*. San Francisco: Jossey-Bass.

Neumann, D. (1996). *Choosing a Divorce Mediator*. New York: Henry Holt.

Olson, W. K. (1991). *The litigation explosion*. New York: NAL/Dutton.

Parsons, R. J. (1991). The mediator role in social work practice. *Social Work, 36*, 483–487.

*Ricci, I. (1980). *Mom's house, dad's house: Making shared custody work*. New York: MacMillan.

*Wallerstein, J., & Kelly, J. (1980). *Surviving the breakup: How children and parents cope with divorce*. New York: Basic Books.

About the Authors

Stephen Erickson, a practicing mediator since 1977, left the practice of law in 1980. Since then he has built a successful private mediation practice in Minneapolis with his partner Marilyn McKnight. His experience as both a divorce lawyer and a mediator allows him to see and teach an innovative and powerful model of mediation that emphasizes clients' needs while at the same time working with the constraints and requirements of the various states' legal systems. His divorce mediation work extends back to the beginning of the field when he worked with Jim Coogler to conduct the first forty-hour divorce mediation training in August, 1980, in Florida. He was also one of the founding members of the Academy of Family Mediators and served as its second president. He has published several articles and coauthored with Marilyn McKnight *The Children's Book* in 1992 and *Family Mediation Casebook* in 1988. In 1996 he received the Distinguished Mediator Award from the Academy of Family Mediators.

Marilyn McKnight is a practicing mediator with a master's degree in Psychology and Human Development. She cofounded Erickson Mediation Institute with Stephen Erickson and has worked as a divorce mediator since 1977. She was president of the Academy of Family Mediators in 1992 and in 1996 received the Academy's Distinguished Mediator Award. As a mediator, trainer, and adjunct professor, she coined the term "client-centered mediation" to describe a mediation process that has its roots in the early mediation movement in which the clients are empowered to work together cooperatively to choose their own divorce settlement. Marilyn is a leader in developing protocols that make the mediation process safe and productive for couples with a history of violence, and her writings on this subject have shaped the field's response to family violence. Marilyn is a frequent lecturer on mediation and for the past seven years has served as Executive Director of Cooperative Solutions, a nonprofit group of mediation centers providing services in rural Minnesota and Wisconsin and a multicultural mediation center in St. Paul, MN.

EDWARD TEYBER

Helping Children Cope with Divorce, Revised Edition

"Realistic, age-appropriate advice for the whole family."
—Child Magazine

"An outstanding book. It reinforces the value of putting children first and acknowledges children's need for both parents during and after divorce. Teyber clearly describes the stress and pain children experience and explains how best to shield them from the parents' own conflicts. . . . Essential reading."
—David L. Levy, president, Children's Rights Council

Paperback   May 2001   272 pages   ISBN 0-7879-5554-X $17.95

CRAIG EVERETT, SANDRA VOLGY EVERETT

Healthy Divorce

For Parents and Children—An Original, Clinically Proven Program for Working Through the Fourteen Stages of Separation, Divorce, and Remarriage

"Healthy Divorce is a very valuable book, containing practical answers to difficult questions."
—Dan Kiley, author of *The Peter Pan Syndrome* and *The Wendy Dilemma*

The authors offer practical advice on using mediation as an alternative to the adversarial court battle; co-parenting to maintain stability for the children after the divorce; and organizing and structuring a happy blended family.

Paperback   July 1998   208 pages   ISBN 0-7879-4381-9 $18.95

HOWARD MARKMAN, SCOTT STANLEY, SUSAN BLUMBERG

Fighting *for* Your Marriage, New and Revised Edition

Positive Steps for Preventing Divorce and Preserving a Lasting Love

"For marital therapists like me who give homework assignments to couples, Fighting *for* Your Marriage *is a gift. And for those couples who want to work on their marriage without a therapist, it is a book I highly recommend."*
—Anna Beth Benningfield, president, American Association for Marriage and
    Family Therapy

The authors present the powerful, proven strategies of the highly acclaimed PREP™ (Prevention and Relationship Enhancement Program) approach for helping couples beat the odds and master the skills that can prevent marital distress and divorce.

Paperback   September 2001   400 pages   ISBN 0-7879-5744-5 $16.95

DONALD T. SAPOSNEK

Mediating Child Custody Disputes

A Strategic Approach, A New and Revised Edition

"The seminal work in systems theory applied to mediation, this will be invaluable to all practicing mediators as well as other professionals involved in custody disputes."
—Library Journal

Donald Saposnek's revised and updated version of his classic primer offers the most current information on issues and procedures concerning child custody mediation and includes important updates on new research and laws. The book offers guidance for developing the essential therapeutic skills and mediation techniques that will help solve problems and create cooperation.

Paperback   May 1998   416 pages   ISBN 0-7879-4051-8 $40.00

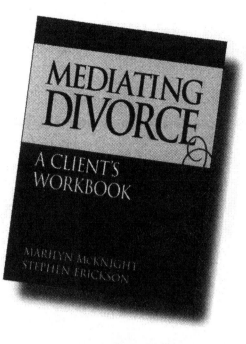